Romantic Organicism

Romantic Organicism

From Idealist Origins to Ambivalent Afterlife

Charles I. Armstrong
Associate Professor
University of Bergen
Norway

First published 2003 by
PALGRAVE MACMILLAN
Houndmills, Basingstoke, Hampshire RG21 6XS and
175 Fifth Avenue, New York, N. Y. 10010
Companies and representatives throughout the world

PALGRAVE MACMILLAN is the global academic imprint of the Palgrave Macmillan division of St. Martin's Press, LLC and of Palgrave Macmillan Ltd. Macmillan® is a registered trademark in the United States, United Kingdom and other countries. Palgrave is a registered trademark in the European Union and other countries.

ISBN 1–4039–0475–8

This book is printed on paper suitable for recycling and made from fully managed and sustained forest sources.

A catalogue record for this book is available from the British Library.

Library of Congress Cataloging-in-Publication Data
Armstrong, Charles I., 1969–
    Romantic organicism: from idealist origins to ambivalent afterlife/Charles I. Armstrong.
        p. cm.
    Includes bibliographical references and index.
    ISBN 1–4039–0475–8
    1. English literature–19th century–History and criticism. 2. English literature–German influences. 3. Philosophy, German–18th century. 4. Romanticism–Great Britain. 5. Philosophy in literature. 6. Romanticism–Germany. 7. Organicism (Philosophy) I. Title.
PR457 .A76 2003
820.9′145–dc21   2002042820

10   9   8   7   6   5   4   3   2   1
12   11   10   09   08   07   06   05   04   03

Printed and bound in Great Britain by
Antony Rowe Ltd, Chippenham and Eastbourne

I (said he) hunt by the eye, like a Grey-hound. I see what my Object is: and dash in a strait line towards it. But you hunt with your nose to the earth: track the Prey thro' every bend & zigzag, in and out thro' the whole maze of Puss' or Renyard's Feet – and at the end what do you catch? – Why the Scent, perhaps, of the Hare or Vermin which I had killed an hour before, after a five minutes' Run.

(Samuel Taylor Coleridge, in a letter to James Gillman, Jr,
24 October 1826)

Contents

Acknowledgements

This book was made possible by a grant from the Norwegian Research Council (Norges Forskningsråd). Thanks are due the staff and students of both the department of Comparative Literature (Allmenn litteraturvitenskap) and the department of English at the University of Bergen, Norway, who have provided me with constructive working environments. I am indebted to the expertise and unfailing encouragement of Ellen Mortensen. Dag Andersson (University of Tromsø), Simon Critchley (University of Essex), Paul Hamilton (Queen Mary and Westfield University), Hans Hauge (University of Aarhus), and Gisle Selnes (University of Bergen) have read my manuscript at various stages of completion, all responding generously with tips and suggestions. I would also like to thank Per Buvik, Rune Falch, Erik Bjerck Hagen, Nils-Øivind Haagensen, Atle Kittang, Ingrid Nielsen, Frode Helmich Pedersen, Stuart Sillars, Nora Simonhjell, Torgeir Skorgen, Lars Sætre, and Tiril Broch Aakre, as well as Emily Rosser and Rebecca Mashayekh at Palgrave Macmillan, for their assistance. I am especially grateful to Inger Margrethe Stoveland, my father Richard J. Armstrong, and all other family members and friends for their support.

An early extract from chapter 2 was presented at a seminar in Norheimsund, and parts of the same chapter have since appeared in the Norwegian article 'Fra kritikk til organisme: Systemtenkning i Kant og den tyske idealismen,' published in *Prosopopeia* (number 2, 2001), 50–8.

An abridged and modified version of a section of chapter 4 has been published as 'The Absolute Implied: Coleridge on Wordsworth and the Bible,' in *Literature and Theology* (Vol. 14, number 4, December 2000), 363–72.

A manuscript based on parts of chapter 5 was presented to the Coleridge Summer Conference at Cannington in 1998, and was subsequently published as 'The Deferences of Friendship: Between Poetry and Prayer in Coleridge's Conversation Poems,' in the *Coleridge Bulletin* (Number 14 (NS), Autumn 1999), 40–6.

1
First Articulations

'Whither is fled the visionary gleam?' asked Wordsworth. 'Where is it now, the glory and the dream?' These beseeching questions, once forwarded by the poet in the wake of the demise of his childhood sense of belonging, might now rightfully be asked with regard to organicism.[1] What on earth has happened to organicism? What has become of the vitality and importance of this idea? One all too obvious answer might be that, like all the dreams which are mere facile illusions, that of organicism has been decisively banished by the cold, clear light of day. Reverie has yielded to lucidity. Yet what kind of lucidity is it that can do without the haloing light of this 'visionary gleam'? Is not, as Poe intimated in the poem 'A Dream Within a Dream', all we see or seem directed – or deranged, perhaps – in some form or another, by dreams? And is not all wakefulness harassed, or even tempted, by a *return* of the obscure, oneiric obsessions of the night?

Nevertheless, organicism has in recent times been written off as an idealistic construction that must be banished to the scrap heap of history. Undoubtedly, it may be said to underlie some of those 'metanarratives' which Jean-François Lyotard has deemed to be inoperative to the postmodern condition.[2] As such it is susceptible to criticism for being a mystifying and often dogmatic form that represses difference and alterity at the behest of ideology. It smacks more of a nightmare, in short, than a desirable dream. Even relatively informed voices, though, continue to hold that organicism is a heritage which has undeservedly lost its centrality in Western culture. The mechanisation and impersonality of modern society has blinded us to the value and importance of a more unified and contextual approach, it is claimed, and this has led to the demise not only of our environment but also of our modes of comprehension and our entire way of life. From this vantage point, the perspective of organicism should be restored to its central and irreplaceable position, and raised from the shades of historical limbo to a more respectable and elevated form of afterlife. For this is a dream, say such dreamers, we should not dream to do without.

Which of these two stances is more justified? And is the current margin-alisation of organicism the prelude to its impending obliteration or to its resuscitation? This study takes its bearings from somewhere between these two positions. It can be rightfully read as a 'deconstruction' of the organ-icist heritage as it shows itself in romanticism and its aftermath, provoked in part by simplistic (and often seemingly unconscious) recuperations of this tradition in modern thought and criticism. Yet at the same time this study can just as correctly be considered a 'reconstruction' of the underesti-mated fecundity and complexity of romantic organicism. If organicism often presents itself as an 'inscrutable workmanship', to use Wordsworth's phrase,[3] this is not simply the inscrutability that is part and parcel of every-day obscurantism. Rather, it is the mark of the complexity and profundity of organicism, and its impatience with superficiality and facile solutions.

The importance of organicism to such writers as Coleridge and Friedrich Schlegel is often underestimated, especially in terms of its relevance to their most profound and noteworthy accomplishments. They offer a wide definition of organicism, which will provide the basis for my argument in this study: organicism is not understood as a fact of nature or as a merely aesthetic phenomenon in their texts, but rather as a *grounding systematics for understanding all holistic structures*. It is, to put matters simply, a way of thinking meaningfully about wholes. For writers such as Coleridge and Schlegel, organicism is also tied to an ever-increasing tendency towards opening up the tradition of the West to the claims of difference and partic-ularity. Not merely through its cultivation of the fragment, particularly prominent in the Jena *Frühromantik*, but also in the organicism which I will show to lie at the heart of that exigency of fragmentation, romanticism bequeaths to us what Maurice Blanchot has called 'this question of discon-tinuity or difference as form [*cette question – la discontinuité ou la différence comme forme*]'.[4] To be sure organicism frequently builds upon a notion of a 'thing as formed matter', which Heidegger, for one, has criticised for being derived from the ontologically restricted nature of technological equip-ment.[5] And the suspicions awakened by the ideological use of organic models in politics are certainly, in some contexts, justifiable. Yet this much-maligned tradition *also* represents a valuable attempt to transcend the growing technicity and instrumentality of the Western tradition, by derailing the mechanistic teleology inherent in the thought of means and ends to a more open-ended model.

In its most radical forms, organicism is thus arguably an important fore-bear of the very tendencies which now, Oedipus-like, rise up to denounce it. What about organicism's relevance for a more restricted concern, namely the interpretation of the era one calls romanticism? Apart from investigations into the nature of its conception of subjectivity,[6] and partic-ularising historical approaches which strive for a form of radical empiri-cism, the most typical contemporary approach to romanticism is by way of the question of language. Paul de Man has been a particularly distinguished proponent of a way of reading that finds romantic texts concerned with their own language. The pre-romantic philosophies of language expounded by Rousseau and Herder provide the basis for a reading that presents the romantics as being conscious of the linguistic underpinnings of their thought, underpinnings that ultimately undermine the absolute ambitions of Hegel and idealism. Yet however fruitful this linguistic approach has proved to be, it has nevertheless resulted in a somewhat distorted image of romanticism. Even if the romantics anticipated the linguistic turn, their achievement was precisely that: an *anticipation* rather than a fully-fledged linguistic revolution. This must be stressed, for the singularity of romanticism is poorly served by making it a mirror image of our later concerns.

Language is always a matter of *articulation* for the romantics, and thus concerns the structuring of relations. In this sense, organicism describes a privileged model as to how language articulates things into a whole: it describes the manner in which language, to borrow the words of Charles Taylor, 'lays out the contours' of that which is spoken of.[7] This sense of articulation as an intra-linguistic structural phenomenon of distribution does not, however, exhaust the matter. For an even more audacious argument can be proffered, according to which organicism is what gives speech, and language in general, its space to unfold. It would figure the very structuring site upon which the links and articulations of the linguistic event are based. Implicitly, this is what the texts of romantics such as Friedrich Schlegel and Samuel Taylor Coleridge seem to imply. They do not think of organic structure as a mode, or possible application, of language; rather, they think of language on the basis of organicism.

This stance is debatable, and can be modified by arguing that language and structure are both equally basic phenomena: they are *gleichursprünglich*, to use a Heideggerian term, and cannot be thought of as independent of one another. As such they both open up, and can only be approached through, relations of difference. Whatever level of generality or priority organicism is said to inhabit, one cannot justifiably claim that it is devoid of difference. Quite to the contrary, despite the holistic aspirations of organicist thought, the particular inflection given to it by romanticism leads precisely to a thematisation of an unbridgeable difference. Unknowable and ungraspable, the centre of the radically organic structure of romanticism can be confronted only in its immediacy from a vantage point beyond all consciousness or perception, in an impossible and heterogeneous relation. As will be demonstrated in chapter 9, the early thought of Georges Bataille and Maurice Blanchot takes its point of departure from this organic *topos*.

Organicism remains relevant, because of the impossibility of the linguistic turn to complete itself, because of its unwillingness – inability, rather – to close its own circle. The claim that modern (or postmodern) linguistic theories have surpassed the idealist dichotomy of subject and object lies at the centre of this problem. Romantic organicism was itself an attempt to transcend this dichotomy. Arguably, its failure to do so – or what might rather be construed as its acknowledgement of the necessarily *impossible* character of such transcendence – actually anticipates what has happened to the more linguistic philosophies of the twentieth century. For the hermeneutical distinction between the natural and the human sciences, as well as the opposition between performative and mimetic forms of language, are arguably evidence of how the subject–object distinction sneaks in through the backdoor whenever one thinks one has banished it from the premises for good. This is one of the many ways in which the problems and positions of organicism have enjoyed a healthy, if somewhat concealed, afterlife in modern theory.

I have tried to identify different inflections of organicism. In its classical form, derived from a long and illustrious tradition, a merely fitting or apt relation is implied, often entailing a sense of measured balance between form and matter. Romanticism often endorses this form of organicism, yet concomitantly frets at its leash. Thus there arises what I have dubbed 'radical organicism', a thinking of structure that does not merely co-ordinate form and matter (or subject and object), but tries to collapse these opposites into an immediate and undifferentiated unity.[8] Radical and classical organicisms are only two major forms of an almost infinitely rich set of possibilities that is exceedingly difficult to define or delimit. This is perhaps not only to be ascribed to historical contingency, but is also due to the fact that organicism, in the words of Frederick Burwick, 'resists definitions which try to identify form as if it were fixed and definite'.[9]

While the resistance of organicism to theoretical formulation risks rendering it invisible and impossible to locate, it simultaneously tends towards making it omnipotent. Nowhere to be found, and therefore impossible to circumscribe, organicism may be presumed to be everywhere at work. Certainly this logic is prevalent for the romantics, for whom the ubiquity and profundity of organicism's employment makes it difficult to demarcate or delimit its significance. It acquires an iconic seductiveness that might lead one to call organicism a dominating *model* for the romantic worldview. Is the body of organicism really a model, though? Even if I have already employed the word 'model', and will continue to do so, this term may be considered to be insufficient since it can be taken to imply an abstract split between thought and world, which is precisely that which is in question in organicism. Likewise, classifying it as a 'metaphor' implies that one is talking about an element of a rhetorical arsenal to be used at will by a linguistic subject, and neglects that the very grounding of a linguistic being in a world encroaches upon the ontological dimension of the problematic of organicism. Although the terms 'model' and 'metaphor' both have the virtue of accessibility over related concepts such as 'arche-type' or 'paradigm', another term – 'ontotypology' – is more precise. To put matters very briefly: according to Martin Heidegger, every age finds its most vital concerns addressed through a comprehensive figure that is pro-pounded jointly by philosophy and poetry.[10] As the neologism (which has been coined by Philippe Lacoue-Labarthe) implies, being and language come together in the ontotypological. Although it is too simplistic and reductive to grant organicism absolute dominion in the age of romanti-cism, it certainly approaches something of the all-pervasive and dominant status of an ontotypological figure – that is, a figure that is utilised in order to lay down the law for the functioning of philosophical, literary, and also political wholes.

This dominance of the organic as ontotypological figure is one of the sin-gularities of romantic organicism, compared to its ancestors and descen-dants. There are others: in this study, I will frequently dwell upon, and return to, three concerns that the romantics articulate through organic images and structures. These three concerns or supplementary limbs are: (a) that of the sacred book – the absolute, and systematic, philosophical-literary text that is romanticism's transformative equivalent to the Bible, and in which the imbrication of literary romanticism, philosophy, and reli-gion rises to the heights of both intimacy and antagonism; (b) the question of the limit-experience (tied to the aesthetic category of the sublime), where the centre of the organic structure reveals itself in a paradoxical and passing experience; and (c) the problem of community, where political and private forms of togetherness are thought of on the basis of an articulated body.

These three concerns are provisional centres, or nodal points, around which my study will circle. Since organicism constitutes a contested and open field, rather than a rigorously unified and delimited body, there is no true story of organicism, no rationale that will save criticism from arbitrary, or at least contestable, acts of inclusion and exclusion. Other important issues and figures will therefore necessarily suffer neglect on the margins of this study. For instance, on the basis of my working definition of organ-icism as concerning the systematical ground for all wholes, I will necessar-ily place a strong emphasis on the functional and philosophical side of organicism rather than its more concretely scientific and biological aspects. Hence my relative neglect of what Wimsatt has aptly called 'that tropical rain-forest of eighteenth-century romantic nature philosophy'.[11] It is also the grounds for pursuing, in my readings of the poetry of Coleridge and Wordsworth, motifs and structures that do not immediately strike one as organic – such as friendship and architecture. The latter readings share a desire to let the romantic organism loose so that it can wander to the *outer-most limits* of its territory, and by allowing it to touch those limits, to dis-cover the extent of its productivity.

In its tendency to overflow preconceived boundaries, we can glimpse something of the latent *monstrosity* of organicism. This more-than-natural monstrosity will be given something approaching a precise, theoretical formulation. Since this study takes its bearings at the intersection between German idealism and English romanticism, and the challenge this intersection raises to conventional dualisms and subject–oriented thought, I have taken Immanuel Kant's meditations on organic form as my point of departure. Although Kant does not represent an unprecedented or exclusive origin for the romantic way of approaching organicism, he and his followers do provide a crucial backdrop for understanding the romantics on this matter. From Kant's Third Critique, I extract three main principles of organicism – hierarchical totalisation, interdependence of parts and external delimitation – which I then try to pursue through their various permutations and agonistic struggles in later thinkers and writers. In chapter 2, an outline of Kant's organicism is followed by a reading of how this problematic is transformed, and given a more central place, in the early idealism of Fichte and Schelling. Fichte's important realisation of the impossibility of an organic transcendence of the subject–object divide might be said to relegate all subsequent formulations to the status of being afterthoughts, or part of the afterlife, of organicism. In chapter 3, I unfold one of the most important sequels to the life of this idea, by relating Friedrich Schlegel's theory of the fragment to his exploding of the notion of organic form.

The second part of my study entails a shift in focus from German idealism and *Frühromantik* to English romanticism. In chapter 4, I follow the immediate *theoretical* consequences the thought of German idealism has for English romanticism on this matter. Here I look into Coleridge's various deployments of organicism, mainly identifying a more conservative tenor in his thought than in that of Schlegel. In the two subsequent chapters, I gradually turn to more exclusively literary matters. In chapter 5, this leads to the identification of more aporetic and exploratory structures in Coleridge than were generally evident in the reading of his theoretical work. Close analysis is here devoted to his early letters, and his conversation poems are scrutinised from the vantage point of an organic theory of friendship. Chapter 6 is devoted to Wordsworth's comparison of his poetry to a gothic church – a comparison which is analysed in a wide context that reveals its complex interconnecting of categories such as religion, poetry, architecture and nature.

I return to more narrowly theoretical concerns in the third part, where I look into organicism's complex survival in modern thought. First, conservative and extreme appropriations of organicism are identified in the early thought of I. A. Richards and Georges Bataille in chapter 7. Then I delineate the conservative organicism implicit in the contemporary hermeneneutical project of Hans-Georg Gadamer. The limits and possible transcendence of organicism is touched upon in that connection, but it is more fully confronted and discussed in chapter 9, where Maurice Blanchot's and Jacques Derrida's more radical interpretations of Martin Heidegger's critique of organicism are put to task. As these two French thinkers have come up with theoretical contributions that are indispensable to how my foregoing chapters interpret idealism and romanticism, a questioning of their own scepticism with regard to organicism is a suitable conclusion to this study.

That final chapter will demonstrate that deconstruction need not entail a simply dismissive relation to organicism. In this respect, the thought of Derrida decisively differs from that of Paul de Man. The latter bases his influential critique of organicism on the premise that romantic celebrations of unity are shadowed by a more fundamental negative awareness of temporal and linguistic discontinuity. This awareness, de Man claims in several texts from the late 1960s and onwards, has to separate the mode of human existence from its inauthentic analogue in organic nature. The tendency 'for the self to borrow, so to speak, the temporal stability that it lacks from nature',[12] is – at crucial moments, singled out by de Man's readings – countered by authentic realisations of human mortality in tune with Heideggerian philosophy.

For de Man, organicism is the root of a fallaciously unifying understanding of time. It is tied to inauthentic hypostatisations of 'origin, continuity, growth, and totalization'.[13] It is also linked to the unifying semiotics of the symbol. In de Man's external deconstruction of the romantic tradition, the symbol and the organism are contrasted with what traditionally have been their poor cousins, namely allegory and the mechanical.[14] Such gestures may have some polemical validity within certain contexts, but they ignore the possibility – which I will pursue at length – of a more *internal* deconstruction of the notion of organicism.[15]

In following such a perspective, my work is indebted to a handful of studies that have worked beyond the simplistic debunking advocated by De Man. Although Philippe Lacoue-Labarthe and Jean-Luc Nancy's book on *The Literary Absolute: The Theory of Literature in German Romanticism* (1978) is a critical study limited to the explication of texts belonging to *German* romanticism, it takes the philosophical elucidation of romanticism in general to a new level. Demonstrating how Jena romanticism responds to the problems opened up by Kant's critical philosophy, Lacoue-Labarthe and Nancy show the interrelation between organicism, an aesthetics of the work, the theory of the fragment, and the modern tendency of literature to reflect upon itself and its own ground. In all these respects, they show how Friedrich Schlegel's early work takes idealist thought to its limits, even before the efforts of the later Friedrich Schelling (which proved so influential for Heidegger and Søren Kierkegaard).[16] My own work differs from this study on at least three general points. First of all, I do not share their confidence in the claim that romanticism – in any country or writer – can be exhaustively described from the philosophical vantage point of transcendental idealism.[17] Although the main focus of my own approach is philosophical and transcendental, I will allow for the imbrication of several modes of discourse and do not claim that an organicist reading of romanticism can be autonomous or completely comprehensive. Second, and relatedly, I do not agree with their thesis that romanticism leaves nature completely behind and opts for a straightforward continuation of the Kantian transcendentalism. I see the idealistic critique of Kant as leading to a situation (evident both in Germany and in England) where the transcendence of the subject–object distinction *also* entails that one must attempt to transcend the distinction between art (or reason) and nature.[18] Third, I will go further than Lacoue-Labarthe and Nancy in attempting to bring forth the inherent tensions and problems of romantic organicism, and I will try to relate these problems to similar and related aporias evident in modern philosophy and literary criticism.

Murray Krieger has pointed in such a direction. His collection of Wellek Library Lectures published under the title of *A Reopening of Closure: Organicism against Itself* (1989) attempts to describe 'the movement of organicism beyond closure, to find in its self-embrace an opening that would expose its apparently monolithic claims to a self-generating opposition.'[19] At first, Krieger finds this opposition on de Man's home ground: in a theory of rhetorical address. Whereas de Man makes a distinction between a mystifying and demystifying rhetoric, Krieger separates a 'theological semiotic' from 'the secular borrowing of certain elements from the theological semiotic'.[20] When romantic and Renaissance poets make use of this semiotic within their poetical texts, it is only in the guise of a metaphor imported from a religious to a secular context which, due to its new surroundings, 'announces its own mock-metaphoric counterthrust'.[21]

Such reductions of organicism to a metaphor, or a 'discursive form',[22] that can be handled as a rhetorical instrument, are questionable at best. For organicism addresses the foundations for the rhetorical situation from which metaphors are articulated. This limitation does not however prevent Krieger from intimating that there are bifurcating paths *within* the organic scheme itself, rather than simply in its rhetorical application. It is here that he makes a decisive contribution to modern criticism on this issue. From a Coleridgean quote on the nature of organicism, he derives an internal tension in the model between unification and balance, and goes on to pronounce:

> It is, then, in the two-sidedness of this dialectic, with the opposition – especially the opposition between the would-be autonomous pull and the would-be totalizing whole – being both indulged and overcome, that the aesthetics of organicism is made by Coleridge, and by those who follow him, to thrive. As I am describing it, built into the mystical dialectic of organicism, with its magical imposition of unity, is a negative thrust that would explode it.[23]

Although Krieger's reduction of the unifying drive of organicism to something inherently 'magical' or theological is suspect, and arguably leads him to downplay the strong political dimension of organicism, he advances a more nuanced and multifaceted understanding of the internal struggles of organicism than perhaps any other critic. My own work will explore in detail, and in context, what Krieger only mentions in passing: the internal tensions of this structure – including those between individual autonomy and totalising unity, and between full unity and mere balance – as they are evident in a wide spectrum of romantic texts and problems.

As Krieger accurately claims, his reading shows that 'De Man's continual and vehement rejection of an organicist romanticism rests ... on his own one-dimensional reading of organicism'.[24] This discovery should make it possible for there to be a certain kind of afterlife for romantic organicism in literary studies: it should, for one thing, facilitate a more informed investigation into the proximity of organicism and modern theory. Something of this kind is attempted by Kathleen Wheeler's *Romanticism, Pragmatism and Deconstruction* (1993), which refreshingly tries to answer the deconstructive critique on the home ground of romanticism. Embracing Coleridge as her 'higher guiding intellect',[25] Wheeler tries to demonstrate the continuity between the goals and intentions of romanticism and those of the modern theoretical movements of deconstruction and pragmatism. She makes valid points on the similarity between romanticism and modern theory in their attempt to transcend dichotomies of thought, and on their similar tendencies to imbricate the activities of literature and philosophy.[26] She is on less solid ground when she argues that Coleridge's organic concept of art

> has been poorly understood, especially in modern theory, as denoting something static and fixed, structural and final. On the contrary, the organic theory of art as expressed by Coleridge and Dewey denotes anything but fixity and finality: it constantly evokes concepts of growth and development, of change, life, movement, and relativity. ... Hence a work of art does not have fixed parts and a static whole or unity. It has the character of living things, things that are in growth, change, development: evolution without any final aim.[27]

Wheeler does not accurately portray the premises of the deconstructive critique of romantic aesthetics, part of which consists in precisely taking issue with the romantic predilection for organic vitalism. Since deconstruction's view of a limited metaphysical approach to the world includes a notion of infinity, it certainly cannot simply be side-stepped by mere gestures towards dynamic development. If Coleridgean organicism is undeniably dynamic and imbued with vitality, its lack of 'any final aim' is surely more open to question. A basic teleological tendency certainly lies at the heart of at least most of his thought,[28] and thus an Aristotelian heritage determines his thought far more than Wheeler allows for. If de Man underestimates organicism's inherent openness towards diversity, Wheeler thus overestimates it. Her exaggerated emphasis on the radicalness of Coleridge's organicism – which has recently been echoed by Seamus Perry[29] – even leads her to equate its *modus operandi* with that of Friedrich Schlegel. I will argue that, quite to the contrary, it is by comparing Coleridge's thought with Schlegel's that one can grasp how moderate his embrace of a pluralistic form of thinking really is.

My approach nevertheless echoes Wheeler's, in that my readings of German idealism, English romanticism and modern theory inform and relate to one another in what decidedly is a *comparative* approach. In an age where the desire for historical exactitude often brings about an unfortunately narrow-minded, and potentially obfuscating, focus on delimited time periods, I have opted for a relatively wide time span. My presentations of some of quandaries of modern theory (bringing in theorists of different nationalities) explicitly places these within the context of the romantic precedent, but the opposite influence – from modern debates on the nature of structure and language – of course equally inform my readings of Coleridge, Wordsworth, Schlegel and the idealists. The modern hermeneutical thesis that any interpretation is only made possible through its own historical embeddedness is, if necessarily subjected to endless negotiations and explications, nevertheless ineluctable.

If romanticism still matters, it is precisely because it is still not a closed and completed issue. Rather than pretending to have recourse to an objective historical depiction of some finished, bygone development, this study takes as its starting point a sense that the questions and texts of romanticism still concern us. Indeed, they still concern the basic manner in which we frame our understanding of past events and works of art. Hence romanticism cannot be exhaustively described from an external and simply objectifying manner, and modern theories of understanding, history and textuality cannot be said to combine in an unquestionable philosophical horizon from which romanticism can be interrogated. Quite to the contrary, modern theories are themselves implicitly or explicitly questioned by the thoughts and writings of, for instance, Schlegel and Wordsworth.

This is what gives the third and final part of this study its impetus: it questions the modern appropriations of organicism, whether they are simply dismissive or more amenable to its sway. Ultimately, of course, the thesis that interpretation cannot stand completely outside the ken of its object implies not only that modern theory in a narrow sense – for instance, in the guise of a supposedly specific and delimited 'literary theory' – is in play, but also that the entire ambience from which this study arises has had more than circumstantial effect in its genesis. Whatever gestures of delimitation and closure one makes, the outside will always have its say.

Part I

German Idealism and *Frühromantik*

2
Absolute Organicism in German Idealism: Kant, Fichte and Schelling

Kant and the question of the whole

One of the major concerns of the texts that are collected under the term of German idealism, as well as those classified as 'romantic', is their sustained attempt to formulate the question of the whole. The nature of wholeness or unity is scrutinised with considerable urgency, in a manner that is far from taking its meaning for granted. Indeed even the meaning of meaning itself is intertwined with this question, as is made clear in an exchange that occurs early in August Wilhelm Schlegel's fictional dialogue 'The Painting', published in 1799 in the *Athenaeum*:

> *Reinhold*: Every craft is blessed with a particular language that is provided with useful abbreviations [*nützliche Abbreviaturen*] in which one can quickly make oneself understood.
>   *Waller*: Unfortunately this specialised language is too often abused, so that one plays at being a connoisseur, while actually only proving that one knows one's alphabet.
>   *Louise*: The descriptions such glib, shoulder-shrugging connoisseurs give of the most elevated and divine matters, are in truth skeletons – images that are struck dead and subsequently hung up to dry in the vaporous store-rooms of their brains [*totgeschlagne Bilder, in der Vorratskammer ihrer dürren Köpfe in den Rauch gehängt*].[1]

The meaning of meaning is a whole, an entirety. To have a full grasp of language, one must not use words without knowing what they mean. It is possible to do so, but in that case one is not entirely in the land of the living – one's language lacks life, but instead becomes empty and skeleton-like.

Poor language lacks the spirit that informs the letter. The distinction between 'Geist' (spirit) and 'Buchstab' (letter) underlies the exchange between Reinhold, Waller and Louise. Indeed, it is a distinction that underlies much of the pre-romantic, romantic and idealist notions of what a whole is. A true whole has spirit, while that which is not a whole (or constitutes a counterfeit unity) lacks it. This is the simplest formulation of the opposition between organic and mechanical unities, and it represents the most elementary form of the idealist attack on the twin threats of British empiricism and French materialism. The empiricism of John Locke or the materialism of Julien La Mettrie is berated for lacking precisely a principle of a spiritual essence, which can give matter life. In the second 'Studierzimmer' scene of *Faust*, Mephistopheles satirises the blindness of scientists and scholars who do not confront this:

> To docket living things past any doubt
> You cancel first the living spirit out:
> The parts lie in the hollow of your hand,
> You only lack the living link you banned.[2]

The scientist who wants to describe a living being will only describe a pseudo-unity if he or she lacks the 'living link' which informs the matter of that being. Without that link, the unity of the being is guaranteed only by external measures, for example, the force of the grasping hand, and does not stem from an intrinsic interrelation. In addition to articulating the distinction between real and false unities, Mephistopheles' truism brings up another side of this question: it addresses the problem of the relation between the parts and the whole. A scientist will go amiss if the 'parts' are grasped in a wrong fashion – indeed he or she lacks the spiritual essence which would 'bind' (the German noun 'Band', used in the original, is related to the verb 'binden') the parts into a whole. That essence does not only *form* the parts, acting on them in purposive fashion; it *con-forms* them in an articulated whole.

Previously, I described the relation between the spirit and the letter as one of 'informing'. Now it evidently has the additional characteristic of being a linkage or act of conforming. But what do these terms mean? And do not wholes that lack a 'living link' in some sense constitute more authentic unities than ones that do, since the former are indeed made up by a single element (pure matter), while the latter are formed by a duality (matter and spirit)? Are not the 'skeletons' evoked by Louise in Schlegel's dialogue more complete than any living being can hope to be?

As shall presently be shown, these questions on the margin of life and death inform, link and rattle their bones in the texts of German idealism. The point of departure for German idealism is commonly situated in Kant's critical philosophy. The latter's Copernican turn, whereby intuition does not respond to the object, but rather 'the object (as object of the senses) must conform to the constitution of our faculty of intuition',[3] is of course an important spur towards the idealist attempt to explain objectivity as generated by the transcendental 'I'. More apposite to my concerns is, however, the way in which Kant's critical philosophy is on the verge of the idealists on the question of the whole.[4] The question of the whole addresses the very centre of idealism, in that it concerns the possibility of establishing a *systematic* philosophy. As has been demonstrated by influential readers such as Heidegger and Nikolai Hartmann, the desire for a system is a defining characteristic of the movement.[5]

This idealist will to system is in many ways anticipated by Kant. The latter considered the critical edifice to be a 'propädeutik', or preparation, for a more complete systematic metaphysics, and did not hesitate to suggest what principles would have to be present for there to be a finished and complete system. The delineation of these principles is to be found in one of the final chapters of the *Critique of Pure Reason*, namely in the third chapter of the transcendental doctrine of method, which has the heading 'The Architectonic of Pure Reason'. The elaboration of what later will become a romantic commonplace, namely the opposition between organic and mechanical unities, is the initial concern of this chapter. According to a practice that is repeated throughout his writings, Kant distinguishes between true systems and those collections of elements that are only aggregates or rhapsodical linkages. The prerequisite for the progress of true science lies, according to Kant, in scientific research being led by an idea. Without such a general, directing and comprehending idea, all knowledge is 'a mere fumbling about with fragments' [*nichts als fragmentarisches Herumtappen*], as it is put in the anthropology.[6]

Thus Kant's starting point is a pure opposition between the systematic and the fragmentary. But what defines the essence of the organic system, as opposed to the fragmentary conglomeration of elements? It is a question of metaphors. Due to the title of the chapter, one might suppose that 'The Architectonic of Pure Reason' would, as is quite common for Kant, have recourse to *architecture* as its primary tropological source. But it soon becomes evident that the 'Architectonic' chapter does not primarily sketch a conception of the nature of the system according to the metaphor of architecture. As with Vitruvius and Alberti, the specifically architectonic shows itself to be dependent upon another model – namely the organic relation. The system proves to be an organic entity, a 'system-creature' of sorts.

In Kant's initial definition of the organic system, no stance is taken with regard to the relation between the elements of the system. A system is quite simply 'the unity of the manifold modes of knowledge under one idea' (653 [A 832/B 860]). Here a hierarchical relation is propounded, where the manifold of knowledge is made to submit to a ruling idea – this is a structure governed by reason, as it is stated a little earlier. If the understanding is the faculty which organises a manifold of impressions in one unified knowledge (*Erkenntnis*) subsumed to a concept, then reason is the higher-level faculty which organises a manifold of knowledge (supplied by the understanding) under the rule of an idea. The ruling idea plays a constitutive role in establishing the system, and is therefore heterogeneous in relation to the elements that take their place within the system.

Added to this premise of a non-symmetrical or hierarchical organisation of the system, there soon follow two more defining characteristics:

> The unity of the end to which all the parts relate and in the idea of which they all stand in relation to one another [*unter einander beziehen*], makes it possible for us to determine from our knowledge of the other parts whether any part be missing, and to prevent any arbitrary addition, or in respect of its completeness any indeterminateness that does not conform to the limits which are thus determined *a priori*. (653 [A 832–3/B 860–1])

The ruling idea must not only subordinate to itself all the elements of the system; in addition it also has to organise them in a specific manner. This internal organisation is defined by both delimitation and interrelationship. The system of reason is thus based on three criteria: totalising unity, delimitation and interrelationship. These are the three limbs the system-creature stands upon, so to speak, and together they constitute a minimal definition of organicism that this study will constantly return to. Coleridge has famously stated that no simile runs on all four legs.[7] Now, the implicit question that the thought of idealism and romanticism will circle around is: can these *three* legs walk in time with each other? Or is the organic system-creature, even when it puts its best foot forward, no more than a hybrid or chimera containing incongruous parts?

I will suspend these questions for the time being. If one turns back to the previous quote one finds a definition of the limit, or border. Delimitation entails that a system can be clearly demarcated and separated from other proximate systems. The critical gesture *par excellence* lies, of course, in a severance or demarcation of one domain from another (the word 'critique' stemming from the Greek 'krinein', meaning to cut). Interrelationship – the relation Kant here calls *'unter einander beziehen'* – is illustrated by an example that possibly alludes to Winckelmann's famous interpretation of the torso of Hercules. Winckelmann claimed to be able to decipher the build of the entirety of the original statue, based on the evidence of the incomplete fragment that survived it.[8]

In Winckelmann's case, one can infer the look of, say, the absent face of the Hercules statue on the basis of its torso. But also the opposite movement – from, for instance, the head or the face to the rest of the body – must be hypothetically possible if the statue is to satisfy Kant's demands of an organic structure. One part of the structure cannot be completely dependent upon another part: both must be dependent upon each other. Here one encounters an important point that underlies the distinction between the idealist and romantic conception of the system, on the one hand, and classical models of organic unity, on the other. The latter models are largely based on causal or logical relations. In a departure from such an approach, Kant's thought contains the seed of a relation that is fundamentally ambivalent: every element is *both* active *and* passive in relation to every other element. This reciprocity is, of course, constitutive of the interlinking between receptive sensibility (passive) and spontaneous understanding (active) in the transcendental doctrine of elements in the *Critique of Pure Reason*. Nevertheless, the principle of interrelationship is only sketched in the 'Architectonic' chapter. The nature of the elements' standing 'in relation to one another' is not made fully explicit. This may be due to the fact that Kant has not yet come to a complete determination of what the singular essence of organicism is – this is a question that is more fully addressed in the later *Critique of Judgement*. In the latter work, one finds the relation expressed in terms of Kant's prevalent distinction between means and ends. In paragraph 66 he writes: 'an organized natural product is one in which every part is reciprocally both end and means' [*Ein organisiertes Produkt der Natur ist das, in welchem alles Zweck und wechselseitig auch Mittel ist*].[9] In an organic system, all the elements are thus both means and ends – the system has its circumference nowhere and its centre everywhere. A truly organic interrelationship is one of reciprocal interdependence.

Thus an outline of Kant's system has been established, based on its three criteria of hierarchical totalisation, reciprocal interrelationship and delimitation. Yet important questions remain to be asked. There is the question of range: what realms does this notion of systematic unity encompass? Where does it apply? And, more immediately, there is a question as to its viability: is Kant's notion of systematic unity coherent? Does it formulate the criteria by which an organic system can be identified, or does it, quite to the contrary, really provide one with the means by which one can interrogate and divulge a certain lack of coherence at the very root of organicism? For all is not as it should be. If the notion of organic unity rests upon the interaction of three different criteria, the nature of that interaction is still not revealed.

Indeed, the criteria may not even harmonise – they may be at variance with one another. This is demonstrated by the late definitions of the essence of organic entities that one finds in Kant's *Opus Postumum*. There the tension between the different criteria for organic unity causes a division of the concept. First there is a definition of the organic body in which the important point is that 'each of its parts, within a whole, is there for the sake of the other'. Then there follows an alternative definition, where it is stated that 'the idea of the whole precedes [*vorhergeht*] the possibility of its parts'.[10] Thus Kant first comes up with a definition based on the criterion of a reciprocal interrelationship, before subsequently providing another definition where the criterion of unified, hierarchical organisation comes to the fore.

A similar clash occurs in Kant's political philosophy. Lurking behind the formulation where it was stated that all the parts of an organic structure must be both means and ends, there is of course a fairly close link to Kant's practical thought. One of the formulations of the categorical imperative famously states that one should always treat a human being not only as the means of one's action, but also as its end. In the basic political system, in the state, this reciprocity can, however, come in conflict with that which gives the system its hierarchical unity. Kant's consternation at the beheading of Louis XVI leads to a theoretical dictum: no people can revolt against their own sovereign. For such a step to be possible,

> there would have to be a public law permitting it to resist, that is, the highest legislation would have to contain a provision that it is not the highest and that makes the people, as subject, by one and the same judgment sovereign over him to whom it is subject. This is self-contradictory ...[11]

Applied to the political realm, the organic system is thus threatened by revolutionary anarchy where the state would be without a governing power. Such an acephalic, guillotined organism strikes Kant as a monstrosity – on this point, his thought parts with that of Sade and, as shall later become evident, with that of Schlegel. Faced with the breakdown of the political system, Kant applies a logic of 'either–or'. The solution lies in privileging one of the legs of the system-creature over another: he chooses the criterion of hierarchical organisation, and discards the criterion of interrelationship. At the crunch, the peaceful coexistence of these two principles is thus demonstrated to be a makeshift solution, a compromise that cannot establish any permanent stability to the system.

A similar lack of stability unsettles the formulation of the precise nature of the *telos* of Kantian thought, that is, of moral freedom. Is moral freedom related to empirical existence, and if so, what is the nature of that relation? Kant's recourse to the terminology of causality in order to determine the influence of the intelligible on the empirical is, of course, proof of his quandary – since the realm of causality is precisely that which is to be transcended. His hesitation as to whether the moral law is grounded in something else, or whether it is an immediate centre in itself, derives from the structural ambivalence inherent in organicism: on the one hand, he needs an absolutely ruling principle, while on the other hand, that principle must communicate with the remainder of the system.

The result is that problems with regard to organic unity infect Kant's thought on moral freedom, as well as his thought on political organisations and natural entities. But what are the limits of such problems? And what, indeed, is the limit of the notion of organic unity in Kant's mature thought? The effects are, in fact, unlimited. Although the organic relation finds its full articulation only in the Third Critique, it has consequences that go beyond the particular context of that work. In the *Critique of Judgement*, organicism plays a familiar and important role: the organic view of nature functions, by virtue of teleological judgements concerning the ends of nature, as a bridge between the Newtonian, causally determined nature of the first critique and the kingdom of ends envisaged by the Second Critique. But organicism has an even more profound role to play for Kant's mature, critical system. The short chapter on 'The Architectonic of Pure Reason' speaks from an overarching vantage point encompassing *all* sciences, and from that position it also encompasses all philosophy, philosophy being described as 'the system of all philosophical knowledge' (657 [A 838/B 866]). Although there is an attempt to exempt the critical philosophy, in an almost surreptitious fashion, from the demand for systematic coherence,[12] there can be no doubt that the interrelationship between the three critiques forms a system of sorts: it is a teleological structure consisting of three elements (the three critiques), progressing from a fundamental element (*Critique of Pure Reason*) via a transitional element (*Critique of Judgement*) to a guiding, purposive element (*Critique of Practical Reason*).

The structure of the whole established by the critical texts is not, however, described by Kant as being an organic relation. In the preface of the *Critique of Judgement*, the organic relation yields to the metaphor of architecture: the Third Critique is constructed like a *bridge* over the abyss separating the two first ones.[13] This metaphor is significant in that it stresses the artificiality of the Third Critique: it is a construction which will not be part of the finished system of metaphysics, but which nevertheless is necessary if one is to avoid 'the ruin of all' [*den Einsturz des Ganzen*] (5 [VI]). Its superfluity for the metaphysical system demonstrates its emphatic subservience in relation to ethics and knowledge: it is neither the seed nor the fruit, neither the means nor the end of the philosophical endeavour, being instead an expendable (yet oddly necessary) supplementary construction in between. If one, in such a manner, takes Kant's pronouncements concerning the ethical bias of his thought seriously, this entails enforcing a strict hierarchical subordination between the roles of the three critiques. One of the criteria for constituting a system, hierarchical unification, is allowed to overrule another, namely the criterion of interrelationship. Schiller's influential stressing of the centrality of the aesthetic, as constituting the essence of the human in its blending of the sensible and the intelligible, can be understood in terms of an alternative stress on interrelation: that which articulates the system is seen as being more fundamental than the system's point of departure and final destination.[14] Another path is, of course, broached by the neo-Kantian stress on the epistemological basis to be found in the *Critique of Pure Reason*. There again, a hierarchical system is evident (granting the First Critique pride of place), by means of a reversal of Kant's own, ethically biased systematics.

The Kantianism one ends up with – whether it be an ethical one, an aesthetic one, an epistemological one, or something in between – is contingent upon what kind of systematics one chooses. This is the reason why any attempt at a reduction of the 'Architectonic' chapter to intra-critical functions, such as reducing the principle of hierarchy to being a subgroup of determinate judgements and the principle of interrelationship to reflective judgements, cannot hold water. The criteria for systematic unity found in the chapter do not form a bastard intermingling of functions found in the various critiques, it is rather those functions which are descendants (or 'mise en abyme' representations) of the all-embracing principles of systematic unity. Or rather they would be, if those overarching principles were not so obviously at odds with any simple thought of 'overarching': for if a conflict between the criteria of interrelationship and hierarchy is unavoidable, then all formation or conceptualisation of systematic unity will be in doubt.

Fichte and the limits of organicism

While Kant typically deduces a chaotic lack of cohesion as being the consequence of an empirical viewpoint, the idealists largely see *nothingness* as its effect. Thus they give the transcendence of empiricism a strictly platonic ring: the goal of philosophical meditation is to surpass the finitude and nothingness of temporality. If Schlegel's particular attainment, as will be shown, is to prove that the organic system cannot escape the fragmentation, then the early work of the idealists illustrate a different trap. They go full circle: if you escape from temporality, you will find beyond nothingness – nothingness again.

The nothingness of organicism is already present in Herder's thought. Together with the biological theories of writers such as Johann Friedrich Blumenbach and Arnold Gehler, and the general reaction to the early flittings of the industrial revolution, his work is one of the primary influences on idealist meditation on the nature of unity. For Herder, organic processes are distinctly temporal: according to a schema inherited from Aristotelian thought, the organism's *telos*, its goal or end, is seen as the beginning of – or even identical to – its death. Being perhaps the eighteenth-century figure who most thoroughly pursues this brand of historical organicism, Johann Gottfried Herder gives it the status of being a universal model which provides the rule for the development of mankind in general, as well as for other general phenomena such as nature, nations, families, art, and science. All these organisms share the same exemplary itinerary: they all 'germinate, produce buds, blossom, and wither away'.[15]

Yet neither Johann Gottlieb Fichte nor his friend and fellow philosopher Friedrich Schelling integrates this tragic temporality into their thought around 1800. In the platonic dialogue *Bruno*, it is precisely the transient nature of organic entities that provokes Schelling to a rare warning against a too complete identification between the nature of such entities and that of the absolute. Organic beings are perishable, he points out, while the absolute is not.[16] In his philosophy of art, Schelling qualifies such transience as being limited to the human realm, and thus implicitly excludes it from being relevant to the divine: 'all that is human, as soon as it has reached the summit in one direction, immediately begins to slide down on the other side'.[17]

In a gesture that anticipates later developments, the idealists will attempt to preserve the notion of the organic system, as it is tenuously handed down to them from Kant, and yet banish all of its connections with temporality. Their immediate touchstone for this transformation is the unclarified ambivalence of the relation between Kant's three critiques. Fichte sees his own thought as an elucidation of that of his predecessor, an elucidation which will precisely bring forth the systematic unity which Kant called for, yet never attained himself.[18] This is to be done while he underlines and strengthens the ethical tenor of Kant's thought, by insisting upon a hierarchical gradation of the faculties.

This particular feature of Fichte's thought is hardly original and not part of his singular contribution to the matter at hand. To describe the transformation the critical philosophy undergoes with Fichte, it is tempting to turn back to Kant's 'Architectonic' chapter and see how he describes scientific progress there. According to Kant,

> since sciences are devised from the point of view of some universal interest, we must not explain and determine them according to the description which their founder gives of them, but in conformity with the idea which, out of the natural unity of the parts that we have assembled, we find to be grounded in reason itself. For we shall then find that its founder, and often even his latest successors, are groping for an idea which they have never succeeded in making clear to themselves, and that consequently they have not been in a position to determine the proper content, the articulation (systematic unity), and limits of the science. (654–5 [A 834/B 862])

According to a traditional formulation inherited by Kant, scientific progress thus comes about by understanding a science even better than its originator did. Such an understanding comes about by one's grasping a central, organising idea which the founder of the science had a vague premonition of, but never managed to express. Such is the origin of Fichte's famous pronouncement that he follows the *spirit* of Kant's texts, if not their *letter*. In this case, the spirit is the conforming idea, the founding centre for the system of transcendental philosophy. It will establish the common ground for practical and theoretical reason, the meeting point of the noumenal will and the transcendental apperception, while at the same time establishing an interrelationship between the elements of the system.

As was the case with Kant's critical edifice, Fichte's project is to establish the foundations of reason, discovering the grounds of possibility for all reasonable activity. Fichte's own name for the system of transcendental idealism is the *Wissenschaftslehre*.[19] Philosophy is to become the science of sciences, an absolute founding of all scientific endeavour. It is perhaps somewhat surprising, though, that this primary, Fichtean science is *not* a subjectivism. Some overlapping with, for instance, René Descartes and Husserlian phenomenology had misled several interpreters on this score. Dieter Heinrich has shown, however, that Fichte's fundamental, and often overlooked, insight is that the subject–object relation cannot function as an absolute ontological basis.[20] Fichte dismisses the relation of consciousness, where a subject senses and thereby gains knowledge of an object, as being a conditioned and secondary relation. The same goes for the practical or pragmatic relation where an acting subject forms, or in some or another way uses, an object. In both cases it is the lack of unity, the lack of a systematic centre which is the problem, and therein lies the source for an irreconcilable dualism between subject and object. Interpretations of Kant which build on this and related dichotomies tend, according to Fichte, to reify the 'Thing in itself' – that is, they tend to overlook its purely negative and virtual status as a limit of experience – and thereby necessarily develop into a solipsistic subjectivism or into scepticism.

Thus the relation of consciousness leads to a division. The upshot of starting from the subject–object dichotomy is either that the subject is severed from the object, or that it leads to another result: a subject separated from, and unconscious of, those preconditions that provide the basis for the knowledge it gains of the object. For if subject and object are separated from one another, then the subject's access to the object must be mediated through a limited and instrumental relation. The subject must have a means, an instrument, by which to grasp and be conscious of the object. But the means themselves cannot be grasped. The thesis, made much of by the modern hermeneutical tradition, according to which an understanding being can never understand the horizon by virtue of which its own understanding has been made possible, is a variation over this idealist theme. One traditional way out of this problem is to call upon the phenomenon of self-consciousness, or the self's questioning of itself, as a solution. The subject becomes its own object. Such a solution might be appealing, yet it is ultimately flawed. For it only ends up moving the subject–object relation to a higher level. If a subject tries to understand the preconditions for the subject–object relation, there will inevitably arise a need to understanding the preconditions for *this* act, and so on *ad infinitum*. Thus an attempt, like that of Gadamer, to understand the historical nature of understanding in terms of such concepts as 'horizon', 'melting' and 'epoch', will necessarily demand an elucidation of the historicity, metaphorical nature and limitations of these particular concepts.[21]

Thus self-reflection cannot rid one of the subject–object split, as it reproduces it only on a higher level. Apart from occasional remarks, for instance in the popularising second introduction to the *Wissenschaftslehre* of 1797, Fichte seems to have had a clear sense that one cannot posit self-consciousness as an absolute ground. The most one can attain within the register of self-reflection is, according to Fichte, an infinite regression. This infinite regression is the essence of Schlegel's conception of irony, as Walter Benjamin demonstrated in his early dissertation on German romanticism.[22]

Fichte's fascination with this mechanism does not match Schlegel's, although it underlies the process of infinite self-determination which Fichte puts at the heart of his practical philosophy. This infinite *Bildung* must have an aim, though, a *Vorbild*, and in order to express it the subject–object dichotomy must be superseded. The manner in which Fichte transcends it is, however, very problematical. Here the idealist *topos* of the so-called 'intellectual intuition' has its place. Although Fichte uses this term less frequently than Schelling does in order to designate the transcendence of the subject-object relation, it does occur in his writings. For the most part it merely serves the negative function of indicating that the absolute is neither purely intellectual (i.e. a conceptual act stemming from the understanding) nor a mere intuition (a reception of a given sensory manifold). The term has a more positive descriptive value in its original, Kantian employment. For Kant, an intellectual intuition designates the act by which a reasonable being that is not finite *produces* its own object. This act of production is distinguished from what can be attained by finite and reasonable beings, such as humans: they necessarily *receive* objects as something *given* in an act of sensation.[23] Even if this does not fully account for the nature of Fichte's notion of the absolute, it does share one thing with the latter: the characteristic of self-positing. This characteristic, the *poiesis* of the absolute, will be of particular importance to the romantic determinations of the creative (rather than reproductive) imagination, which typically designate the poetical act as a reproduction of the absolute's production. Fichte is not satisfied with this, though. For insofar as the intellectual intuition constitutes a self-representation where the self becomes conscious of itself as its own object (as it undoubtedly does in Kant), it of course falls short of transcending the subject–object dichotomy.

In Fichte's case, this line of reasoning leads to the realisation that the phenomenon of the intellectual intuition doesn't explain organic unity: it is, quite to the contrary, the other way around. The intellectual intuition must, according to the *Wissenschaftslehre* of 1804, be understood in terms of a *'unity in duality'* and can therefore only be explained in terms of an 'inner organic unity of a necessary connection' [*innre organische Einheit eines nothwendigen Zusammenhanges*].[24]

Since the absolute must be understood in terms of organic unity, the entire problem of the ambivalence of the different criteria of the organic system resurfaces. Fichte's absolute (defined as the aim of all self-determination) plays the same role as the idea that hierarchically configures the whole does in Kant's organic system. From the very first, Fichte's thought takes an original and important turn by insisting that this central idea does not simply precede or establish the interrelationships internal to the system: it is also definitely marked by that interrelating. Reciprocity touches the centre. This happens from the first versions of the *Wissenschaftslehre*, even before his *explicit* endorsement of organicism in the *Foundations of Natural Right* (the *Grundlage des Naturrechts*) of 1797.[25] The criterion of interrelationship is applied to the founding centre that gives the system its hierarchical totalisation. If it were not applied, then the centre would simply be a forming principle, informing the pure mass of the elements, and one would have fallen back into the trap of the subject–object dichotomy.

Fichte's radical move, his transcendence of the subject–object relation, is thus intimately linked with his organicism. Now the organic system's criterion of interrelationship bears on the criterion of hierarchical organisation. And yet, even in Fichte's case, the coexistence of these two is not without its uncertainties and problems. This is demonstrated by his notoriously numerous rewritings of the *Wissenschaftslehre*, where he vacillates between different alternatives. On the one hand, apart from numerous lapses where self-consciousness is given an absolute status, there is the most well-known definition of the centre as an 'absolute I'. Even if the absolute I is not identical to the empirical 'I' – that is, the instance which faces and determines an object or 'Not I' – it is nevertheless implicit that the relationship between subject and object is resolved by a hierarchical movement. As in Hegel's dialectic, the absolute is a negation or an appropriation of nature. Hence there is no fundamental reciprocity, no real interrelationship, at the basis of the organic system.

On the other hand, though, Fichte wants to preserve a certain amount of reciprocity even in his definition of the absolute centre of the *Wissenschaftslehre*. In his early writings, he argues for his system's precedence over logic on the grounds that logic is purely formal, and therefore cannot explain or generate the content it is applied to. Differing from logic, the first principles of the *Wissenschaftslehre* have both form and content. The same tendency evinces itself in another fashion, when Fichte describes the absolute as a 'subject–object', using a rule between the connected terms in order to demonstrate their interconnection.

A complete interpenetration of form and matter is the limit of organicism. Fichte does not shirk the consequences of such an interpenetration. They are expressed with admirable lucidity at the very beginning of his career, in the 1794 version of the *Wissenschaftslehre*:

The absolute 'I' is simply identical to itself. Everything in it is one and the same 'I', and belongs (if it is permitted to express oneself so inappropriately) to one and the same 'I', wherein there is neither anything to distinguish nor any diversity. The 'I' is everything, and it is nothing – because *for itself* it is nothing [*das Ich ist Alles, und ist Nichts, weil es* für sich *nichts ist*], and can neither distinguish any act of positing nor anything posited in itself.[26]

Lacking the distinction between subject and object, between 'I' and 'Not I', the absolute is beyond all relations of comprehension or determination: thus it cannot be something *'für sich'*, for itself. Here one glimpses why Fichte not only calls the organic relation a reciprocal balance or a *'Wechselwirkung'*, but also – more radically – a *'Verschmelzung'*.[27] In the latter term, an undifferentiated unity is heralded which simply does not have any distinct elements to balance. The criterion of delimitation evidently must give way, if the criteria of hierarchy and interrelationship are fully deployed. In this meltdown into undifferentiated continuity, German idealism finds its final consummation, its dead end; everything is identical, everything is unified, and nothingness has annihilated nothingness. The attempt to avoid nothingness, by spatialising and detemporalising organicism, only serves to demonstrate that even a purely atemporal structure cannot avoid it.

The halfway house of philosophy: Between allegory and symbol

The conceptual preconditions for the organic unity of the transcendental system are thus laid down by Kant, and deployed by Fichte. Together they expose organicism to fundamental, and arguably fatal, problems. To a certain degree, one might say that the organism is *already dead* when it is handed down to the other idealists and romantics. Fichte and Kant have already revealed its dead end. Yet it will enjoy a multifarious and eventful afterlife: for this is by no means *the end* of organicism. However shadowy and insubstantial a creature it has revealed itself to be, the system-organism will enjoy considerable employment long after Fichte.

From the aporias developed by Fichte, I will now turn to the consequences for the problem of representation, as it unfolds in both Fichte and Schelling's writings in around 1800. The full complexity of their grasp upon this problem is understandable only through the prism of organicism, and it has escaped influential commentators such as Paul de Man and Andrew Bowie. Contrary to Bowie's reading,[28] it will be demonstrated that the symbolic mode is far from having unlimited dominance in Schelling's writings. As de Man has pointed out with regard to Fichte, one has to allow for a form of radical disruption – of allegory – in the idealist confrontation with the problem of representation. But this is not due, as de Man claims, to Fichte having a notion of the absolute as something linguistic.[29] Rather, the problem of language takes place only within the confines allowed it by organicism: language both represents and fails to represent the absolute, in an ambivalent relation to which organicism holds the key.

In order to approach this question, let us first return to the matter of nothingness: if the absolute is nothingness, where does that leave philosophy? From what vantage point can one gain a comprehensive perspective on the system desired by philosophy, if the centre of that system is a vanishing point? There is a variety of ways to confront this problem, and the idealist response to it is far from unequivocal. One of Fichte's more popularising works, *The Vocation of Man*, tries to avoid the issue by turning it into a struggle between epistemology and ethics. The text presents nothingness as the predicament of epistemology: the attainment of knowledge is said to be 'absolutely empty', a position which 'abolishes and annihilates all existence'.[30] The practical and ethical relation of acting upon the world is presented as being a higher, more advanced stage: 'we raise ourselves from this abyss and maintain ourselves above it, solely by our moral activity'.[31] But since the goal of mankind's ethical relation entails a domination of the natural world whereby 'all that pertains to sense vanishes into nothing',[32] the consummation of that relation would entail precisely the same lack of determination as that from which it tries to escape.

If ethical action merely is a deferral of the absolute, what about the act of philosophising, then? Fichte's writings are characteristically imbued with an unprecedented eagerness to grapple with the issue of philosophy's legitimacy and limits. The very first explication of his system, the brief *Concerning the Concept of the Wissenschaftslehre* which functioned as an advertisement for his first lectures at the University of Jena, is, in fact, more preoccupied with expressing the limits and preconditions for there being a *Wissenschaftslehre*, than presenting the system itself. The text demonstrates that the philosopher must always be caught by the ironies of all reflection (*Reflexion*) and representing consciousness (*Vorstellung*):

> we can be conscious of all the intellect's modes of activity (which are supposed to be exhaustively described within the *Wissenschaftslehre*) only in the form of representation [*Vorstellung*], that is, only insofar as and in the manner that are they are represented.[33]

Even if Fichte's thought is reflective and representational, 'it by no means follows that everything which is reflected *upon* is also nothing but an act of representing'.[34] Fichte's immediate purpose here is to distance himself from Reinhold's philosophy of consciousness. He is trying to defend the thesis, that even if the mode or medium of philosophy is consciousness, consciousness is not its object. But the ramifications hold good even with regard to his later writings: his texts and lectures can, at best, function as secondary copies of the system itself.

For can the philosopher, insofar as he or she exists in an empirical and non-absolute context, really claim to have access to the absolute centre of the philosophical system? The practical relation of determining and denying nature's given objectivity is possible only in the deferral of this abyssal ground. And in thinking and writing, the philosopher is involved in such a practical relation. Fichte is more consistently perspicacious than Schelling is on this issue. The latter identifies the task, the 'intellectual intuition' of the philosopher, as an act of reflection[35] – but as we have seen previously, self reflection is caught in the conditioned dichotomies of form and matter, subject and object.

Even if the philosopher must describe the absolute centre of the organic system, then, he must – for Fichte – situate himself in the position of heterogeneity and difference that is necessarily implied by his own distance from that centre. Thus a paradox, or at least what might sound like a paradox, becomes clear: organicism is far from precluding heterogeneity and difference. Quite to the contrary, it is precisely an insistent development of the workings of organic unity that leads to a strong emphasis on heterogeneity in Fichte's writings. Precisely because the absolute is a fusion of form and content, there is an insurmountable difference between it and the empirically existing subjects and objects. By insisting upon the criterion of interdependence, Fichte is forced to acknowledge the gulf existing between the empirical 'I' and the absolute. This acknowledgement takes place instead of another possibility, namely, a one-sided favouring of the criterion of hierarchical organisation which could lead to the degeneration of the absolute into an ideological idealisation of the empirical subject.[36] It is precisely such a development Fichte's contemporaries would seem to have been hinting at, when they gave him the nickname 'The great "I" of Oberlausitz'. But the empirical self cannot function as a symbol which manifests the universal in the individual, since the universal cannot be described as being a self which is related to an object by the relation of consciousness. Nor is the universal a dialogical relation of subjects – that is, a subject–subject relation – since all subjectivity implies an object. In Fichte's pithy words: 'no subject, no object; no object, no subject'.[37]

Ineluctably, this insistence upon the heterogeneity between the subjective and the absolute causes a series of fundamental problems. This is true, for instance, with regard to how the absolute *generates* subjectivity and objectivity, and even more pressingly so with regard to the self-reflective dimension of Fichte's own philosophising. For if philosophy makes use of concepts, and concepts (according to the tradition Fichte is writing within) establish a subject's determination of an object, then philosophy is by definition unable to express the absolute. Philosophy is caught in a trap which he memorably formulates as the attempt 'to comprehend what is absolutely incomprehensible, precisely as absolutely incomprehensible' [*das schlechthin unbegreifliche zu begreifen, eben als schlechthin unbegreiflich*].[38] The absolute cannot be expressed or grasped as an object, precisely because it is the precondition for the possibility of all objectivity. This denial of the continuity between the subject–object relation and the condition of its possibility will cause Fichte to favour an allegorical mode: the sensual expression of the absolute can never be identical with the absolute itself. In *Concerning the Concept of the Wissenschaftslehre*, he points out that however perfected the *Wissenschaftslehre* might turn out to be, there 'will always remain gaps to be filled, proofs which require improvement, and terms which have to be more precisely specified'.[39]

Schelling's originality, in this context, comes from choosing another strategy than Fichte's. He does not condemn philosophy to the same infinite self-determination that marks all reasonable activity, or simply preclude the absolute from all kinds of presentation. Rather, Schelling insists upon the fact that, if the given is given by the absolute, it must at the very least bear a trace of its origin. The difference between Fichte and Schelling lies – as Hegel pointed out in his *Differenzschrift* – precisely in how Schelling opens for the possibility of the empirical managing to express the absolute.[40] In a clear follow-up of Kant's Third Critique, the symbolic relation, where the universal and transcendental manifests itself in the particularity of the empirical realm, is applied by Schelling with regard to organic, natural objects and products of art. This hypothesis of an identity between the absolute and its diverse manifestations is taken to extreme lengths in Schelling's philosophy of identity in the first years of the 1800s, where all individual entities are posited as being *actually identical* to the absolute. Once this possibility is broached, idealism will always be able to embrace a certain degree of radical empiricism – much to the confusion of later commentators.[41]

Were Schelling's philosophy of identity to be fully implemented, it would entail one-sidedly favouring the criterion of interrelationship, to the demise of the criterion of hierarchical organisation. This position is, however, never fully implemented in Schelling's writings. The symbolic always finds it counterpart, if only intermittently, in tendencies towards annihilation, destruction or even 'deconstruction' of the finite and empirical.[42] Schelling thus also embraces a differential, or allegorical, relationship between the empirical and the absolute. At its most extreme, his notion of an absolute indifference – which also crops up at this time – implies such a negation of the given that it could, were it fully embraced, entail the destruction of all particulars.

This hierarchical strain in Schelling leads him to agree with Fichte in lamenting the fetters placed on philosophical speculation by language. For Fichte, language necessarily is 'the *expression of our thoughts through arbitrary signs*', and those – such as Herder – who have claimed that thought is impossible without such signs, have completely overestimated the role of language: 'Language has, according to my conviction, been given far too much importance.'[43] Schelling takes a similar stance. In the early *Of the I as Principle of Philosophy*, he claims that the great philosophers have had to fight with their language in order to express the supersensible. Even if he repeats this position elsewhere, a similar hesitation as that which was evinced with regard to allegorical and symbolical modes also comes across in Schelling's stance with regard to language. In *The Philosophy of Art*, it is precisely the capability of language to express ideas – the fact that 'the most appropriate symbol of the absolute or infinite affirmation of God ... is language'[44] – that enables him to place the verbal arts at the top of his hierarchy of the arts. As we shall see in the following chapter, Schelling is not alone in granting such a divine status to art. In Schlegel's hands, though, the potential monstrosity of the divine art will be fully unleashed, and the relations between philosophy, art, and religion will become far more problematical.

3
Prefaces to the New Gospel: Friedrich Schlegel and the Fragment

Revelations of the other: The mediator and self-sacrifice

There are close links between idealism and the phenomenon known in Germany as the *Frühromantik*. The latter term is primarily used to describe the writings of a circle of writers – including the Schlegel brothers, Dorothea and Caroline Schlegel, Friedrich Novalis, Johann Tieck and Friedrich Schleiermacher – associated with the *Athenaeum* journal in Jena, from 1798 to 1800. Both Fichte and Schelling had close contacts with the group, and they also had considerable influence on its thought. In the following chapter I will try to close in on Friedrich Schlegel's theory of the fragment dating from this period, primarily by looking at its relationship to the absolute system-organism of idealism. The fragment will not prove to be a simple denial of the system, but rather a more inclusive operating of the manifold of possibilities evinced by the preconditions of the system. Simplifying somewhat, one might say that the fragment embodies the system's dispersal from within.

In this respect, Schleiermacher's polemical tract called *On Religion* (1799) is instructive as a contrast, since it fits better with the image of Schlegel often prevalent among outsiders, than Schlegel himself does. Schleiermacher, like all the writers influenced by organicism and Kant's Third Critique, is primarily interested in finding a means of accessing an absolute state of unity. He distinguishes two opposite tendencies in mankind, that is, two antagonistic drives:

> The one strives to draw into itself everything that surrounds it, ensnaring it in its own life and, wherever possible, fully absorbing it into its innermost being. The other longs to extend its own inner self ever further, thereby permeating and imparting to everything from within, while never being exhausted itself.[1]

These centripetal and centrifugal forces represent little more than a version of the idealistic dichotomies of the receptive and the spontaneous powers of the subject (mirrored, on another level, by the opposition of 'I' and 'Not I'), tendencies which Fichte ascribed to the theoretical and practical powers of reason, respectively. Schleiermacher differs from that tradition in one significant detail: he is not primarily interested in seeking for a reconciliation of the two tendencies in the faculty of the transcendental imagination. The fusion of the two is not explained philosophically, but rather taken for granted. 'Religion' is the name he gives the fusion of theoretical and practical reason, a fusion that nevertheless stands outside the theoretical and practical realms, as something heterogeneous to them which grants them their direction.[2] The heterogeneity of this realm does not, however, mean that it is completely inaccessible: certain individuals can achieve initiation into its secrets. Such an individual is a mediator (*Mittler*) who subsequently functions as an example to be followed by others.

Religion thus manifests itself in the intersubjective realm, in a peculiar form of *socius* – this is indeed a precedent for Emile Durkheim's later version of an absolute *sociologism*. This stress on collectivity is not without precedent in Jena romanticism, for instance in Schlegel's writings. There is a pervasive recourse to *Geselligkeit* – that is, sociability or conviviality – as the means for the *Bildung* of the absolute, and this recourse resonates with the definition Fichte gave, on one occasion, of the God as being identical with the congregation (the *Gemeinde*). A fulfilled, collective humanism – the vision of which of course represents a central part of romanticism's often underestimated inheritance from the Enlightenment – is identified with the absolute. Here it represents a singular form of the general problematic of presentation or *Darstellung*, the quasi-manifestation of the absolute, which we have already encountered in idealism – it is also an important parallel to the metaphysical interpretations of intersubjective relationships that I will later trace in Wordsworth and Coleridge. Accepting one-sided and individualist misrepresentations of the development of idealism, readers of English romanticism have tended to overlook how close the similarities are between the latter and their German contemporaries on this question.[3]

Let me return, though, to Schleiermacher and *On Religion*. According to a hardly inconspicuous play on words, the mediator not only provides a mediation between a person and the absolute, but does so by virtue of having attained the mediate position (*Mitte*) which fuses the two basic drives. In Schleiermacher's treatise, the mediator represents a particular transformation of the priest, but typically of German theology inspired by the Pietists this is a *private* priest, who executes 'a private affair' [*ein Privatgeschäft*] (90),[4] and thus operates outside all institutionalised forms of community. He also operates without recourse to scripture: no ontological primacy is granted to any sacred book in this religion, since any 'holy writing is merely a mausoleum of religion' (50). Such are the limitations of the 'dead letter', that it can only give access to a 'weak reproduction' [*schwacher Abdruck*] of the unique reality of that religion (ibid. [68]).

Schleiermacher places particular emphasis on the singularity of the private relation involved here. He claims that every true religion is formed by a foundational intuition (*Grundanschauung*) of the unified cosmos, but that every such intuition must necessarily be unique. Furthermore, the connection of that intuition to a systematically organised dogma is, even if it constitutes a necessary stage, always at variance with its essence:

> Intuition is and always remains something individual, set apart, the immediate perception, nothing more. To bind it and to incorporate it into a whole is once more the business not of sense but of abstract thought. The same is true of religion, it stops with the immediate experiences of existence and action of the universe, with the individual intuitions and feelings; each of these is a self-contained work without connections with others or dependence upon them; it knows nothing about derivation and connection, for among all things religion can encounter, that is what its nature most opposes (26).

The reason for this breach between the centre of the religion and its subsequent systematisation is not completely explained by Schleiermacher. Here Friedrich Schlegel, Schelling and Fichte are really more lucid, in their understanding of the paradox of the absolute, despite their far more positive approach to the organism-system. For the many invectives against system-builders in *On Religion* cannot conceal the fact that Schleiermacher's vision is indeed a systematic one itself, based on an ideal of an organically united whole. Both the structure of his ideal community and his intuition of the universe as a living unity cannot be comprehended except in terms of the absolute system-work. The individuality of the *Grundanschauung* thematises an irreducible empiricism dogging all access to the absolute, but this aspect is – as we have seen earlier – a commonplace of idealism.

Thus Schleiermacher's thought is profoundly systematic, but unconsciously so, and, despite its own pretensions, it does little more than repeat Fichte and Schelling on this fundamental point. Schlegel's singular contribution will be to take a more subversive turn, exploring the margins and problems of the system rather than claiming to escape it altogether by way of a leap of faith. Schleiermacher nevertheless has a large influence on the latter figure, in how he replaces the sublime as a privileged access to a revelation of the absolute with an intersubjective scenario following the same mechanism.[5] Like the sublime object, the mediator grants access to the absolute, and, as in the case of the sublime, this experience subsequently shows itself to be 'a passing condition. A person should then see with his own eyes and should himself make a contribution to the treasure of religion' (50). The mediator's role is only preparatory, and is soon replaced by a more personal kind of experience.

Evidently, even the revelation through a mediator cannot do without the stigma of the inessential that is the hallmark of all representation: here Schleiermacher's conventional critique of writing as being 'a weak reproduction', cited above, cannot really provide means to privilege the intersubjective realm over the mediation of the book. Indeed, in the description of the Christian Bible, in the fifth and final speech of his treatise, Schleiermacher does not entirely dismiss the possibility of a book functioning as what he calls (alluding to the *logos* rather than to the discipline of logic) 'a logical mediator' [*einen logischen Mittler*] (121 [170]). What would seem to call for such a movement is the fact that the manifestation of the absolute through the mediator is not, in Schleiermacher's thought, an everyday occurrence. It is certainly not facilitated through the event of everyday language, through 'common conversation', but rather through 'all the effort and artistry of language' (74). In its artistry, the Bible has the means for something at least approaching a mediating and elevating form of communication.

Friedrich Schlegel confronts this problematic in his collection of fragments entitled *Ideas*, where he draws widely and explicitly upon Schleiermacher – describing, for instance, Fichte's teachings as 'religion in the form of philosophy'.[6] Schlegel goes further than Schleiermacher does, by simply identifying the mediator's role as being that of an *artist*. Even a clergyman is an artist:

> The priest as such exists only in the invisible world. In what guise is it possible for him to appear among men? His only purpose on earth will be to transform the finite into the infinite [*als das Endliche zum Ewigen bilden*]; hence he must be and continue to be, no matter what the name of his profession, an artist. (*Ideas*, no. 16)

The artist has the formative power – the power to form (*bilden*) the conditioned to the absolute. One of the most significant manners in which this can be done is through literature – and a new Bible.

The figure of the mediator acquires new characteristics in Schlegel's *Ideas*. Schlegel differs from Schleiermacher in stressing the auto-destruction of the *Mittler*, in a way that causes the sublime to be equated with self-sacrifice. A need to draw out the implicit negativity in Schleiermacher's text is already evident in Schlegel's earlier review of *On Religion*. There he claims, in a sweeping and unmistakably impish vein, that the significant points of Schleiermacher's treatise consist in presenting a case for 'the impossibility of presenting religion, the purely negative view on the divinity, the necessity of mediation, and the naturalness of melancholy'.[7] There is negativity in Schleiermacher's text from the very beginning. But insofar as the latter's version of the mediator states that the effect of negativity is only a 'passing condition', only the initiate who is affected by the absolute *via the mediator* is deemed to embody something provisional. Negativity is, one might say, but a passing phase.

Schlegel goes further than this. In his version, the transitory nature of the surrogate object is integrated into its very being and is not merely part of its reception: the mediator is someone who 'perceives the divinity within himself and who self-destructively sacrifices himself [*sich selbst vernichtend preisgibt*] in order to reveal, communicate, and represent ... this divinity' (*Ideas*, no. 44). Another fragment states the same point in a more polemical vein: 'The artist who doesn't sacrifice himself completely is a contemptible slave' [*Der Künstler, der nicht sein ganzes Sein preisgibt, ist ein unnützer Knecht*] (*Ideas*, no. 113).[8] This self-destructive imperative is adumbrated in the 131st of the *Ideas*, where it is stated that it is the vocation of the artist to commit self-sacrifice. For the 'annihilation of the finite', also called 'enthusiasm of annihilation', is the 'hidden meaning of sacrifice'. This sacrifice is not seen as something inherently Christian, as in Schelling, since it here is linked to the Roman Decii and, beyond that, refers to the Greek practice of 'consecrating oneself to the gods of the underworld' (*Ideas*, no. 131). Apart from practising a typically romantic reinterpretation of primitive ritual, Schlegel is – to put it crudely – playing a Fichte to Schleiermacher's Schelling here. He is stressing the heterogeneity (and thus the principle of hierarchical totalisation) rather than the symbolic connection (latent in the principle of interrelationship) between the given and its absolute precondition.

On the other hand, a more inclusive approach which comprehends a *plurality* of forms of mediation – not only through intersubjective pedagogy, but also, as we have seen, through artistic means – is a hallmark of Schlegel's appropriation of *On Religion* in *Ideas*. This is also evident in how he responds to Schleiermacher's denial of that nature can function as a mediator to the absolute. In Schleiermacher's scheme of things, intersubjectivity is given precedence over any relation to nature or the world in non-subjective form,[9] and consequently all natural religion is dismissed as inessential. Schlegel's follow-up to this move is ambivalent. The *Ideas* vacillate, at times seeming to preclude any mediation via nature, and on other occasions straightforwardly insisting upon it. One fragment, for instance, states that direct access to the absolute is impossible, but that there nevertheless exists a privileged form of mediation:

> We cannot see God but we can see godliness everywhere [*Gott erblicken wir nicht, aber überall erblicken wir Göttliches*] – first and foremost in the heart of a thoughtful man, in the depths of a living human creation [*eines lebendigen Menschenwerks*]. Nature, the universe, can be felt and conceived of without mediation: but not God. Only a man among men can write divine poetry, think divine thoughts, and live religiously. (*Ideas*, no. 44)

This passage is ambiguous, to say the least. It starts off by claiming that the absolute is in itself inaccessible and only available through a mediation that passes through *all* things: 'everywhere'. Yet it would seem that the immediacy of the experience of nature is what precludes it from being a true mediator: the absolute is accessible only by indirect means. Schlegel seems to imply the Kantian distinction between the immediate intuition and mediate concept here: one can approach the absolute only where some mediate instance beyond the given, and sensibly available, manifold is present as a spiritualising and formative power. The latter force would only be granted through an encounter with a human *Mittler*.

It would seem, then, that Schlegel endorses Schleiermacher's privileging of the human, of *Menschheit*. The next fragment insists that if one seeks a 'vital centre', the centre that binds the whole into the indivisible unity of a true individual, then one should seek for it 'only in ... another man' (*Ideas*, no. 45). And yet, as we saw above, 'we can see godliness everywhere'. A counter-movement is therefore possible, and indeed it does occur in the 47th of the *Ideas*: 'God is everything that is purely original and sublime, consequently the individual himself taken to the highest power. But aren't nature and the world also individuals?'[10] In the fragmentary tension of these mutually contradicting sentences, it becomes evident that not only mankind and art, but *perhaps* also nature, provide a step beyond – neither subjectivity nor objectivity has any unconditional claim to precedence in relation to what is beyond both subjectivity and objectivity.

This plurality of routes to the absolute is the grounds for Schlegel's own summing up (in 'Literature', an article published in 1803) of the second half of the *Athenaeum* as mainly having consisted in 'the forceful defence of the symbolic *forms*, and their necessity, against the profane mind'.[11] A manifold of forms, all representing divergent and singular approaches to the absolute, are allowed to coexist. The same article differentiates this later stage of the *Athenaeum*'s activities from an earlier one, in which 'criticism and universality' were the main ends.[12] In order to facilitate an understanding of this earlier phase, and what one might call the *fragmentation* of the absolute, I will now turn to some of Schlegel's earliest publications.

The two systems: Organicism and history in Schlegel's early philology

In his pre-*Athenaeum* writings dating roughly from 1794 to 1797, the contrast between the ancient and the modern is a central concern for the young Friedrich Schlegel. At this stage he is primarily a scholar of antiquity, specialising in literature. As Winckelmann revolutionised the study of ancient painting and sculpture, it is Schlegel's ambition to lay a new, innovative foundation to the investigation of classical *literature*. The manner in which he goes about to attain this objective does not, however, consist in a simple transfer of Winckelmann's methods. Although there is a large debt to the latter's holism, it is quickly integrated in, and surpassed by, Schlegel's distinctive preoccupation with the nature of systematic structure. This is evident in the latter's main work of the period, the characteristically ambitious and unfinished tome called *The Greeks and Romans* (1797). There the unearthing of a connection between the political and the artistic realms among the Greeks leads to a reflection on the essence of the common, structural unity which brings them together: 'The art, customs, and states of the Greeks are so intimately interwoven, that knowledge of these things cannot separate them from one another. And in general the Greek formation of character [*die Griechische Bildung*] is a whole, in which it is impossible to gain completely proper knowledge of any single part on its own.'[13]

To grasp this whole, one must fastidiously follow a critical methodology. The Kantian heritage becomes apparent, when Schlegel warns against a scientific endeavour not starting from a unifying principle: research that is oblivious to the 'necessary laws of formation of art' [*notwendigen Bildungsgesetze der Kunst*] is inevitably forced to 'grope in the dark, and have no guide to allow it to infer the unknown from the known' [*im dunkeln tappen, und keinen Leitfadem haben vom Bekannten aufs Unbekannte zu schließen*].[14] One has to proceed in Schlegel's prescribed manner because of the *organic* structure of the object to be studied – as such, it is unlike the mechanical agglomeration that is modern poetry. The literature of the Greeks is a '*beautiful organisation*, where even the smallest part gains the necessity of its existence and freedom through the laws and aim of the whole'.[15] Not only is every part of the whole free, an independent unity in itself, but also the structure of the whole is delimited and closed upon itself. Thus one has a structure that follows the Kantian prerequisites for an organic unity. It has a hierarchical centre (the laws of formation, or '*Bildungsgesetze*', mentioned above), and is also characterised by the principles of mutual interrelationship and delimitation.

Not only is the literature of antiquity such a unified whole – so is every authentic work of art. In a characteristic passage, which anticipates Wordsworth's famous dictum 'We murder to dissect', Schlegel denounces the 'critical anatomist' who analyses the work only in terms of its parts (its 'elementary bulk' [*elementarische Masse*]). Such an approach does not really lead to an analysis of art, 'for the work of art no longer exists' after such treatment.[16] Strictly speaking, though, the perfect work of art does not even exist *prior* to analysis. The Greeks only reached 'a conditioned, *relative maximum*' – art in general is 'infinitely perfectible and an absolute maximum is not possible for its constant development'.[17]

In this notion of an infinite progression, one can detect a Kantian understanding of history that rescues Schlegel from a stolid and reactionary classicism. Yet history is not simply to be described as following a straight line of enhanced perfection, for Schlegel also entertains a myth of the

Fall of sorts. Even the *relatively* perfect work of art is, at this stage of his thought, only a thing of the past. The relative peak of the ancients has been replaced by a faulty, modern literature: 'In the strictest sense of the word, not even a single modern work of art has reached the peak of aesthetic *fulfilment.*'[18] According to a theme that has its particular variations not only in Schlegel, but also in Schiller and Hegel, modern literature's predominant subjectivity upsets the perfect balance characteristic of the works of antiquity. Rather than postulating, *à la* Schiller, an infinite progression towards a higher fusion of the subjective and the objective, or a Hegelian *Aufhebung* of art through philosophy, Schlegel's strategy in *The Greeks and Romans* is to call for an aesthetic revolution 'through which the objective [*das objektive*] would become dominant in the modern'.[19]

As in Schelling's later philosophy of art, the complete work of art is a work to come, a work surpassing the precedents of both classicism and present modernity. And yet, according to the logic of Schlegel's thought, even such a work could only represent a *relative* perfection. Schlegel's historicism relativises the prospect of his own revolution. His endorsement of a potentially crippling historicism is evident in the fact that he not only wants to grasp antiquity as an organised whole (for instance, through a taxonomy of genres); he also wants to grasp the past as an organic development *in time*: 'just as the organic seed fulfilled the circular course of its formational drive through constant evolution – grew happily, blossomed lushly, ripened quickly, and withered suddenly – so too every poetical mode, every age, every school of poetry.'[20]

One might suggest, then, that Schlegel's problem is that he wants to embrace *both* Herder *and* Kant. He explicitly praises Herder's writings in a note to this text, citing how they 'in general beautifully defend well-considered experience against one-sided reason'.[21] Yet, at the same time, his recourse to *Kantian* precedents and methodology is tangible throughout. While Herder presents a temporally unfolding process that can potentially be radicalised into the eternal repetition of the same, Kant provides him with a simulation of perfection, the spatialisation of the organism. Schlegel himself is somewhere between these two. Thus we have the outline of a exceedingly familiar tale of time versus the atemporal, or historicism versus transcendental idealism.

Things are not, however, quite that simple. For in another text of this period, 'On the Value of the Study of the Greeks and Romans' (1795–96), Schlegel's divided loyalties do not reveal themselves by the endorsement of two different views (one historical and one ahistorical) on the object of his criticism. Quite to the contrary, two different *histories* – two different versions of temporal unfolding – are the upshot of his vacillation. Both are explicitly designated as systems: on the one hand, there is 'the system of the circular course' [*das System des Kreislaufes*], and, on the other, 'the system of the infinite progression' [*das System der unendlichen*

Fortschreitung].[22] The development of Greek art is described as being circular (reaching extinction in the achievement of its *telos*), while modern art follows an entirely different trajectory of unending development. The latter is derived from Kant's notion of infinite perfectibility, based on an imperfect saturation of the form (stemming from the realm of freedom) in its matter (the empirical world), while the former follows a structure of complete saturation more in keeping with a strand of Herder's thought.

The difference between these two structures (a difference Schlegel declares not to be absolute, but which he has no means to bridge) does not lie in that one is temporal, while the other is not: *both* represent development in time. Their opposition stems from what one might call the question of saturation or formation. While infinite perfectibility includes an element of reserve whereby the heterogeneity of form and matter (spirit and time-bound empiricism, respectively) is never *completely* suspended, the other structure is terminated by the complete informing of matter. In other words, the structure of modernity preserves an element of hierarchy whereby form never becomes one with its object, while that of antiquity entails a complete interrelating of the two. This is of course also, as Schlegel points out, an economy of desire: the 'satisfaction' and 'complete pleasure' of the ancient works are contrasted with the reserve of modern writings which 'take more than they give'.[23]

Hence the struggle is not simply between the historical and ahistorical, but rather between two different deployments of organic unity. One of these systems is rooted in a radical notion of interdependence, while the other is strictly hierarchical. All of this happens on the limits of organicism. There can be no doubt that Schlegel inherits the basics of conception of an organic whole: his conception is, as we already have observed, a structure based on the principles of hierarchical totalisation, interrelationship and delimitation. In this he is far from original, but a singular awareness of the inherent tensions in this conception is what quickly jettisons Schlegel beyond the less conscious founderings and equivocations typical of Kant and the idealists. Ultimately this awareness will lead to the paradoxical workings and unworkings of the fragment, during the early stages of the *Athenaeum* journal. Yet already in 1796, in two texts that have been relatively neglected, it provides a vantage point for decisive and illuminating interventions into politics and poetics. As I will now show, these texts stage a confrontation with Kant, on the subject of republicanism, and a confrontation with Aristotle concerning the nature of the epic.

The polyp and the fiction of the sovereign: Schlegel on poetics and politics

In effect, the view of history Schlegel inherits from Kant in his early writings is like that of an unsolvable plot – a plot that is an organic whole, and yet, due to the particular inflection organicism acquires in the eighteenth century, lacks a real ending. The plot of history has an *end*, a purpose (*Zweck*), which rules its unfolding, and yet there is no possibility of achieving that end through the actual unfolding of time.

Having this view of history's plot at hand, and being a classical scholar, it is perhaps inevitable that Schlegel takes another look at Aristotle's *Poetics*. It is an encounter that takes place in the essay 'On the Homeric Poetry' of 1796. The immediate cause for this text is F. A. Wolf's epoch-making philological work *Prolegomena ad homerum* from the previous year, where Wolf argues that the *Iliad* and the *Odyssey* are in fact collective products of an oral tradition.[24] Indeed, the subtitle of Schlegel's essay is 'In Consideration of Wolf's Investigations'. Schlegel's main concern lies elsewhere, though. After an introduction on the changing role of the poet in ancient Greece, he criticises Aristotle's scant writings on the nature of the epic plot. He finds fault with the author of the *Poetics* for having projected the plot structure of the tragedy onto the epic poem. Schlegel claims Aristotle has overlooked the fact that the epic has its own singular manner of unfolding:

> Unjustly he demands of the epic poem the presentation of a fulfilled action, and believes – or wishes, rather – that he can find this in Homer .... Thus he becomes for thousands of years the inexhaustible source for all the fundamental misunderstandings that stem from confusing the tragic and epic modes with one another.[25]

There is no resolution in the plots of Homer, 'but a thoroughly undetermined and thus infinitely progressing expectation of sheer fullness [*bloßer Fülle überhaupt*]'.[26] Still, every point of the epic narrative 'simultaneously includes tension and satisfaction'.[27] Evidently, this is only a *relative* satisfaction, which nevertheless does not rule out, at the same time, that 'every incident is a member of an infinite series [*einer endlosen Reihe*], the result of prior events and the seed of future ones'.[28] The originality of this scheme stems from its superimposing, in a manner quite equivalent to the view of history that we discussed above, a structure of immanence onto a structure of infinite progression.

If Schlegel's conception of the epic plot were only to be read in light of its immediate context, as an original interpretation of the Homeric epic, it would represent little more than a curiosity, since the scarce references to Homer are hardly compelling. The essay becomes more interesting when viewed as a rigorous application of radical organicism to the workings of plot. Aristotle's teleological plot structures are unashamedly hierarchical structures, based on his metaphysics. The resolution, or *lysis*, of the plot is, in his understanding, the teleological completion and apex of a process; it is the point at which form has completely saturated content. Schlegel's alternative structure is a result of the idealist and pre-romantic rebellion against the abstract separation of form and content, which we elucidated in Kant and Fichte. If there is a more thorough informing of form and matter, then there cannot be a single centre to the plot. It must be imbued with an equal amount of its end, of its formative goal, at every stage of the process. Ultimately this leads Schlegel, as we have seen, to the concept of the *series*. Every part of the series is at the same level, every part of the plot-organism has an independent value as an end in itself. Or, as Schlegel puts it, finding some relevance in Aristotle's passing remarks, if not in his overall conception of the epic:

> He very aptly remarks that the *Iliad* and the *Odyssey* contain several parts that are *independent wholes in themselves* [*für sich bestehende Ganze*]. For the epic poem is, if I may express myself in such a manner, a poetical polyp [*ein poetischer Polyp*] where every small or large member (which can be separated without mutilation or disintegration from the matured whole into simple, and no longer poetic or epic, components) has a life of its own, and indeed even as much harmony as the whole.[29]

This conception of narrative structure will also inform Schlegel's later reading of a modern novel, that is, his interpretation of Goethe's *Wilhelm Meister's Years of Apprenticeship*. There, the organic structure of the work is precisely what will legitimatise isolating one single part: 'where everything is at the same time both means and end, it would not be wrong to regard the first part, irrespective of its relationship to the whole, as a novel in itself'.[30] In a broader context, his use of the metaphor of the polyp in the above quote is significant. Being an organism that can be divided infinitely and yet survive as new, separate organisms (separate animalcula), it represents an apt figure for the monstrosity that can be evoked by a radicalised form of organicism. Once the principle of interdependence is taken seriously, it contains the seeds of an uncontrollable proliferation of independent parts. One is not far from the fragment here. The paradoxical status of the parts of the polyp – being fragments, as parts of a whole, and yet nevertheless complete in themselves and hence separable from the whole – already contains the germ, so to speak, of the fragment as it is conceived of in Schlegel's later, more widely read texts.

Before I look at those texts, though, the matter of politics must be addressed. We have already observed that Friedrich Schlegel's understanding of antiquity made no strict separation between poetics and politics. Indeed, the first version of *The Greeks and Romans* granted politics an absolute status encompassing all other realms.[31] In an early text such as 'On the Limits of Beauty' (1794), political freedom and cultivation of the arts are explicitly linked, and the basis of political freedom is formulated in a manner which is directly inherited from Kant's ethical vision of a kingdom of ends. Thus the perfect state is said to consist of a community where there is 'a public love, where everyone finds an infinite and reciprocal pleasure in one another'.[32] A distinctive shift is evident in the use of the word 'love' rather than the more Kantian 'respect', a shift manifesting the influence of Schiller's criticism of Kant in 'On Grace and Dignity' (1793). But the important aspect here, in this context, is the founding of collectivity in a relation of mutuality. The relationship between 'free humans' is one of 'reciprocity' [*Wechselwirkung*].[33] Even if Schlegel at this point endorses a radical republicanism, this relation of reciprocity is implicitly supplemented by a hierarchical principle that suffuses organic structures and supplies their parts with vitality.

The manifestation of this hierarchical principle in the political realm is, according to a peculiarly Schlegelian twist, always *provisional*. In that sense it works, in principle, in the same manner as modern art – which is merely 'interesting' art in its subjective and mannered singularity, and not a full representation of the absolute. As Schlegel puts it: 'But always what is interesting in poetry only has a *provisional validity* [provisorische Gültigkeit], like a despotic government.'[34] Both despotic government and modern poetry represent unbalanced systems, where the lack of a reconciliation between form and matter, coupled with the need for a certain formative and linking power, results in provisional structures which are only makeshift solutions while one waits for the arrival of the absolute organism.

The provisional authority of the ruler of any political structure is the main point by which Schlegel, in the essay 'Attempt on the Concept of Republicanism' (1796), attacks Kant's forays into political philosophy. As we have observed, the clash between the king and the insurgent movements within the population of France provoked Kant to declare that no sovereign can be legitimately dismissed by its people. Faced with the aporia of an irreconcilable clash between the manifestation of the hierarchical grounding of the political organism, on the one hand, and the principle of the mutual interrelationship between the members of that organism, on the other, Kant chose to unconditionally embrace the forces of hierarchy. Schlegel cannot live with this and argues for a more flexible solution. He points out that a temporary state of lawlessness can be a legitimate option, since every sovereign is a necessary but nevertheless *fictional* representative of the general will. For, according to what one might note is a distinctly Kantian logic, there is no real manifestation of the absolute in the ruling power, prior to the complete (and yet infinitely remote) fulfilment of the kingdom of ends:

> The individual and the general are always separated from one another by an infinite abyss, which one only can cross by a mortal leap [*einen Salto mortale*]. Nothing else is possible here, than by way of *fiction* to allow an empirical will to count as a *surrogate* for the a priori thought, and absolutely general, will; and since a real solution to the political

problem is impossible, one must be satisfied with the *approximation* of this practical 'x'.[35]

The ruler is only an expedient fiction, only a representative, and when the conflict between the general will and the sovereign becomes obvious, there must be a clause in every state constitution that allows for a dismissal of the sovereign. Revolution is allowed when the empirical fiction of the republic differs too emphatically from its idea. Such a revolution is only a temporary measure, and is therefore legitimate, unlike the *permanent* state of being without a sovereign (which Sade endorsed at this time). The latter is denounced by Schlegel as being 'a spurious and *permanent insurrection*; for the genuine and politically viable one is necessarily transitory'.[36]

In effect, the Schlegelian modification of Kantian republicanism comes down to the importation of a new measure: the transitional. As we have seen, the provisional surrogate for the absent absolute is not a phenomenon that is restricted to the political dimension of Schlegel's writings. The classic work of art is, for instance, deemed to be a necessary, but nevertheless relative, manifestation of an absolute that cannot really manifest itself at all. Further on, beyond the horizon of Schlegel's text, this phenomenon relates to the sublime object and to the simulation of the absolute in the philosopher's act of self-consciousness: all these manifestations of the absolute, of the centre of the system-organism, are, in a sense, fictions. The fictional nature of the centre is due to the fact that it is *necessary* according to the principle of hierarchy, and yet *impossible* according to a strict deployment of the principle of mutuality. It is a compromise solution, and like all compromise solutions it inevitably risks becoming biased: it risks no longer managing to defer the imbalance which it is constructed to avoid. The potential imbalances of the political realm are addressed in 'Attempt on the Concept of Republicanism', when Schlegel points out that there are two different, yet possible, political poles of republicanism:

> In republicanism there is, to be sure, only *one* principle of the political fiction, but there are *two* different *directions* of this one principle. In their widest possible divergence these do not only constitute two pure types, but also two opposing *extremes* of the republican constitution: the *aristocratic* and the *democratic*.[37]

The workings of the organic system-structure open, of course, for considerable leeway as to how one is to confront this compromise. In the quotation above, one can envisage a balance – a golden mean. But a more complete unity, a fusion rather than a balance, can also be called for. Thus in a later context, in an *Athenaeum* fragment, Schlegel will echo Novalis and state that the perfect republic 'would have to be not just democratic, but aristocratic and monarchic at the same time'.[38]

The fragment and the new Bible

The texts scrutinised so far in this chapter – Schlegel's early, philologically and politically-oriented texts – provide an important context for understanding how his later concern with the fragment in Jena is inherently related to a meditation on the foundations of the system-organism.[39] One finds an early reference to fragmentation in the most surprising of places. In Schlegel's essay on the place of woman in ancient Greece, 'On Diotima' (1795), woman's lack of philosophical prowess is defended in terms which address themselves to the contemporary rage for systematic philosophy in Germany. The spirit of the system is not identical to philosophy, claims Schlegel, it is only a part of what in general characterises the specifically philosophical. Furthermore, one shows good sense – a kind of intellectual probity – by not endorsing the desire for complete systems, and rather indulging in the lyrical gift which he claims to be inherent to femininity:

> As long as the uniquely true system has not been revealed, or as long as it has only been imperfectly presented, the systematic procedure remains more or less divisive and isolating. Philosophising in a lyrical manner, devoid of systematic coherence, at least does not ravage the whole of the truth quite so much.[40]

So long as the system is not complete, all versions of it will be biased infringements upon the true unity. Such a view no doubt smacks somewhat of an idle dilettantism, since it seems to be abrogating responsibility for what, after all, might be construed as being a both possible and necessary task. Yet is it really possible? When one takes into consideration that Fichte, as we have observed earlier, explicitly states (in 1794) that philosophy – due to inescapable aporias – will *always* have more work to do, that it will always be trying to catch up with an unachievable absolute, then the non-systematic approach no longer simply represents an easy way out. Rather, it represents an attempt to show restraint rather than arrogance before an impossible exigency.

This probity, tied to an insistence on the necessarily provisional and incomplete nature of all thought, is one dimension of the theory of the fragment as Schlegel later deploys it. The fragment bears witness to the absence of the system, the absence of the book which would contain the whole. Thus it represents a sceptical critique of all philosophy's ideological pretensions to the absolute, a logical insurrection: 'As a temporary condition skepticism is logical insurrection.'[41]

But the fragment does not simply amount to being a sign of incompleteness. Schlegel's approach to the system is insouciantly paradoxical, both endorsing and dismissing it concomitantly. If all systems have a flaw, a necessary particularity that undermines their pretensions to universality, it is nevertheless true that the piece or individual always has a tendency towards totalisation in itself. As Nancy and Lacoue-Labarthe have pointed out, 'the fragment both is and is not System'.[42] It is, as we have seen, not system, namely, it signals the postponement and tarrying in the space of the system's absence. In addition, though, it is *also* the fulfilment of the system. In this second characteristic it is like the symbol (or rather: it *includes* the symbol, although there is no complete dialectical *Aufhebung* here), as it is envisaged by Schelling and Goethe, and later by Coleridge. For the fragment is a projection of 'the real form of universal philosophy' [*die eigentliche Form der Universalpoesie*],[43] the universal poetry – according to the famous 116th *Athenaeum* fragment – being the romantic form which will comprise both modernity and classicism. All the fragments work together in order to form the comprehending system. Thus the fragments of the Jena group constitute an objective equivalent of the subjective 'system of fragments' evident, for instance, in memorabilia.[44]

In other words, true fragments can be construed as being fragments *for* the system, building blocks for an as yet unfinished edifice. But their existence is not only devoted to being members of the grand 'dialogue' which makes 'a chain or garland of fragments'.[45] For they also have a separate individuality of their own. Schlegel's famous comparison between the fragment and a hedgehog humorously brings this dimension forth: 'A fragment, like a miniature work of art, has to be entirely isolated from the surrounding world and be complete in itself like a porcupine.'[46] As a small work of art, the fragment is a microcosm – not a mirror of the world, but a world in itself, albeit in diminished dimensions. Having both separate value as organic wholes, as well as contributing to a larger and more comprehending whole, the fragments constitute perfectly formed works: 'A work is cultivated [*Gebildet*] when it is everywhere sharply delimited, but within those limits limitless and inexhaustible; when it is completely faithful to itself, completely homogeneous, and nonetheless exalted [*erhaben*] above itself.'[47] In following this double logic of autonomy and heteronomy, the fragments are identical to what Schlegel, in a typical cross-fertilisation of the poetic and political, calls a republican form of speech. This latter kind of speech is 'a speech which is its own law and end unto itself, and in which all the parts are free citizens and have the right to vote'.[48]

According to an inherent tendency, then, the fragment is thus both a unit that is part of the all-encompassing whole, and a monument to the absence of the whole. If the former dimension of the fragment entails a seed towards completion, a step forward in what might be called the pilgrimage towards the system-temple of the absolute, then the latter dimension entails a resistance towards that progression. The structure is akin to that which Schlegel himself finds, in an earlier text, in Herder's fragments: 'The "for" and "against" in the fragments is sometimes similar to the gait of a pilgrim, who goes three steps forward and then two steps backwards.'[49]

The unresolved coexistence of these two modes is an uneasy one, and would be unbearable to Hegel, but is in consonance with the duplicitous logic which I have shown to be at work in Schlegel's pre-*Athenaeum* writings. Another name Schlegel gives this mode of writing is *wit (Witz)*: he writes that there is an 'architectonic' form of wit which 'has to be properly systematic, and then again it doesn't; with all its completeness, something should still seem to be missing, as if torn away'.[50] Wit is a form of the productive imagination, the capability to link elements into a larger whole, which yet stops short at grasping the whole.

A further complication must be added: the fragment is not only the instantiation of the system and its incomplete prelude – it is also its subsequent parody. If authors, like all organic entities, 'sink into obscurity after reaching their greatest heights',[51] then this is also true of the system-organism. This movement will later be developed by Bataille and Blanchot in their conception of the writing which comes after the completion of the whole.[52] In Schlegel, one catches sight of it in his defence of Aristophanes in 'On the Aesthetic Value of Greek Comedy' (1794). There comedy is defended as being the genre of completion: in a perfect state (Kant's kingdom of ends) all wills will be free and there will be no negativity to overcome. Tragedy will no longer have any function to play in such a society. A new, true comedy will become the central genre:

> Thereupon pure joy, without the additive of evil that now is necessary for comedy, would have enough dramatic energy in itself. Comedy would be the most perfect of all poetical works of art, or rather, the ravishing would take the place of the comical and would, when it first existed, endure forever.[53]

Remnants of this divine comedy are to be found in one of the Lyceum fragments, which describes the moment of *Witz* not as movement of combination, but rather as the explosion subsequent to the synthesis of imagination.[54] Another fragment states more pithily that 'Wit is an explosion of confined spirit' [*Witz ist eine Explosion von gebundnem Geist*].[55]

Only by way of an understanding of multiplicity of the fragment, and its manner of engaging and dispersing the system-organism, can one approach Schlegel's particular conception of the absolute work of art. In this conception, he follows a tradition in German idealism, initiated by Lessing's call for a new gospel, where one tries to conceive of a new and secular form of Bible. We shall later see this tradition having consequences in British romanticism, too. In a German context, Schlegel here enters into a dialogue with Schleiermacher, which we already have touched upon. He is also very close to Schelling, who very closely links art and religion at the time.

Just like Schelling, Schlegel views the absolute work of art as coming about as a result of an encounter between art and philosophy. Also like

Schelling, he does not provide an unequivocal view of how art and philo
sophy should relate to each other. But there are differences between the
two of them. Whereas Schelling first gives precedence to art in the *System of
Transcendental Idealism* and *Bruno*, and then goes on to declare the sovereignty of philosophy in *The Philosophy of Art*, Schlegel never comes to such
clear-cut decisions. While the former changes his views from work to work,
the latter seems change *his* within a matter of pages.

This becomes evident if we return to Schlegel's *Ideas*, and their dialogue
with Schleiermacher. The *Ideas* polemically ignore the reservations of
Schleiermacher in *On Religion* with regard to sacred books, envisaging
instead a great system of books manifesting the absolute. For Schlegel, this
system is organised in the same manner as the totality of the texts of classical literature. Although the latter collection of texts comprise a diverse
manifold of works, they still

> form an organic whole [*bilden ein organisches Ganzes*], they constitute,
> properly viewed, only a single poem, the only one in which poetry itself
> appears in perfection. In a similar way, in a perfect literature all books
> should be only a single book, and in such an eternally developing book,
> the gospel of humanity and culture [*das Evangelium der Menschheit und
> der Bildung*] will be revealed. (*Ideas*, no. 95)

The same fragment points out that 'Even what we now call the Bible is
actually a system of books'. This reference to the Bible demonstrates that
for Schlegel, the issue is not – as for Schleiermacher – whether the holy
scriptures of Christianity, or of other religions, are to be granted an
absolute status or not. That issue has become irrelevant. Instead Schlegel
devotes himself to what he considers a more pressing concern: what will
the nature of the new, absolute literature be? If it is to include all purportedly 'profane' works, as well as the entire system of classical literature,
how is it to constitute an elevated unity?

Schlegel's actually seems to put this question to rest even earlier, in 1798,
in the first batch of fragments published in the *Athenaeum*. There, the Bible
is compared to the person who becomes a king, but makes a far more inept
king than private citizen: 'Can we say the same of the Bible? Is it also just
an admirable everyday book [*liebenswürdiges Privatbuch*] whose only fault is
that it should have become the Bible?'[56] In another fragment, reference is
made to Lessing's call for a new gospel, *the* book of the Enlightenment,[57]
and Schlegel playfully juxtaposes such a work with Kant's most famous
text: 'According to this ideal, what book is more fit to be chosen by the
philosophers for their bible than the *Critique of Pure Reason*?'[58]

Although some philosophers, even today, might be inclined to take this
last question at face value, Schlegel is obviously poking fun at the pretensions of philosophy. For him, as indeed also for Schelling during this

period, the absolute work of art cannot be a purely philosophical work. It must fuse philosophy and literature. This fusion can be attained in vastly different ways, though. One of them follows Schleiermacher's example: in the *Ideas* a proto-dialectic is envisaged, whereby the fusion of two different entities will produce a higher, and third one, which will comprehend and yet supersede both its constituents. The task would appear to be a simple one: 'Join the extremes and you will find the true middle.'[59] The extremes to be fused are identified as philosophy and poetry, the former being an 'idealism' while the latter is a 'true realism'.[60] As long as they are not fused, 'there still is no religion'.[61] The two of them are really 'depending on one's point of view, different spheres, different forms, or simply the component parts of religion' [*je nachdem man es nimmt, verschiedne Sphären, verschiedne Formen, oder auch die Faktoren der Religion*].[62] This stance was already latent in one of Schlegel's *Athenaeum* fragments preceding Schleiermacher's *On Religion*, which envisaged there being something 'Divine' which is 'higher than any poetry and philosophy'.[63] But another of the *Ideas* complicates matters by suggesting another relationship between the three fields or spheres: 'Whoever has religion will speak in poetry. But to seek and find religion, you need the instrument [*Werkzeug*] of philosophy.'[64]

Schlegel presents a similar view in a later article entitled 'Literature'. In a gesture that inverts Schelling's demoting of art to the role of an *organon* or instrument for philosophy, he gives poetry the pride of place:

> *Poetry* will be the centre and goal of our meditations. For that is precisely the position we believe it occupies the whole of art and science. Even philosophy is only an organon, or a method to establish the genuine, i.e., divine, mode of thinking [*doch nur Organon, Methode, Konstitution der richtigen, d.h. göttlichen Denkart*] which constitutes the essence of true poetry. Thus philosophy is only an educational establishment, a tool, and means [*Bildungsanstalt, Werkzeug und Mittel*], for what poetry is in itself.[65]

Poetry is the goal of philosophy, its end, if one is to believe Schlegel here. Yet it is hard to make this statement cohere with the complex set of positions we have already encountered. For although the relationship between literature and philosophy thus is a constant concern in Schlegel's writings of the *Athenaeum* phase, his stance is profoundly unstable.

What is recurrent is that philosophy is in a state of lack. Fichte's *Wissenschaftslehre* is described as being one of the three (together with the French Revolution and Goethe's *Wilhelm Meister*) 'greatest tendencies of the age'.[66] In the original (and usually overlooked) draft of the passage, though, he adds that all three are 'tendencies without a thorough execution'.[67] Schlegel is not taken in by the feint by which the philosopher's intellectual intuition would provide a crowning monument of a general edifice incorporating all other spiritual activities and sciences. He does not endorse Fichte's occasional claim, that the intellectual fuses the practical and the theoretical and thereby grants access to the absolute precondition for both these realms. Instead, the intellectual intuition is denigrated for being a narrowly *theoretical* concern: 'The intellectual intuition is theory's categorical imperative' [*Die intellektuale Anschauung ist der kategorische Imperativ der Theorie*].[68]

Once the categorical imperative and the intellectual intuition are seen to be only similar to one another, rather than united, the philosopher no longer has immediate access to the absolute. Indeed, Schlegel finds the typical philosopher wanting, precisely because of his inability to *de facto* achieve the transcendental position which is sought: 'Every philosopher has his impulsive moments that frequently are real limitations for him, and to which he accommodates himself, etc.'[69] This lack means that philosophy can be *characterised* – its individuality can be clearly criticised and delimited from without. According to Schlegel's essay 'On the Essence of Criticism', the task of such characterisation belongs to the critic. The latter must describe the 'precise peculiarity' of the philosopher's system, and the 'movement and articulation' [*Gang und Gliederbau*], that is, the diachronic development and synchronic articulation, of his thought.[70] Uniting history and philosophy, criticism thus incorporates them both into a higher viewpoint. Schlegel does admit, though, that this objective is 'not easy', indeed there is 'nothing harder'.[71] One of the *Athenaeum* fragments simply states that 'one can never be too critical'.[72] An act of criticism, or the work of a critic, cannot therefore be said to *complete* that which is in fact a necessarily incomplete process. In addition, the process of criticism can be integrated into other activities – for instance, into art.

A few years later, on the other side of the English Channel, an adamant follower of German thought will develop his own idiosyncratic blend of art, philosophy and self-characterisation. His name is Samuel Taylor Coleridge, and his great, though inevitably unfinished, achievement has the title of *Biographia Literaria*. Is the latter work related to, or even a manifestation of, the fragmentary as conceived of by Schlegel? This is one of the questions I will turn to in the next chapter.

Part II
English Romanticism

Part II

English Romanticism

4
Organic Vagaries: Coleridge's Theoretical Work

Keeping things whole in *Biographia Literaria*

Commentators of Coleridge's *Biographia Literaria* (1817) have to a large degree been divided between adulation and contempt – between awestruck admiration for the way in which the work lays the foundations of a philosophically informed criticism, on the one hand, and scathing criticism of how those same foundations are borrowed, and at times simply stolen, from earlier German sources, on the other.[1] What seems to have not been fully comprehended, though, is how Coleridge displaces and selects from those German precedents. This displacement is related to his gradual transition from pantheism to a relatively dogmatic form of Christianity – a transition authoritatively explored by Thomas McFarland.[2] But other displacements have been ignored. In this chapter I will home in on one in particular, by providing an elucidation of how Coleridge largely suppresses the radical consequences of the organicism of German idealism.

The fragment disappears when organicism makes its journey across the English Channel. It is expunged from the organism of thought, repulsed from within like a malevolent virus, which has invaded, and subsequently been turned back by, the defensive forces of thought. This immunising repulsion is almost completely tacit, almost completely withdrawn from the surface of Coleridge's discourse. Yet its ramifications are as consistent as they are wide-reaching. Those ramifications can be witnessed in strategic places in his texts, like the occasionally recurring symptoms accompanying a life-long struggle against a dormant disease.

The importance of organicism for the *Biographia Literaria*, one of the classics of English literary criticism, is an established fact. Indeed, Walter Jackson Bate has noted its ubiquity in all of Coleridge's critical work:

> The concept of organicism pervades every aspect of his practical criticism – language, idiom, metaphor, semantics, larger problems of form and genre; the psychology of the 'creative imagination', of taste, of

sensibility; the relation, in the drama, of expression to character and of both to over-all structure ...[3]

In the *Biographia Literaria* organicism is manifest in the pervading interest in the unification of opposites. It is present from the early references to how Bowles' sonnets 'reconciled the heart with the head',[4] through the exploration of metre's 'interpenetration of passion and of will',[5] to the grand theme of the unification of philosophy and poetry. Even the dichotomy of imagination versus fancy that informs the whole book – arguably through the dual focus of philosophy (volume I) and practical criticism (volume II)[6] – is essentially reducible to an application of the opposition between organism and mechanism to the mental faculties. Fancy's passivity, its inability to do more than 'receive all its materials ready made from the law of association',[7] entails that it can be no more than an 'aggregate power'.[8] This construction of unorganised totalities is contrasted with how the active imagination always 'struggles to idealize and to unify'[9] impressions into organic wholes. In addition, the imagination 'dissolves, diffuses, dissipates, in order to re-create'[10] in manner which is in harmony with the development of temporal organisms. The distinctively literary use of these faculties is explored in the second part of the *Biographia*. There imagination is described as 'the power of reducing multitude into unity of effect, and modifying a series of thoughts by some one predominant thought or feeling'.[11]

One of the clearest anticipations of this use of organicism as the hallmark of a well-constructed work of art, is to be found in Coleridge's 'Essays on the Principles of Genial Criticism' (1814). These essays are heavily marked by Coleridge's admiration for Kant's Third Critique. Their most succinct definitions of beauty show that imagination's aesthetic role consists in creating a beautiful (and organic) unity. Coleridge suggests that the 'most general definition of Beauty' is 'Multëity in Unity'.[12] A more expansive definition reflects more closely the Kantian roots of Coleridge's thought at this juncture:

> *The sense of Beauty subsists in simultaneous intuition of the relation of parts, each to each, and of all to a whole: exciting an immediate and absolute complacency, without intervenience therefore of any interest sensual or intellectual.*[13]

Although the style is unmistakably Coleridgean here, both the terminology and general gist of the argument are far less exclusively so. Kantian influence is evident in the emphasis on epistemology ('intuition'), disinterestedness ('complacency') and the renunciation of sensuousness.

Within a wider context, Coleridge's conception is not even all that distant from the very first known instance, in the history of Western thought, of an organic definition of artistic unity. This first definition belongs to Plato's dialogue *Phaedrus*, in a passage that is significantly vague. A fine discourse, Socrates states,

> must be organised, like a living being, with a body of its own, as it were, so as not to be headless or footless, but to have a middle and members, composed in a fitting relation to each other and to the whole.[14]

Here Socrates does not explain exactly *what* the relation between the parts, and between the parts and whole, should be. The vague call for a 'fitting' relation in no way excludes something like the purely mathematical 'golden section', where a line is divided in such a manner that the shorter segment has the same relation to the longer section as the longer section has to the whole. But since this kind of relation is purely mathematical, rather than based upon a relationship of ends and means, it is more characteristic of classicist poetics than romantic organicism.

How romantic is Coleridge? Does his notion of organicism easily concur with the traditional, classical precedent, or does he, on the contrary, approach something like the explosion of organicism explored in Jena romanticism? If one returns to the *Biographia*, one finds Coleridge gesturing to tradition in precisely the spot where he makes explicit his preference for a conservative form of organicism. This occurs in the second part of the book, in the elucidation of the ideal poetical form:

> The philosophic critics of all ages coincide with the ultimate judgement of all countries, in equally denying the praises of a just poem, on the one hand, to a series of striking lines or distichs, each of which absorbing the whole attention of the reader to itself disjoins it from its context, and makes it a separate whole, instead of an harmonizing part; and, on the other hand, to an unsustained composition, from which the reader collects rapidly the general result unattracted by the component parts.[15]

There have been few critics more 'philosophic' than Friedrich Schlegel, and yet the first class of poems mentioned here seems akin to Schlegel's conception of the fragment. As we have seen, the theory of the fragment was derived from a thorough meditation on the limits of organic form. The monadic self-sufficiency of every part of an organic whole was precisely what opened for Schlegel's famous comparison of a fragment to a hedgehog and 'a miniature work of art'.[16] It also provided the logic for his reading a separate part of *Wilhelm Meisters Lehrjahre* as a complete work in itself.[17] Are such examples reducible to the logic, described by Coleridge here, of 'absorbing the whole attention' in a manner in which 'disjoins' from 'context', making a 'separate whole, instead of an harmonizing part'? And does not Coleridge's conviction, expressed in the *Biographia*, that the

'fairest part of the most beautiful body will appear deformed and monstrous, if dissevered from its place in the organic Whole',[18] express a view
directly contrary to the German's positive evaluation of the fragment?
Perhaps – yet Coleridge's language is sufficiently vague to force one to defer
judgement for the time being.

One might be tempted to interpret Coleridge's scepticism towards too
independent parts as stemming from a suspicion of too hierarchical structures. If a part becomes isolated, it may overshadow the remainder of a
structure. Yet the evidence for Coleridge's allowing for, indeed insisting
upon, hierarchy is very strong. Later on in the *Biographia*, for instance, one
is told that '*all* the parts of an organized whole must be assimilated to the
more *important* and *essential* parts'.[19] The distinction between the 'important' and 'essential' parts and those of lesser significance shows the unbalanced nature of Coleridge's organic whole.

The suggestive term of 'keeping' is repeatedly introduced in the
Biographia, as a means of explaining this structure. A distant relative of the
Heideggerian notion of 'gathering', it demands some scrutiny. In one of
the final addenda to the *Biographia*, in the third of 'Satyrane's Letters',
Coleridge comments on a view of the German town of Ratzeburg, where
the 'rich light ... not only was itself in harmony with all, but brought all
into harmony'.[20] This unified prospect of the town is described as being
'perfectly beautiful, and the whole [was] softened down into *complete
keeping*, if I may borrow a term from the painters'.[21] The problem of the
harmonising of parts is also crucial to Coleridge's discussion of poetry. In
his discussion of Wordsworth's poetry, one of the deficiencies of the verse
of Coleridge's friend is said to be 'incongruity' or 'the sudden superiority'
of one passage over one connected with it. In order to describe a more continuous style, Coleridge again compares poetry to painting:

> the business of the writer, like that of a painter whose subject requires
> unusual splendor and prominence, is so to raise the lower and neutral
> tints, that what in a different style would be the *commanding* colors, are
> here used as the means of that gentle *degradation* requisite in order to
> produce the effect of a *whole*.[22]

The effect of a whole is here presumably created because an unnecessarily
uneven structure, where some colours would be 'commanding', is avoided
and instead replaced by a more balanced structure where there is only a
'gentle' form of degradation. In such a slightly unbalanced structure, the
degraded elements are 'raised' almost to the level of the dominant ones. A
certain equality is also suggested in Coleridge's first use of the word
'keeping', which occurs early in the second part of the *Biographia*, in a discussion of the possible introduction of heterogeneous materials to a work
of poetry:

In short, whatever *specific* import we attach to the word, poetry, there will be found involved in it, as a necessary consequence, that a poem of any length neither can be, or ought to be, all poetry. Yet if an harmonious whole is to be produced, the remaining parts must be preserved *in keeping* with the poetry; and this can be no otherwise effected than by such a studied selection and artificial arrangement, as will partake of *one*, though not a *peculiar*, property of poetry. And this again can be no other than the property of exciting a more continuous and equal attention, than the language of prose aims at, whether colloquial or written.[23]

Coleridge's emphasis on the words 'in keeping' alerts us to the fact that there is more at stake here than merely the convenient usage of a conventional phrase. The non-poetical is *in keeping* with the poetical, when they are subjected to 'selection' and 'arrangement': both a process of exclusion of unfitting material and an internal organisation of the elected materials is needed. The internal organisation is a hierarchical one, as the non-poetical elements must be adjusted to the poetical ones, in a manner anticipatory of Russian Formalism.[24]

The absolute book: Coleridge on Wordsworth and the Bible

One of the major ironies of the *Biographia Literaria* is, of course, that it denounces the fragment in the very act of manifesting it. Some commentators have sought to circumvent this problem, arguing for the organic unity of the work, but Coleridge himself did not dissimulate the incompleteness of the text. In the famous fictional letter written to himself, which interrupts the thirteenth and final chapter of the first part of the work, he tells his alter ego: 'You have been obliged to omit so many links, from the necessity of compression, that what remains, looks ... like *the fragments of the winding steps of an old ruined tower*.'[25] At this point one can catch a whiff of Coleridge's suppressed, or unconscious, involvement in the kind of radical organicism explored by Jena romanticism. Yet where Friedrich Schlegel, as we have seen, consistently granted the necessity of the provisional, Coleridge will always choose another path. In the *Biographia Literaria* he admits the makeshift character of his reflections, but claims to present the perfected system 'if God grant health and permission ... in a work I have many years been preparing'.[26] The deferred work referred to here is Coleridge's *Magnum Opus*. It will never actually be completed, and this fact of course throws some ironical light on Coleridge's constant references to the possibility of an absolute work. Yet the irony is offset somewhat by the fact that those references never draw their weight and authority *exclusively* from the imminence of the *Magnum Opus*. Even if all Coleridge's writings are written, as it were, in the shadow of its unfinished monument, the neighbouring edifices of Wordsworth's *Recluse* project, and the Bible, often supersede the *Magnum Opus* as paradigmatic expressions of the absolute.

The odd coupling of *The Recluse* and the Bible at this juncture comes down to Coleridge's variations on the theme of the absolute science. In his persistent search for a new absolute work, combining literature and philosophy, his thought here paves the way for Wordsworth's ambitious poem. The precedent of the German idealists and their search for a similarly absolute work certainly anticipates Coleridge's thought on this matter. Later on, I will look into how Coleridge conceives of this matter in *The Philosophical Lectures*, where the fundamental relation is between philosophy and religion. In the *Biographia Literaria*, he is at a transitional stage: philosophy is finding a new partner or wrestling mate. The text is heavily marked by his early, teutonically inspired, search for a marriage between philosophy and literature. If Wordsworth is proclaimed as being 'capable of producing the FIRST GENUINE PHILOSOPHIC POEM',[27] this is of vital importance. For poetry is both the epitome of philosophy and its wedded partner:

> No man was ever yet a great poet, without being at the same time a profound philosopher. For poetry is the blossom and the fragrancy of all human knowledge, human thoughts, human passions, emotions, language. In Shakespeare's *poems*, the creative power, and the intellectual energy wrestle as in a war embrace. Each in its excess of strength seems to threaten the extinction of the other. At length in the DRAMA they were reconciled, and fought each with its shield before the breast of the other.[28]

Coleridge is implicitly proposing that Shakespeare is the precursor for Wordsworth's imminent reconciliation of the poetical and the philosophical. Yet Shakespeare does not function as an exclusive touchstone for the canon, as he will later become for Harold Bloom.[29] Shakespeare is only one example, albeit an important one, among the many to be summoned by Coleridge as instances of great historical role models for the philosophical poem. An added twist is supplied by the fact that, for Coleridge, philosophy is not fully self-identical and therefore constitutes a problematical component in this ideal fusion. For, ultimately, 'philosophy would pass into religion, and religion become inclusive of philosophy', according to one of the more cryptic comments towards the end of the first part of *Biographia Literaria*.[30]

Thus it seems as though the combining of religion and poetry is at stake here, rather than the marriage of philosophy and poetry. If one were to follow through such reasoning, it would not be the works of Shakespeare, but rather the Bible that would represent the absolute of literature. Indeed one finds Coleridge making something like such a claim earlier on in the

Biographia Literaria: 'To give the history of the bible as a *book*, would be little less than to relate the origin or first excitement of all the literature and science, that we now possess.'[31] The Bible's original value, in this quote, *may* be read as simply consisting in its historical priority, that is, as being the first real book of knowledge and literature. Such an interpretation is favoured by way in which Coleridge qualifies his argument with the words 'or first excitement'. Yet Coleridge also seems to have wanted to grant the Bible an *ontological* priority, an ahistoric validity as an infallible source of revelation.[32]

This transcendental priority of the Bible acquires more of an overt articulation in Coleridge's later works, but it surfaces even in the *Biographia Literaria*. Here one finds his ambitious *Magnum Opus* described as being written 'with, and as the introduction to, a full commentary on the Gospel of St John'.[33] It seems safe to infer that this pronouncement implies that the utmost a philosophical disquisition can attain, is to become an instrument to the meaning and message of the Bible. In his tract roughly contemporary with the *Biographia Literaria*, laboriously dubbed *The Statesman's Manual, or The Bible the Best Guide to Political Skill and Foresight* (published in December 1816), such a view seems to be expressed. Yet even here matters do not progress with impregnable lucidity. On the one hand, the Bible is indeed granted a transcendental authority: 'The imperative and oracular form of the inspired Scripture,' Coleridge writes, 'is the form of reason itself in all things purely rational and moral'.[34] As reason is indeed a formal faculty in itself, laying down the rule and the parameters of the understanding according to Coleridge's Kantianism, it is indeed high praise – if veering towards the tautological – to be deemed the 'form of reason'. The very next sentence of *The Statesman's Manual* withdraws slightly from such an audacious claim, as if a certain dizziness has been experienced on the verge of a profound precipice:

> If it be the word of Divine Wisdom, we might anticipate that it would in all things be distinguished from other books, as the Supreme Reason, whose knowledge is creative, and antecedent to things known, is distinguished from the understanding.[35]

The argument of Coleridge's text takes for granted that the Bible is indeed 'the word of Divine Wisdom'. Reason is deemed 'creative' here, in terms of a god's constitutive reason (which Kant disallows human validity), whereby every act of knowledge makes a reality identical with its own known object, rather than merely being more or less adequate to that object. If the Bible operates in a similar manner, its word is not truth as a *mimesis* of some given reality, but rather as a legislative act: what the Bible says, becomes true. Other books have to make do with the imitative status that is the result of the understanding's forming of true or false judgements.

A variation on this same point is made further on in Coleridge's argument, where he claims that 'what is *expressed* in the inspired writings, is *implied* in all absolute science'.[36] If the distinction between creative and imitative judgements concerns the difference between the fallible and infallible, this latter point adds a new dimension: even an absolutely true science, at the highest level of reflection, would not measure up to the scripture. Such a science would be separated from its object, as an imitation is from its model, even if it were indisputably perfect. It would be a representation, and not a present manifestation of truth, such as the Bible is. For the latter would *make* the truth, and not merely dispel any impediments to its revelation.

Truth simply self-made: this is, of course, too good to be true. For if the Bible were only the coming to be of truth, it would be nothing: pure creation cannot be fixed, and is thus not amenable to literary expression. Stéphane Mallarmé's desire for a work expressing no more than the empty whiteness of an unblotted page addresses this paradox. Thus, inevitably, Coleridge's pure creative effusion is transformed into a collection of writings, a book, a system – and that very system does not preclude the existence of something else outside and other to itself. First of all, there is the significant manner in which Coleridge very quickly addresses the danger of fundamentalism. The Bible does not speak immediately to mankind, after all:

> In the Scriptures therefore both Facts and Persons must of necessity have a two-fold significance, a past and a future, a temporary and a perpetual, a particular and a universal application. They must be at once Portraits and Ideals.[37]

As well as demanding an interpretative vigilance, in the distinction of this 'two-fold significance', the Bible does not constitute the only means of revelation. It is the privileged means of revelation within the cultural domain, but nature itself is also a source. In *The Statesman's Manual*, Coleridge refers explicitly to the traditional idea of 'another book, likewise a revelation of God – the great book of his servant Nature'.[38]

Not only is revelation divided into two different books – that of nature and that of the Bible – but in addition the form of the latter is complicated by the fact that it constitutes an articulated system. In seeing the Bible as a system, Coleridge follows the example of the idealists. Predictably, organicism provides the form for the system – the organic body is the ontotypological figure, or 'metatype' (to borrow Stephen Prickett's term), that even the Bible must conform to.[39] To read the Bible in fragments is like tearing out separate limbs from a living body, 'plucking away *live-asunder*, as it were, from the divine organism of the Bible, textuary morsels and fragments'.[40] The later *Confessions of an Inquiring Spirit*, written in 1824, describes the Scripture in a similar vein, eulogising 'the whole Body of Holy

Writ, with all its harmonies, & symmetrical gradations ... this breathing Organismus, this glorious *Panharmonicon*'.[41]

Confessions of an Inquiring Spirit is remarkable for its attempt to balance philological historicism with reverence for the Bible's divine status, but in doing so it further weakens any claims the Bible might have to being an immediate expression of truth. The argument of the *Confessions* utilises the purported organicism of the system-book of the Bible as a means of avoiding the pitfalls of extreme fundamentalism. A distinction is made between more or less authentic passages in the Bible, according to the same structural logic that discriminated between the more or less central parts of a poem in the *Biographia Literaria*. The writers of the scriptures are not absolutely infallible in 'matters altogether incidental and foreign to the objects and purposes of their inspiration'.[42] Coleridge himself generally devotes far more time to the biblical writings of St Paul and St John than to any other sections of the Bible, and he insists that the more peripheral scriptural passages have to conform to holistic interpretation:

Does not the universally admitted Canon of Interpretation, that each part of the Scripture must be interpreted by the Spirit of the Whole, lead to the same *practical* conclusion as that for which I am now contending? – Namely, that it is the Spirit of the Bible, and not the detached words and sentences, that is infallible and absolute![43]

The parts of the book that do not conform to the totality are on one occasion rather ignominiously compared to 'a petty breach or a rat-hole in the wall' of a grand temple.[44] The stance that permits Coleridge to allow for such extraneous or alien matter to be contained in an organic unity might seem surprisingly inclusive. On the other hand, the implied overlooking, or even exclusion, of such matter in the actual practice of a holistic interpretation certainly points towards a totalitarian structure where the whole is far from dependent upon all of its parts.

In comparison to the view of *The Statesman's Manual*, the authority of the Bible is markedly weakened in the *Confessions*. Not only are many parts of the Bible written off as being incidental, but even its very priority is denied – at least as an instrument for instruction. It is no longer considered a flawless guide to absolute truths, surpassing even transcendental philosophy. Indeed, faith should precede access to the Bible: it is Coleridge's conviction, 'that in all *ordinary cases* the knowlege [sic] and belief in the Christian Religion should precede the study of the Hebrew Canon'.[45] One should study 'the sacred volume in the light and in the freedom of a faith already secured', as it is not identical to Christianity but rather 'the most precious Boon of God next to Christianity itself'.[46]

Thus the view of the Bible previously offered in *The Statesman's Manual* – as being expressive of self-evident truths – is debunked. Yet Coleridge nevertheless persists in asserting that the two testaments grant 'all the revealed Truths',[47] however tortuously and suspiciously one must approach their manifestation. He also persists in the view, likewise introduced in *The Statesman's Manual*, that religion is the fusion and sublation of philosophy and poetry. 'Religion,' he writes,

> is the Poetry and Philosophy of all mankind; unites in itself whatever is most excellent in either, and while it at one and the same time calls into action and supplies with the noblest materials both the imaginative and the intellective faculties, superadds the interests of the most substantial and homefelt reality to both, to the poetic vision and the philosophic idea.[48]

The most interesting consequence of this passage is that it implies that the Bible has already accomplished what Coleridge wants from Wordsworth. For if Wordsworth is capable of writing a 'PHILOSOPHIC POEM', or of creating 'a union of deep and subtle thought with sensibility'[49] this has already been attained by the Bible.

Coleridge's acclaimed interpretation of Wordsworth acquires a different slant if one looks at it in the context of this biblical criticism. The praise of the Bible's characteristic virtue of adding 'substantial and homefelt reality' to poetry and philosophy, in the quote above, might have been gleaned from the pages of the *Biographia Literaria* singing Wordsworth's praises. Although the latter is criticised, on one occasion, for the '*matter-of-factness*'[50] to be found in some of his poems, Coleridge elsewhere singles out 'the perfect truth of nature in his images and descriptions'[51] as especially commendable. Furthermore, what he identifies as Wordsworth's characteristic fault, 'the INCONSTANCY of the *style*'[52] of his poems, is not essentially different from what one finds in the most elevated tomes of all. For we have already seen that Coleridge was forced to admit the existence of inconsistencies and trivialities in the Bible.

Ultimately, though, one might be tempted to distinguish firmly between Wordsworth's efforts and those of the biblical authors on the basis of Coleridge's distinguishing definition of the poetic faculty. The definition at the end of the first part of the *Biographia Literaria* famously calls the poetic (and secondary) imagination an 'echo' of human perception (the primary imagination), which again is 'a repetition in the finite mind of the eternal act of creation in the infinite I AM'.[53] If poetry, at its acme, is '*creation rather than painting*'[54] – a productive act rather than a mimetic copying – this production is nevertheless at a position twice removed from divinity. Yet the Bible itself is, according to the *Confessions of an Inquiring Spirit*, not simply equal to the word of God. Although we are very far from the scepticism evinced by Schleiermacher in *On Religion*, Coleridge does insist that the Bible is secondary to God's own immediate self-presence, since it is subject to the 'written letter' and therefore not identical to the 'Light higher than all, even THE WORD that was *in the beginning*'.[55] Although Coleridge would rather not believe there to be any lack of conformity between the two, this is always possible:

> If between this Word and the written letter I shall any where seem to myself to find a discrepance, I will not conclude that such there really is; nor on the other hand will I fall under the condemnation of them that would 'lie for God', but seek help as I may, be thankful for what I have, and *wait*.[56]

Just as perception and poetry can be at fault, so can the Bible.

There are also other, more positive grounds for seeing a certain similarity between Coleridge's conceptions of Wordsworth and the Bible. According to one radical statement, the poetry of Wordsworth can leave perception completely behind – thus effectively going beyond the parameters provided by the definition of it as an 'echo' of perception. Just as the Bible 'shows clearly and certainly, and points out the way that leads to' the '*summum bonum*, or ultimate good' of the ideas,[57] the poet has access to symbols which can sidestep the limits of perception and instead express the ideas more directly. That is why Wordsworth's 'Intimations' ode is said to be 'intended for such readers only as had been accustomed to … venture at times into the twilight realms of consciousness'. The latter realms are described as areas where 'the attributes of time and space are inapplicable and alien' and yet which 'can not be conveyed, save in symbols of time and space'.[58]

Even if one cannot say there is any simple identity, then, it seems clear that Coleridge's understanding of the Bible and that of the poetry of his friend overlap in many ways. Later I shall confront Coleridge's attempt to interpret philosophy through the appropriating perspective of Christian theology. What makes him founder on that issue will prove to be the same as what undoes his attempts to both grant the Bible an absolute status as the Book of books and give Wordsworth's *Recluse* the honour of being the first genuine philosophic poem: it is the mutual contamination and interlinking of the realms of poetry, philosophy, and religion, across any simple boundary markers. The grid or model that is supposed to arrest and fix these realms in a hierarchical and delimited structure is that of the organic body. I will have to continue my elucidation of Coleridge's conception of organicism, though, before it can become clear why his attempts at organisation are confounded.

Nature's two-step in the *Theory of Life*

More explicit and well-formulated theoretical expressions of Coleridge's conception of organic unity than we have encountered so far can be found around the same time as the *Biographia*. The ambitious *Theory of Life*, probably written a year earlier (1816) but published posthumously, combines a large amount of speculative zoological systematisation (mainly grafted from the work of Schelling and Heinrich Steffens) with advanced meditations on structural cohesion.[59] In countering materialistic or mechanical explanations of life, Coleridge makes the point that a living phenomenon cannot be completely explained by any single element of its own constitution. Hence life cannot be reduced to digestion, or to the performance of any single organ:

> a physiological, that is a real, definition, as distinguishable from the verbal definitions of lexicography, must consist neither in any single property or function of the thing to be defined, nor yet in all collectively, which latter, indeed, would be a history, not a definition. It must consist, therefore, in the *law* of the thing, or in such an *idea* of it, as, being admitted, all the properties and functions are admitted by implication. It must likewise be so far *causal*, that a full insight having been obtained of the law, we derive from it a progressive insight into the necessity and *generation* of the phenomenon of which it is the law.[60]

This linking of the law with the causal generation of the living entity provides the occasion for what one might, rather anachronistically, call Coleridge's most articulate renunciation of a purely synchronic structuralism. For structure, he claims, is not self-explanatory. It can only be explained by referring to the genesis that lays its foundations:

> I repel with still greater earnestness the assertion and even the supposition that the functions are the offspring of the structure, and 'Life the result of organization', connected with it as effect with cause. Nay, the position seems to me little less strange, than as if a man should say, that building with all the included handicraft, of plastering, sawing, planning, & c. were the offspring of the house; and that the mason and carpenter were the result of a suite of chambers, with the passages and staircases that lead to them. ... But if I reject the organ as the *cause* of that, of which it is the organ ... I might admit it among the *conditions* of its actual functions ...[61]

This point is derived from a more general critique of materialism, as are other typical romantic gestures such as the favouring of process over product, and actions over fixed states of being. When all is said and done, Coleridge really desires the transcendence of the dichotomies such arguments build upon. But he has no means of achieving it: when he makes an attempt, he usually ends up echoing the German idealists, making vain appeals to the intellectual intuition. The unifying and originating intellectual intuition is however out of bounds for the *Theory of Life*, since this text is exclusively concerned with the explanation of living entities, and therefore one has to make do with a dualistic explanation. At first, though, a simple and unified definition is given. In Coleridge's organic vitalism,

> the most comprehensive formula to which the notion of life is reducible, would be that of the internal copula of bodies, or (if we may venture to borrow a phrase from the Platonic school) the *power* which discloses itself from within as a principle of *unity* in the *many*.[62]

Immediately following this definition, though, monism yields to dualism. For if the power of life is a 'link that combines the two [i.e. the whole and the parts], and acts throughout both', it will necessarily have to differ according to how it affects either of the two. The ensuing definition distinguishes between the parts' dependence upon the whole, on the one hand, and the inverse relation – the whole's dependence upon the parts – on the other hand. These two relations are not the same:

> But a whole composed, *ab intra*, of different parts, so far independent that each is reciprocally means and end, is an individual, and the individuality is the most intense where the greatest dependence of the parts on the whole is combined with the greatest dependence of the whole on its parts; the first (namely, the dependence of the parts on the whole) being absolute; the second (namely, the dependence of the whole on its parts) being proportional to the importance of the relation which the parts have to the whole, that is as their action extends more or less beyond themselves.[63]

Two separate relations of dependence, both formulated in terms of means–end relations, are thus presented. A notion of organicism as constituting a form of *polarity* is one of the defining characteristics of both Coleridge and Schelling's thought, and in the former's theory of life these two relations together form the basic, complementary polar forces.[64] Elsewhere, they are called the 'tendency to individuate' and the 'tendency to connect'.[65] In giving the parts an *absolute* dependency on the whole, Coleridge effectively denies them the possibility of independence. All parts are but subjects in this kingdom of ends. Indeed, we are not really speaking of a kingdom of ends at all, in Kant's precise meaning of the phrase, since such a kingdom demands that every member is an absolute end in itself. In Coleridge's displacement of idealist organicism, only the whole – which is not embodied absolutely in any part – is a means in itself.

Yet this does not mean that all parts are equally abject. For though all parts are equally dependent upon the whole, the whole is unevenly dependent upon different parts. There is a hierarchy of parts, according to the extension of their power, or according to what Coleridge (echoing Steffens) elsewhere calls the power of 'individuation'. The hierarchical system structured by different levels of individuation turns, on closer scrutiny, to be a new version of a familiar system, namely the Aristotelian chain of being. Mankind is both the highest link of this vertically extended chain, and the point at which it crosses over into its outside, transcending or overcoming itself:

> In the lowest forms of vegetable and animal world we perceive totality dawning into *individuation*, while in man, as the highest of the class, the individuality is not only perfected in its corporeal sense, but begins a new series beyond the appropriate limits of physiology.[66]

These are the rudiments of 'the great scale of ascent and expansion',[67] which shares with Steffens the originality of conceiving vegetable and animal life as parallel forms, thus equally developed although of different essence, rather than following the traditional subordination of plant to animal.[68]

The latter minor disturbance to the Aristotelian scheme is of negligible importance in itself, but it is symptomatic of a sophistication which Coleridge introduces into the systematics of his physiology, a sophistication which perhaps expresses a slight murmur of discontent with the foundations of this thought. The problem is of course that Aristotle's chain of being is so strictly hierarchical precisely because it originates in a metaphysics of form and matter. Aristotelian thought creates hierarchy by making levels where each lower level provides the matter for the form of a higher level, the latter form then again becoming the matter for the next level. Coleridge wants to formulate an organicism that at least does not subjugate matter to form, and even preferably (but impossibly) a conception of unity which is not the unification or organisation of separate parts. He ultimately desires what he elsewhere defines as 'not an intense Union but an Absolute Unity',[69] but he cannot do without Aristotle's levels or his form-matter opposition. Only the latter, which also implies a subject–object dichotomy, can provide him with a scheme which will be attuned to his Christian conception of the human as the privileged and unique part of God's creation. In the late work of Coleridge, this ultimately leads him to leave the most important tenets – and in effect, though not always, the radical organicism – of idealism behind.[70] This is a gradual process, as one finds him insisting upon an absolute subject–object of self-consciousness as late as in the *Logic* completed in 1822, thus allowing an element of reciprocity affect the very centre of his system.[71] The later *Aids to Reflection* describes the absolute in more strictly hierarchical and conventional terms. It is identified as being 'a *Subject* (*i.e.* a sentient and intelligent Existence)'.[72]

One is faced with a thinker who wants, indeed really needs, a transcendence of the form–matter and subject–object distinctions in order to achieve a true organicism. Yet at the very same moment he must deny such a transcendence. In the *Theory of Life* this leads to a rather baroque aberration, when Coleridge embraces Aristotle's very hierarchical conception of a chain of being but with an important afterthought. He introduces an idiosyncrasy – something slightly *fishy* (for this is indeed, as it will soon become evident, a matter of the fish) – which does not belong to Aristotle or to Aristotelian metaphysics.

The text of the *Theory of Life* utilises the image of climbing a ladder as a metaphor for how life gradually ascends to higher and higher levels. Nature does not 'ascend as links in a suspended chain, but as the steps in a ladder'.[73] At every new level, new rungs are added to those already attained below. Coleridge's basic three steps (reproducing a staple triad of the German *Naturphilosophie*) are collated with spatial dimensions:

first, the power of length, or REPRODUCTION; second, the power of surface (that is, length and breadth), or IRRITABILITY; third, the power of depth, or SENSIBILITY.[74]

The human body includes all these as fully-fledged constitutive forces, while the insect world inhabits the realm of irritability (and thus also includes reproduction) and vegetables are exponents of reproduction and nothing else.[75]

The transitions, or borderlines, between each of the levels complicate this three-tiered scheme. The most intricate transition is supplied by the species of fish, which Coleridge (in concordance with Steffens) places as the lowest form of manifestation of sensibility. As well as representing a progression from the irritability of the insect world, though, fish *also* represent regression. In order to explain this surprising anomaly, Coleridge resorts to an anthropomorphism:

But as if a weakness of exhaustion had attended this advance in the same moment it was made, Nature seems necessitated to fall back, and re-exert herself in the lower ground which she had before occupied, that of ... the power of reproduction. The intensity of this latter power in the fishes, is shown both in their voracity and in the number of their eggs .... [Thus] the fish sinks a step below the insect, in the mode and circumstances of impregnation.[76]

This curious passage can only invoke the fictional (it is 'as if' nature were exhausted), in order to attempt to explain the non-linear progression of nature. Perhaps the fictional mode is the only apt response to the monstrosity of what is suggested. One must, as it were, allow nature to put its best foot forward, even when it stumbles: it would be unseemly and hubristic to suggest that nature is anything else than infinitely resourceful –

that it, in fact, can lose what it previously has gained – except under the cover of fiction. The unbelievable can be ventured in fiction, since it is the nature of the latter, as Coleridge famously claimed, to operate under the suspension of disbelief.

Another way by which Coleridge avoids the potential sacrilege of offending Mother Nature, is by circumlocution. By evasively wrapping criticism in praise, nature's odd deficiency is converted to a notable virtue:

> But nature never loses what she has once learnt, though in the acquirement of each new power she intermits, or performs less energetically, the act immediately preceding. She often drops a faculty, but never fails to pick it up again. She may seem forgetful and absent, but it is only to recollect herself with *additional*, as well as *recruited* vigour, in some after and higher state; as if the sleep of powers, as well as of bodies, were the season and condition of their growth.[77]

Nature thus forgets in order to remember, loses in order to gain all the more, every step backward thus not excluding, perhaps even facilitating, another step forwards. This is 'the usage (I dare not say law) according to which Nature lets fall, in order to resume, and steps backward the furthest, where she means to leap forward with the greatest concentration of energy'.[78]

Even if she is something of a queer fish, then, Mother Nature does get the job done. Just as each individual has both centripetal and centrifugal principles, both an urge towards individual self-sufficiency and towards immersion in the whole, evolution combines progress and retrogression. The balance between these two tendencies constitutes a diachronic implementation, on a large scale, of Coleridge's organicism. Just as his general organicism, as sketched in the *Theory of Life*, only gives progression towards the universal an absolute status, his conception of historical development similarly gives progressive accumulation priority over any forgetting on the part of nature. Indeed, instances of the latter may be interpreted (although Coleridge merely mentions the fact, without attempting to prove it) as dialectical negations, providing the tension and dissonance necessary for any true progression to take place.

The step back is really only half a step. In the *Biographia Literaria*, this is the gist of a much-quoted passage comparing the reader's progress to the motion of a snake: '[A]t every step he pauses and half recedes, and from the retrogressive movement collects the force which again carries him onward.'[79] The problem not answered by such statements is, of course, how the rebounding movement forward can somehow have any more energy than the 'retrogressive' movement that precedes it. On the one hand, there is a sort of feigning of a *perpetuum mobile*, whereby the progressing instance generates its own energy. On the other hand, there is implicitly – and indeed explicitly in the quotes of the *Theory of Life*, cited above – an admission of insufficiency and dependency. For the organism (or life, the reader, etc.) has to move backwards, in order to acquire the resources which it has neglected the first time around. An economy of equalisation and equivalence, rather than the gift of an original productivity, is the law of the latter movement.

Exclusion excluded and assimilated: *The Philosophical Lectures*

Does nature lose force along the way, or is it unbounded in its energy and ability for inclusion? This question will crop up in another form – loosened from its natural basis – in another work of Coleridge's from this time. From December 1818 to March 1819, he held weekly lectures in London on the history of philosophy. These lectures approached the same problems that occupied him in the slightly earlier *Biographia Literaria* and *Theory of Life*. In general, though, a transition is being made in Coleridge's thought at this point, as his major works from now on – *Aids to Reflection* (1825) and *Church and State* (1829) – primarily deal with the beliefs and institutions of Christianity. It is no accident, then, that the *Philosophical Lectures* are perhaps primarily interested in stressing the hegemony of religion over philosophy: they mark a transition from Coleridge's philosophical criticism to a phase dominated by theological speculation, and also attempt to provide a justification for this change in emphasis.

The lectures also cover some of the ground already broached in the *Theory of Life*, but with a wider scope than that of physiology. Philosophy, in Coleridge's understanding of it, can transcend the limits inherent to physiology and vitalism, for it has access to mankind's deeper nature, a nature beyond nature. If the theory of life places the human at the acme of the physiological system, the lectures on philosophy try to follow how that acme transcends such a system:

> I think too highly of my responsible nature to confound it with a something by which I am not distinguished from the merest animal. Whatever life is, in its present state it cannot be brought to account for that which more especially constitutes us Man [*sic*].[80]

By avoiding a thorough vitalism, Coleridge modifies Schelling's nature philosophy, since the latter's central premise of human consciousness developing continuously from inanimate and unconscious nature is discarded. Stressing the breach between the empirical and the supersensual, and localising man's essence in the latter as fundamentally an ethical matter, *The Philosophical Lectures* are far more dependent on Kant than on any of his idealist followers.

Kant's complex relation to religion had involved a double strategy. On the one hand, *Religion within the Limits of Reason Alone* circumscribed the scope of religion according to the limits set up by critical philosophy, while, on the other, the First Critique in many ways represented an attempt to save some of Christianity's central beliefs from materialistic critique. Philosophy had both to save and delimit religion. For all his Kantian leanings, Coleridge has another understanding of these matters. His departure from orthodox Kantianism takes its bearings on the subject of the ideas of reason. As numerous commentators have pointed out, Coleridge goes far beyond Kant in granting the ideas a constitutive rather than a merely regulative function.[81] He also relegates philosophical knowledge to being merely adequate to the understanding, and grants religion access to valid (though paradoxical and mystical) knowledge of the ideas of reason. Philosophy can only 'point' to them, since they are actually 'unattainable' without what Coleridge calls the *supplement* of religion.[82] All 'the great moral truths' (Kant's ideas) are 'given from without', and the manner in which such gifts are conveyed is revelation. Only religious acts, as opposed to philosophical thought, are present at the bestowal of such gifts. Yet philosophy is necessary for the formulation of what place these gifts have within a cohesive, reasonable system of thought.

This supplementary structure is heavily weighted, in Coleridge's implicit polemic, to the favour of religion. But his evaluations can of course be reversed. Even if philosophy is dependent upon the data of religion, religion would be helpless to comprehend itself without the aid of philosophy. The immediate presence granted by the former is helpless without the articulating discourse and systematics of the latter. Thus considerable room is opened in Coleridge's lectures for manoeuvres with, and speculations on, the unstable relation of dependency between the two realms. In many ways, this is the central focus of the lectures, and inevitably Coleridge musters up the resources of organicism to manage its operations.

The editor of *The Philosophical Lectures*, Kathleen Coburn, has claimed that the lectures argue that philosophy 'satisfies that need up to the limits of human knowledge, religion beyond those limits to the limits of human faith and will and beyond these to divine grace'.[83] This is an accurate description of one of the central problems of the lectures, but in what manner can it be said that Coleridge thus proves that 'philosophy and religion [are] reconcilable'?[84] In order to find out how he envisages the balance of authority between philosophy and religion in this text, one must place that balance in the context of what he always takes as the blueprint for all harmonisation of differing entities: namely, his thought on organic unity.

Coleridge is engaged in constructing a meta-system in the lectures, a system delimiting and hierarchising the main areas of human endeavour and knowledge, in a manner not totally dissimilar to Kant's sketch in 'The Architectonic of Pure Reason'. This overarching system is shown to be both intermittently revealed, and subject to numerous deformations and occlusions, throughout the history of philosophy. An early, privileged uncovering of the system is said to take place in ancient Greece:

> Speusippus, the nephew and immediate successor of Plato, deserves especial honor from us ... as the first man who attempted an encyclopaedia in the genuine sense of the word; that is, a co-organization of the sciences, as so many INTER-dependent systems, each having a specific life of its own but all communicating with philosophy as the common centre or brain, if I may say so ...[85]

Philosophy or metaphysics is thus proclaimed to be the first and fundamental science, the science of sciences. All other sciences are interdependent, but are especially dependent upon philosophy, the centre of the whole organism of knowledge.

For Coleridge, though, this self-sufficient system does not tell the whole story. Although metaphysics is completed and exhausted already in antiquity, it is dependent upon an outside. Even if 'all the forms of philosophy that are properly philosophy' were 'developed previous to the appearance of our Lord',[86] the revelation and doctrine of the latter are not irrelevant or extraneous to the realm of philosophy. Even if philosophy is the totalising centre of the body of sciences, it is nevertheless far from being self-subsistent. Philosophy is dependent upon religion for its own foundation. Yet sublating philosophy completely, and without reserve, to religion, is no less pernicious than doing the opposite. The most important historical instance of an attempt of assimilating religion to philosophy is, for Coleridge, represented by Neoplatonist or 'eclectic' philosophy, while the schoolmen of the Middle Ages are berated for the inverse error of trying to transform philosophy into religion. If the Neoplatonic thinkers tried, on the behalf of philosophy, to 'make religion its property',[87] the scholastics erred just as much, although it was 'far more excusable in the circumstances',[88] by staking out the opposite course.

Since there is no sure-fire rule for how to formulate the proper relation between philosophy and religion, one and the same response to that relation may be appraised positively one moment, and negatively the next. In *The Philosophical Lectures* this is what happens with the scholasticism of the Middle Ages. As I have just noted, he criticises the scholastics for collapsing philosophy into religion, thus committing the inverse of Neoplatonism's error. But the scholastics' desire to 'convert philosophy into religion'[89] can be described in a number of ways, and Coleridge significantly hedges his bets on this matter. Elsewhere their error is interpreted in wanting to 'have a religion without a philosophy',[90] which would seem to indicate that the conversion of philosophy to religion would have a cataclysmic and eradicating effect on the very existence of philosophy. But can there be subsumption without any preservation? Would not philosophy survive *within* religion in some manner, as a tacit and irreducible premise for its own self-presenting? According to one formulation in *The Philosophical Lectures*, immediately following the lectures that expressly deal with scholasticism, there is no real survival of philosophy within scholasticism and precisely this constitutes the fatal error of the scholastics. Ideally, the prototypical thinker co-ordinating philosophy and religion would be like an astronomer, surveying the harmony of the planets:

> Thus the astronomer places himself in the centre of the system and looks at all the planetary orbs as with eye of the sun. Happy would it be for us if we could at all times imitate him in his perceptions – in the intellectual or the political world – I mean, to subordinate instead of exclude. Nature excludes nothing. She takes up all, still subjecting the highest to the less so and ultimately subjecting all to the lower thus taken up. But alas! The contrary method, exclusion instead of subordination, this and its results, presents the historian with his principal materials in whatever department his researches are directed. Thus in our own past route [i.e. in the philosophical lectures presented up to this point], we find a long period from the first Christian century to the sixth, distinguished by a vain attempt to substitute philosophy for religion, and following it a more injurious endeavour to make religion supersede philosophy.[91]

The final clause reiterates and amplifies Coleridge's critique of scholasticism, and does so on the basis of the scholastics' excluding rather than subordinating philosophy. But this critique is completely reversed further on in the lectures:

> Were it only therefore for their endeavours to reunite reason and religion by a due subordination of the former to the latter, we owe a tribute of respect to the schoolmen from the thirteenth and fourteenth centuries.[92]

Here it is precisely that which previously caused Coleridge to dismiss scholasticism, which now forces him to praise it. But he interprets its gesture differently: either scholasticism eradicates philosophy, or it preserves it intact within the body of religion. Scholasticism, one might hazard, is unreadable because its very gesture is ambivalent. It is the queer fish of philosophy.

The cause for confusion lies in the ambivalence of the sublation involved, an ambivalence which Hegel celebrated in his use of dialectical subsumption or *Aufhebung* (which combined preservation on a higher level with both transformation and eradication). Insofar as Coleridge's texts are infected by this ambivalence, they are plagued with the same contingencies that riddle Hegel's works: stress is laid almost randomly on one or the other of the sublation's aspects, opening up ample room for ungrounded decisions and opportunism. If the dialectic never works in the same manner, the strategy chosen at any particular moment is liable to be contingent and prey to outside interests.

Coleridge attempts to escape the law of this ambivalence in *The Philosophical Lectures*, stressing that subordination is *not* exclusion. One might object, though, that the reason why scholasticism is described, on different occasions, as both being and not being a true subordination of philosophy, is that subordination always involves or implies an element of exclusion. From the instance or exemplar that is central, to all that which is lower down in the hierarchy, there is a gradual lessening of centrality which can be calculated in its diminishing force. Thus at the limit there will be a quantitatively almost non-existent intensity which will open for exclusion or at least qualitative demarcation.

The necessity of exclusion might be said to be what *The Philosophical Lectures* explicitly deny, yet implicitly affirm. Even if it seems, at times, that Coleridge wants to reduce Kant's three principles of organic unity (hierarchical totalisation, interdependence and delimitation of an exterior) to a duo, he cannot fully avoid following the father of the critical philosophy on this issue. More explicit evidence of how Coleridge cannot do without exclusion is provided elsewhere. In two short, unpublished texts of the same period as the lectures, 'Patriotism' and 'On Election',[93] Coleridge expressly grants what is denied in the lectures: exclusion is indeed a trait of all nature. In a comparison between the 'Body Moral' of elected human souls (granted spiritual afterlife in heaven) and 'the Organic Body' everywhere evident in nature, the principles of the former are elucidated according to their similarity with the latter. If some souls are deemed not worthy to gain access to heaven, it is because heaven is structured like a natural and organic body, where 'the separative and eliminative process is no less necessary than that of assimilation'.[94]

In the brief fragment on 'Patriotism', Coleridge explores the acts of exclusion characteristic of various religious communities throughout the ages. In a step which in some respects is anticipatory of the work of René Girard, Coleridge names this form of exclusion a 'sacrifice', applying the term beyond its literal meaning. The fragment implicitly argues for a linear, historical development in the deployment of exclusion. Furthest away from the modern stance is the oriental principle where all are sacrificed to a 'PERSONAL ONE'. The next step on the ladder is provided by antiquity – which Coleridge, in a belligerently conservative spirit, equates with the French revolutionaries on this matter – where all individuals are sacrificed to the 'ABSTRACT ALL'.[95] In the modern Christian era, the principle is one in which every one 'sacrifices to every other what is necessary for the

Constitution of a Whole'.[96] In this final stage, there is evidence of a new sense of mutuality absent in the earlier societies. Yet the voluntarism implied by the claim that 'the Integer consents to become a Part in order to preserve itself as an Integer',[97] suggests that Coleridge is still thinking in uncharacteristically Hobbesian terms of a collectivity formed by atomic individuals forging a social contract. The main gist is, however, the same as in the *Theory of Life* and 'On Election': exclusion is, it would seem, an inescapable fact of life.

Body politics in *Church and State*

The ruling metaphor of 'On Election', where a 'Body Moral' is understood in terms of an organic body, is replaced by the more traditional metaphor of a 'Body Politic' in Coleridge's late meditation *On the Constitution of Church and State* (1829). In this tract he declares that

> with, perhaps, one exception [namely, the religious use of 'the Word'], it would be difficult in the whole compass of language, to find a metaphor so commensurate, so pregnant, or suggesting so many points of elucidation, as that of *Body Politic*, as the exponent of a State or Realm.[98]

Not only the state, but also the church, is a body politic of this kind. *Church and State* is an interesting text, not only because it formulates the organic nature of the church and state (particularly the former) in an abyssal manner, but also because the relation between the two leads Coleridge to theoretical formulations of considerable conceptual complexity.

At first sight, his conception of the state would seem to be extremely fragmentary. The totalising, hierarchical part of society is seemingly eradicated (he dismisses a 'constitutional pure Monarchy' as an *'ens rationale,* unknown in history'[99]). As a result, he proffers a seemingly democratic model akin to some of the early political thought of Friedrich Schlegel (though, as we have seen, the latter contained opposite extremes). Instead of a ruler, one has a constitution:

> First then, I have given briefly ... the right idea of a STATE, or Body Politic; 'State' being here synonymous with a *constituted* Realm, Kingdom, Commonwealth, or Nation, *i.e.* where the integral parts, classes, or orders are so balanced, or interdependent, as to constitute, more or less, a moral unit, an organic whole; and as arising out of the Idea of a State I have added the Idea of a Constitution, as the informing principle of its coherence and unity.[100]

Here Coleridge's thought is obviously in conformity with the inheritance of idealist organicism: a whole has interdependent parts, but also an ideal and totalising centre. What is the relation, though, between the interdependency and the hierarchy, between the mutuality of the parts and the founding rule of the centre? Coleridge's later thought is consistent on this matter, and hence one finds him taking no other route here, than he did in the *Biographia Literaria* and the *Theory of Life*. Provocatively, the 'final cause of the whole' of a state is articulated as being the clerisy's ability to 'form and train up the people of the country to obedient, free, useful, organizable subjects'. This condition implies 'living to the benefit of the state' and being prepared 'to die for its defence'.[101] The individual must be willing to surrender his or her life for the benefit of the state. Never, perhaps, is the hierarchical tendency of Coleridge's organicism more blatantly prominent than on this matter. The connection with his comments on Lessing's *Ernest und Falk*, where he insists that the subjects exist for the state, rather than the other way around, is obvious:

> I hold, that ... Men were made for, i.e. have their final cause in, the State, *rather* than the State for *the* Men ... I say *rather*, because both may be true. Not only is the Whole greater than a Part; but where it is a Whole, and not a mere All or Aggregate, it makes each part that which it is.[102]

These matters were stated even more emphatically in *The Philosophical Lectures*, where it was remarked that a 'man is unworthy of being a citizen of a state who does not know the citizens are for the sake of state, not the state for the sake of the immediate flux of persons who form at that time the people'.[103] The grounds for such an argument is the state's organic nature, for in that which is 'truly organic and living, the whole is prior to the parts'.[104] When organicism is coupled, in this manner, with an insistence upon the individual's duty to sacrifice itself for the sake of the whole, one is of course far removed from modern democratic ideals. Although Coleridge's organicism opens up for the individual's being an end in itself in the state, this is only as a relative end. Walter Jackson's Bate is therefore quite simply wrong when he claims that Coleridge is unlike 'many organicist thinkers' in providing 'no basis at all for totalitarianism, for the individual is the ultimate purpose of the state'.[105]

The body politic of the church is organised differently from that of the state. Just as the latter has its constitution as its totalising fulcrum, and indeed can have a monarch as its 'visible head',[106] the former also has an organic and centred structure. But the nature of the embodiment of the spiritual centre of the church is problematical, and subject to much discussion in *Church and State*. For the centre is, in concordance with the tenets of idealism, heterogeneous to the structure it organises. This may be stated negatively: the 'Church of Christ' has an 'absence of any visible head or sovereign' – there is a 'non-existence, nay the utter preclusion, of any local or personal centre of unity, of any single source of universal power'.[107] This would seem to provide one with a completely dispersed scheme, devoid of a centre, yet such an appearance is, of course, misleading. For even if there is no visible centre, there may be one on another level, and indeed Coleridge soon after calls Jesus the 'invisible head' of the church.[108]

Coleridge finds grounds for his polemic against Catholicism in this heterogeneity of the centre. Much of his argument is concerned with allowing a place for a religious group within a state (specifically the Catholics within the English state) *as long as* they do not allow their religious leader (for instance, the Pope) to usurp the authority of the secular instance in charge of their state. His dual approach, separating church and state as almost completely alien realms, is well designed to accommodate a particular form of Catholicism. A less benevolent tone is struck towards Catholicism, however, in the internal analysis of the body politic of the church. For the Catholics' acknowledging of the Pope as the spiritual centre of the church is vigorously attacked. Indeed, Coleridge goes so far as to claim that the Pope is identical with the Antichrist. In itself, this fact provides sufficient justification for the Reformation:

> that if by Antichrist be meant – what alone can rationally be meant – a power in the Christian church, which in the name of Christ, at once pretending and usurping his authority, is systematically subversive of the essential and distinguishing characters and purposes of the Christian church: that *then*, if the papacy, and the Romish Hierarchy as far as it is papal, be *not* Antichrist, the guilt of schism, in its most aggravated form, lies on the authors of the Reformation. For nothing less than this could have justified so tremendous a rent in the Catholic church with all its foreseen most calamitous consequences.[109]

The error of Catholicism is formulated linguistically as a being prone to understand Christian *symbols* incorrectly, in taking them in 'a literal *i.e.* phaenomenal* sense', and thereby 'interpreting *sensually* what was delivered of objects *super*-sensual'.[110] The division between the noumenal (super-sensual) and phenomenal (sensual) is a commonplace of idealism, yet its deployment here is not without its strategic subtleties.

Significantly, a literal interpretation of the symbol is not dismissed here in favour of a purely *metaphorical* one. For the 'mistaking of symbols and analogies for metaphors' has, according to Coleridge, been 'a main occasion and support of the worst errors in Protestantism', almost in the manner of an inverted mirror image of the Catholic fault.[111] Coleridge's own stance seems to lie in the vague borderland between pure literality and pure metaphor, according to the principle of identity in difference which is so typical of thought taking its bearings from Neoplatonism or organicism. This corresponds to the halfway house position German idealism took between symbolic and allegorical modes. Similarly, Coleridge's warnings against taking any worldly representation of Christ as absolute is correspondent to Friedrich Schlegel's critique of Kant's granting the political ruler transcendental authority. The need for the absolute is present, yet there is never any full, sensory manifestation of that absolute.

We have previously encountered Coleridge's earlier grappling with the question of precisely how religion and philosophy are transcendent. Arguably, there has been some progression in *Church and State* as regards the formulation of the relation between the secular and the religious. In *The Lectures of Philosophy*, we saw Coleridge vacillate between hypostatisations of Kant's ideas (transformed into an autonomous and fundamental religious realm by Coleridge) and conflicting attempts at constructing an organic (or quasi-dialectical) relation between reason and faith. Coleridge is both more circumspect and more audacious in *Church and State*. The difference between the religious and the secular bodies politic is insisted upon, and yet a tenuous connection is nevertheless upheld – as in the implicit compromise between the literal and metaphorical modes.

Coleridge somewhat surprisingly reaches for the word *friend* at this juncture. The religious and transcendental is, he claims, the friend of the empirically present. This word is first proposed in a discussion of the difference between the actual church of a state and the transcendental, super-sensual church I have been inspecting so far:

> In relation to the National Church, Christianity, or the Church of Christ, is a blessed accident, a providential boon, a grace of God, a mystery and faithful *friend*, the envoy indeed and liege subject of another state, but which can neither administer the laws nor promote the ends of this other State, which is *not* of the world, without advantage, direct and indirect, to the true interests of the States, the aggregate of which is what we mean by the WORLD – *i.e.* the civilized world.[112]

This is an odd form of friendship, with distance and mystery as some of its defining characteristics. It is a conception of friendship which is somewhat adjusted by a later description of the Christian Church as 'the appointed Opposite' to all kingdoms and states, a collectivity which is 'the *sustaining*, *correcting*, *befriending* Opposite of the world!'[113] In this latter quote, the more personable verbs ('sustaining', 'correcting') are coupled with Coleridge's privileged term for polar complementaries ('Opposite'), thus creating an impression of a closer and less heterogeneous relation. As I shall demonstrate in my later reading of Coleridge's early letters and conversation poems, however, it is precisely in the tension between such proximity and the distance of mystery and the gift, that Coleridge's early work identifies the essence of friendship.

From the ruined tower to the aphoristic *Aids to Reflection*

Before I backtrack to the conversation poems and Coleridge's early conception of friendship, a reading of how he applies the systematics of organicism to the formal properties of his own writings is in order. There cannot
be any doubt that, in his critical and theoretical writings, 'Coleridge's
endeavour', as one commentator puts it, 'was always towards system'.[114]
But this system is nowhere attained. It remains a planned projection, an
unfulfilled desire, a dream. Thus one paradoxically meets a writer everywhere criticising the incomplete and the unfinished, in texts which are
themselves markedly piecemeal or lacking in structure. This is a paradox
Coleridge could not but be aware of, as contemporary critics were quick to
find fault with the structure and scope of his texts. On the fly-leaf of *The
Statesman's Manual* (Copy G), one finds the following impassioned response
to one specimen of such criticism:

> Now surely a series of Essays, the contents [and purposes] of which are
> capable of being faithfully and compleatly [*sic*] enumerated in a sen-
> tence of 7 or 8 lines, and where all the points treated of tend [to] a
> common result, cannot justly be regarded as a motley Patch-work, or
> Farrago of heterogeneous Effusions! even tho' the form and sequence
> were more aphorismic *kai asunarteton* [i.e. 'and disconnected'] than is
> really the case. ... Here are from 14 to 18 entire Works, produced by my
> labors – and nevertheless I must be the wild eccentric Genius that has
> published nothing but fragments & splendid Tirades – [115]

No doubt the exaggerated nature of the criticism involved here makes it all
the easier for Coleridge to defend himself against it. Yet his own demands
for systematic coherence are rather daunting, and certainly call for far more
than simply writing something more organised than 'Tirades'.

One of Coleridge's more famous statements on this question is to be
found in the *Biographia Literaria*. The grand finale of the philosophical
exposition which concludes the first part of the work is suddenly cut short
by a fictional letter from a friend (a letter which Coleridge famously
boasted having written himself 'without taking my pen off the paper
except to dip it in the inkstand'[116]). The friend berates Coleridge's philosophical chapter on the imagination – a chapter that Coleridge had not, in
fact, written – on two grounds. One is that the chapter would add too
much obscure, philosophical speculation to a book which, after all, is
meant to be an introduction to a volume of Coleridge's poetry. The other
reason we have encountered before:

> I see clearly that you have done too much, and yet not enough. You
> have been obliged to omit so many links, from the necessity of compres-

sion, that what remains, looks ... like the fragments of the winding steps of an old ruined tower.[117]

The motifs of the fragment and the interrupted step thus coalesce at this crucial point of the *Biographia Literaria*. Oddly enough, the upshot of the letter is that Coleridge decides to 'content myself for the present with stating the main result of the Chapter'[118] – that result being his famous distinctions between fancy and imagination, and between primary and secondary imagination. These distinctions, then, are compressions of a compression, or fragments of a fragment, if one is to follow the terminology of the letter of the fictional friend.

Ironically, then, the *Biographia Literaria* has to revert to fragmentary writing at the very heart of its argument, the essence of which is a denial of fragmentation. Coleridge is forced to make similar, denigrating admissions with regard to all of his other major works. Often, he simply takes recourse (as we have seen earlier) in evoking the *Magnum Opus*, as a sort of *deus ex machina* which one day will appear on the literary stage and put paid to all obtuseness and incompleteness. On other occasions, he simply admits to the unfinished nature of his writings, as if to disarm any criticism from the outset. *Church and State*, for instance, is described in an advertisement as being 'Epistolary Disquisitions, or Extracts from a series of Letters'.[119] A more defensive manoeuvre follows: 'To say it is *patchy*', Coleridge argues, 'is but another less courteous way of conveying the same description. For the Work purports to be a Pasticcio.'[120]

Aids to Reflection is Coleridge's text that most unabashedly presents itself as a hodgepodge of different writings. In its first version, published in 1825, the work contains several extracts detached from the texts of Archbishop Leighton (1611–84), accompanied by commentaries from Coleridge's own pen. In the second edition, of 1831, the text is radically revamped, and Coleridge's own meditations – in the form of isolated aphorisms collected under three headings – take centre stage with less timidity. Confronting the discrepancy between the two different versions, Coleridge in fact argues that the later text is *not* an organic growth or development of the first version: 'the present Volume owed its accidental origin to the intention of compiling one of a different description', and therefore one should not 'speak of it as the same Work. It is not a change in the child, but a changeling.'[121] The reason one nevertheless speaks of first and second editions of the *Aids* is, of course, that the two texts manifestly share quite large amounts of material – some repeated verbatim, some edited. As a changeling, then, the text is partially identical to the other 'child' it was erroneously swapped with at its (mythical) birth. The other, first edition is both other and same – the two of them are doubles that both have separate identities, yet are completely the same on some accounts.

They are, indeed, like fragments – or rather, like aphorisms, if one uses the definition of the aphorism supplied by *Aids to Reflection*. In producing an obviously cut-up and not simply continuous text, Coleridge is here forced to make a positive evaluation of fragmentation. Perhaps as a result of his investigations into the independence and connection of different sciences, as separate systems organically linked together, he here gives a positive description of the isolated textual morsel. His facing up to the necessary sacrifice inherent in all religions, in 'Patriotism' and 'On Election', may also be taken to be a precedent to this change of mind. Coleridge's definition of the aphorism takes its bearings from etymology:

> Aphorism, determinate position, from the Greek, ap, from; and horizein, to bound or limit; whence our horizon. – In order to get full sense of the word, we should first present to our minds the visual image that forms its primary meaning. Draw lines of different colours round the different counties of England, and then cut out each separately, as in the common play-maps that children take to pieces and put together – so that each district can be contemplated apart from the rest, as a whole in itself. This twofold act of circumscribing, and detaching, when it is exerted by the mind on subjects of reflection and reason, is to *aphorize*, and the resultant an *aphorism*.[122]

The aphorism, then, is organically constructed insofar as it is (a) clearly delimited, and (b) a whole in itself. It would seem that the order of priority between these two principles of organicism has – if one takes the second one as a version of the principle of hierarchical totality – been reversed from their normal one. For often delimitation is an afterthought that is omitted (or even, as we have seen, repressed) in definitions of organic wholes. Here it is granted pride of place, while complete elision is the fate of another of Kant's three principles, namely mutual interrelationship.

Yet *Aids of Reflection* is very far from being devoid of an organising principle. The aphorisms do not follow each other in an order quite as haphazard as that which would seem to be the rule for, say, Schlegel's *Athenaeum* fragments. Coleridge's text is divided under three main headings (with intermediate phases in between). These are 'Prudential Aphorisms', 'Moral and Religious Aphorisms' and, finally, 'Aphorisms on that which is indeed Spiritual Religion'. The basis for the three groups is provided by Coleridge's rather idiosyncratic departure from his normal dichotomy of understanding and reason. Here one is instead faced with a trichotomy, with the three different types of aphorisms following three different faculties:

> Thus: the prudential corresponds to the sense and the understanding; the moral to the heart and the conscience; the spiritual to the will and reason, *i.e.* to the finite will reduced to harmony with, and in subordina-

tion to, the reason, as a ray from that true light which is both reason and will, universal reason, and will absolute.[123]

The distinction between conscience and reason is provoked, in this text, by Coleridge's reaction to the contemporary weakness for a religiosity of good deeds and nothing more – an atrophied, anti-intellectual version of the idealist emphasis on the primacy of the moral law.

The later, spiritual aphorisms are on a supposedly higher plane than the moral ones, which again have reached a more elevated coign of vantage than the prudential aphorisms. Even if each aphorism is a whole in itself, the more general collection is nevertheless organised in a ladder-formation akin to the Aristotelian chain of being we found appropriated in the *Theory of Life*. Thus *Aids to Reflection* must be deemed a hierarchical organisation of aphorisms and detached comments, not a genuine collection of independent and mutually interdependent fragments. Despite raising the theme of 'Reciprocal Action or the Law of Reciprocity', which Coleridge, in a nod to his German antecedents, also calls *Wechselwirkung*,[124] true reciprocity is not the formal law of the text itself. Coleridge here bases himself on a traditional and strictly hierarchical conception of organicism, and must be said to inherit rather than solve the problems of that tradition.

Indeed, Coleridge comes closer to the literary organicism of his German predecessors in an earlier text. On the face of it, his journal entitled *The Friend*, running for twenty-eight issues between June 1809 and March 1810, would seem an unpromising work in which to look for a radically organic mode of writing. Yet Coleridge's problems with presenting popular and readable issues of the journal result in constructive and uncompromising self-reflection. For instance, when criticised for allowing individual essays of *The Friend* to run over from one issue to another, Coleridge points out the arbitrary format of the issues in general, calling them 'the Procrustes Bed of 16 pages'.[125] Jestingly, he compares his use of this format with the form of the most rudimentary of organic entities, the polyp: '*most often* I will divide them polypus-wise, so that the first Half should get itself a new Tail of its own, and the latter [half] a new Head'.[126] Interestingly, the artificial addition of material is here compared to the most natural of phenomena, indicating just how flexible and wide-reaching a model organicism can be.

Elsewhere there is a more definitive comparison between the individual essays of *The Friend* and organic individuals: 'Each Essay will', Coleridge writes, 'be found compleat [*sic*] in itself, yet an organic part of the whole considered as one disquisition.'[127] Here it is not quite clear whether individual wholeness is part of organicism itself, or something which threatens to disturb its singular form of unity. The connecting adverb 'yet' remains taciturn and potentially ambivalent on this point. If one grants that Coleridge here fully embodies the 'whole in the part' dictum of organicism, the essays of *The Friend* can be said to be the fullest, and most positive, embodiment of radical organicism, on the level of form, of his entire output. Does this mean that the essays are like *friends* to one another? And exactly what would such a claim entail? Although it might be a little far-fetched to infer that friendship provides the formal mode of organisation, as well as the title and an underlying theme, to the essays in *The Friend*, I shall presently show that Coleridge early on developed an understanding of friendship which displayed considerable structural sophistication.

5
Early Affinities: Friendship and Coleridge's Conversation Poems

Pantisocracy and the mourning of Southey

Those of Coleridge's early poems that have been loosely grouped together under the common name of 'conversation poems' arguably constitute an early instance of the radical informality pursued by the modern lyric. With one exception, they were all written between 1794 and 1799, and were to have a considerable influence on Wordsworth. Yet Wordsworth is not the only figure who had a close link with Coleridge at the time. In a manner not completely unlike that of the romantics in Jena, Coleridge briefly had a group of friends and writers living close by in the West Country. At least intermittently, this group constituted something of a literary coterie or circle with close bonds of both friendship and writing. With Dorothy Wordsworth, Charles Lamb and various spouses and relatives, Coleridge and Wordsworth formed a closely-knit unit, particularly during when Coleridge was living at Nether Stowey.[1] This informal community was a shadowy remnant of Coleridge and Southey's preceding and more ambitious plan to form a small, completely democratic society on the banks of the Susquehanna in Pennsylvania – the so-called 'pantisocracy'.

I am going to read the conversation poems through the prism of this community. In order to gain a sense of what kind of community we are dealing with, the actual reading of the poems will be deferred for the moment. For although the conversation poems strive for an immediate form of communication, this does not mean that they are self-evident utterances. They are mediated expressions and harbour – as I will show – something radically inaccessible at their very centre. As Jacques Derrida's recent work on the politics of friendship (which I will return to in chapter 9) has shown, there is an otherness at the heart of friendship. Although Coleridge's organically conceived theory of friendship does not perhaps go quite as far as Derrida, it is important to see that it too transcends intimacy and privacy. With Coleridge, too, the friend must be something of a stranger.

Coleridge's conception of friendship comes from the ashes of pantisocracy. The precise theoretical foundations of the pantisocratic scheme are less accessible in the extant literature than the external history of how it flourished and then ran aground in tandem with Coleridge and Southey's early friendship. The scant documentary evidence that survives suggests that the two instigators were far from agreement on all the details of their venture. If Southey 'out-paced Coleridge in extravagance of commitment',[2] it is nevertheless true that Coleridge was more circumspect with regard to the dangers inherent in all concessions to the conventional morality of the day. Unlike Southey, he would not countenance any form of servitude – neither through the use of hired employment nor in the treatment of the wives.[3] The central tenet by which the scheme differed from the more popular utopianism of William Godwin was with regard to property – indeed, in one letter Coleridge described pantisocracy simply as 'the System of no Property' (90),[4] in another as 'a scheme of emigration on the principles of an abolition of individual property' (96). The goal of such abolition was ultimately to 'remove the *selfish* Principle from ourselves' (163).

The possibility of selflessness is one of the fundamental tenets of the pantisocratic scheme. But it is a highly idiosyncratic form of selflessness, for the members of this community are also described as being ends in themselves. It is precisely the inherent freedom of such absolute ends that is violated when servitude is admitted. The labour of animals can be employed to 'our own Benefit', but not the labour of other human individuals: 'To be employed in the Toil of the Field while *We* are pursuing philosophical Studies – can Earldoms or Emperorships boast so huge an Inequity? ... A *willing* Slave is the worst of Slaves – His *Soul* is a Slave' (122). Hence the selflessness of the pantisocratic member is of a peculiar kind: it is a kind of *freedom in selflessness*. Concomitantly, it is not a state of being fully unattached. Although Coleridge criticises the fetters of domestic relationships, whereby wives are treated as possessions, he nevertheless embraces a certain form of domesticity. In its current state, domesticity may be 'morbid' and one of 'our most perilous Temptations', yet ideally it is an immeasurable boon: 'Domestic Happiness is the greatest of things sublunary' (158). But as to where the border between pure and impure domesticity, as that between pure and impure selflessness, lies, Coleridge is consistently, and perhaps necessarily, vague.

Does this entail that the pantisocratic ideal is really an impossibility? As early as in February 1796, Coleridge seems to hint as much: in a letter to his publisher, Joseph Cottle, he describes the pantisocratic venture as 'a scheme of Virtue impracticable & romantic' (185). Six months earlier, he envisages its realisation as being 'distant – perhaps a miraculous Millennium', and writes to Southey: 'What you have seen, or think that you have seen of the human heart, may render the formation even of a pantisocratic *seminary* improbable to you' (158).

If pantisocracy is impossible, and even a weakened application of it is improbable, this might explain why no coherent or detailed description of it will survive Coleridge and Southey. Coleridge plans to write a manifesto or treatise on it, and mentions his plans for writing 'the book of Pantisocracy' (115) in an early letter to Southey. This book – and not the later descriptions of a planned epic poem, or the plans for an absolute poetico-philosophical work inspired by his exposure to German romanticism – is in effect the first manifestation of Coleridge's planned super-work, of which the late notes for the *Opus Maximum* are but the last of a series of unsuccessful heralds. In its earliest formulations, the book is envisaged as being a polemical rejoinder to the work of Godwin. In the same early letter, Coleridge confidently plans to write something that will not only 'have comprised all that is good in Godwin' (115) and the latter's *Political Justice*, but also managed to surpass Godwin. Yet within days, buoyant optimism yields to a more despairing tone. In the following passage, the problems of his friendship with Southey are hard to separate from worries concerning the very foundations of the pantisocratic system:

> I have told you, Southey! that I will accompany you on an *imperfect* System. But *must* our System be necessarily imperfect? I ask the Question that I may know whether or not I should write the Book of Pantisocracy – I can not describe our System in circumstances *not* true: – nor can I *omit* any circumstances that *are* true. Can I *defend* all that are *now* true? Is it not a pity, that a System so impregnable should be thus blasted? (120)

Although not even a satisfying rudimentary sketch of the pantisocratic system survives in the letters between Southey and Coleridge, those very same letters nevertheless reveal the centrality of *friendship* to pantisocracy. Friendship is projected both as an ideal form of community, in terms of a politics of friendship,[5] *and* as a provisional construction based upon the actual relations between the two letter-writers. For Southey and Coleridge were friends – in fact, they were to be the most intimate of the all pantisocratic friends, the most equal among equals: 'Surely, Southey! we shall be frendotatoi meta frendous. Most friendly where all are friends' (103).

The quantitative relativity of friendship, hinted at in this last quote, indicates that Coleridge's ideal community is far from being constituted on the basis of equality or mutuality only. The pantisocratic collectivity has a centre from which all other relations disperse themselves, and from which one can organise something of a hierarchy of friendship. In an early letter to Southey, Coleridge starts with the metaphor of the heat granted by the sun, according to one's relative proximity to it, in order to describe this system:

> Warmth of particular Friendship does not imply absorption. The nearer you approach the Sun, the more intense are his Rays – yet what distant

corner of the System do they not cheer and vivify? The ardour of private Attachments makes Philanthropy a necessary *habit* of the Soul. I love my *Friend* – such as he is, all mankind are or *might be*! The deduction is evident –. Philanthropy (and indeed every other Virtue) is a thing of *Concretion* – Some home-born Feeling is the *center* of the Ball, that, rolling on thro' Life collects and assimilates every congenial Affection. (86)[6]

In this centrifugal process of gradual assimilation, friendship comes first – because it is close to home. The friend is one's neighbour, and therefore one's affections begin with him or her. Metaphorically speaking, all other affections are forms of friendship, but depleted or weakened forms of it, lukewarm compared to the intense heat of the most intense closeness. Does this imply that one can come too close? Does friendship risk burning up, if one comes too close to the central sun? I will suspend this question for the moment.

In making friendship a privileged metaphor for community, Coleridge is denying distance. The vain abstractions and generalities of Enlightenment ethics, and particularly those of Godwin, are being corrected by a recourse to the near, to the neighbour. The essence of this tendency is later summarised by Coleridge in terms stressing the primacy of family relations: 'if you love not your earthy Parents whom you see, by what means will you learn to love your heavenly Father who is invisible?'[7] As the invisible manifests itself only by way of the visible, and the distant by means of the near, all community – however universal and wide-reaching it might desire to be – must begin in 'home-born Feeling'.

Yet this very beginning is divided. The reference to the affections' being 'home-born' is a lead to this division. For the friend is close to home, and yet not simply a family member. The borderline between home and neighbourhood is often blurred in Coleridge's discourse of the 1790s, most commonly by way of a blurring of the borderlines between the terms 'friend' and 'brother'.[8] His brother George, for instance, is also a 'friend', according to the letters,[9] while his neighbour at Nether Stowey, the tanner Tom Poole, is described as a 'Brother of my Choice' (246) and as a 'Brother of my soul' (289). In addition, Poole is a 'Friend of my Soul' (246). The linking of the communal bond to the 'soul' alerts one to the location, the virtual *topos*, of the proposed kinship or friendship. It is a friendship or brotherhood of the inner – in this profound intimacy, soul mates have a common fund or space of interiority, removed from the superficial civilities that otherwise dominate the intersubjective domain.

This interiority is not only named the soul; it is also called the *heart*. It is a 'friendly Heart' (231) that is the cause of kindnesses, and when Coleridge gives up on his friendship with Southey, he can say in retrospect that 'I *locked up* my heart from you' (167). Once refused access to this inner shrine of friendship, Southey has to make do with outer formalities:

You gave me your hand – and dreadful must have been my feelings, if I refused to take it. ... But is shaking the Hand a mark of Friendship? – Heaven forbid! I should then be a Hypocrite many days in the week – It is assuredly the *pledge of Acquaintance, and nothing more.* (167)

Friendship facilitates habitual access to the other's heart, and this is why Coleridge (in the same letter) laments that his friend has 'left a large Void in my Heart – I know no man big enough to fill it' (173). Banished from this space, Southey has *'fallen back into the Ranks'*, no longer a friend: 'You were become an Acquaintance, yet one for whom I felt no common tenderness. I could not forget what you had been' (166). Thus Southey is situated in a strange, twilight space in Coleridge's affections, where the sun of friendship has sunk down beyond the horizon, yet leaves the dim afterglow of its memory. If Coleridge allows him 'to sink into that Class' other than friendship, specifically into that class named 'Acquaintance', he does so only by leaving a mark or interior wound. There survives a mnemonic remainder in the interior of the heart, straddling the interiority of friendship's heart with the outer distances of mere civility. This interior wound is not without relevance to the project of the conversation poems, since most of them come about *after* Coleridge has renounced Southey and given up on the entire pantisocratic scheme. Even if Kelvin Everest is correct in linking the conversational poems written during Coleridge's stay in Nether Stowey with the earlier ideal of the pantisocratic community,[10] the former cannot be a complete renaissance, or perfected repetition, of the latter. The incomplete mourning of Southey's friendship and its legacy mark the later conversational poems with a void at their heart.

Love, paternity and the essence of friendship

Even before Southey's intimate companionship is gained and lost, the nature of friendship's interiority is a contentious theme for Coleridge. In order to grasp not only the content, but also the limits and heterogeneous abysses of his conception of friendship in the 1790s, a wider compass than his relations to Southey is required. While his neighbouring companionship with Thomas Poole plays the role of supplanting the faulty precedent of Southey, essentially prefiguring his later relation to the Gillmans, Coleridge's correspondence with George Coleridge and Mary Evans intercalates a more uneasy and ambivalent note into his thoughts on friendship.

The latter two relationships show how exteriority affects and questions the heart-felt interiority of friendship. The figures of the lover and the parent hover in the backdrop here, as bordering alternatives to the friend. In the case of Mary Evans, the limits of friendship are marked by her act of denial. Towards the end of 1794, Coleridge is forced to renounce any hope of success in his courtship of her. She regards him 'merely with the kindness of a Sister', according to his own analysis of the relationship, and although he thinks of her 'with the purity of a Brother' it is with 'more than a Brother's ardor': he has a 'disquieting Passion' which he has to tame (130). In even his 'wildest day-dream of Vanity', he claims, he has never supposed that her feelings for him go beyond those of 'a common friendship' (144).

In the latter quote, two different problems with regard to Coleridge's conception of friendship are touched upon: commonness and dreaming. One is classical: the qualitative distinction between a 'common' and a rarer, more elevated form of friendship is broached in such precedents such as Cicero and Montaigne.[11] We have also come across this distinction earlier, in Coleridge's hope that he and Southey will be the 'Most friendly where all are friends'. With regard to his relations to Mary Evans, it would seem that love and friendship are not quite differentiated from one another: he has brotherly feelings towards her, but too much 'ardor', while she might conceivably have reciprocated his advances if only her friendship were not 'common'. The basic distinction here is not one between friend and lover, but between common friendship and ardent friendship, both of which can be described in family terms (that is, described in terms of 'brotherly' or 'sisterly' emotions).

The other problem concerns the activity of dreaming. The ardour of friendship is linked to dreaming in another of Coleridge's letters to Mary Evans. This letter stems from the time before she rejected him, a period when their relations were even more unresolved than they would become later. He signs a letter dated 7 February 1793 with an extended, flirtatious finale, which compares his own written words to opium:

> Are you asleep, my dear Mary? – I have administered rather a strong Dose of Opium –: however, if in the course of your Nap you should chance to dream, that
> > I am with the ardour
> > of fraternal friendship
> > Your affectionate S.T. Coleridge,
> you will never have dreamt a truer dream in all *your born days*. (50)

Apart from Coleridge's obvious self-irony, it is worth noting how the mechanics of how the dream are tied to a transgression of limits here. This transgression has a certain legitimacy, for it is covert: the dream is that which *might* cause Mary Evans to 'chance to dream' that Coleridge feels the 'ardour of fraternal friendship'. Not only is the whole scenario diverted to a hypothetical mode, it is also couched in ambivalent terms. For what is the ardour of fraternal friendship? The question hinges upon the precise point where that ardour is 'more than a Brother's' and yet pure as a brother's. The reason Coleridge can flirt with abandon here is that the limits between friendship and sexual love are not precisely drawn. The *dream* is precisely what grants access to that borderline area where transgression is not transgression, and friendship is not common friendship. Indeed, in a letter to Southey from December 1794, after he has shelved his love-interest in Mary Evans, Coleridge again locates friendship's transgression in the dream – in a 'Dreaminess of Mind':

> I am well assured, that she loves me as a favorite Brother. When she was present, she was to me only as a very dear Sister: it was in absence, that I felt those gnawings of Suspense, and *that Dreaminess of Mind*, which evidence an affection more restless, yet scarcely less pure, than the fraternal. (145, emphasis added)

Here fraternity and friendship are said to be definitively surpassed by the dream. Even the rare and elevated form of friendship, the one where one is a 'favorite Brother' or a 'very dear Sister', is something other than the more ardent state introduced by the dream. Yet ambivalence is still preserved, if one looks closer. For what are 'those gnawings of Suspense' that accompany the dreaminess of mind? Does the suspense only concern the beloved's affections for the lover, or does it also encompass the lover's affections for the beloved? Concomitantly, is Coleridge's affection 'restless' because it is a desire that demands to be assuaged, which relentlessly seeks an outlet that is not forthcoming? Or is it deemed restless because it entails a state of meandering beyond the stolid affection of present friendship, to the fervid desire of absent love, and back again?

The context of Coleridge's letter does not allow one to decide on these matters. Precisely how much, and how simply, Coleridge's text hovers on the borderline between friendship and love is not clear. Suffice to say, love and friendship share borders thanks to their both being based on 'affection' or 'ardour'. Although the problem of the closeness of love and friendship surfaces only in the context of Coleridge's complex feelings for Mary Evans, the very existence of such borders opens up the possibility of there being a latent homoerotic dimension in what is a predominantly *fraternal* understanding of friendship.

Friendship consists of feelings of affection, but not exclusively so; it is also characterised by at least one more ingredient, variously denominated in Coleridge's letters. In order to close in on it, I will return to his lamenting to Southey the loss of their friendship. The phrases put in quotation marks cite Southey's own words:

> Southey! I *have* 'lost Friends' – Friends who still cherish for me Sentiments of high esteem and unextinguished Tenderness. For the Sum Total of my Misbehaviour ... is Epistolary Neglect. I never spake of them without affection, I never think of them without Reverence. Not 'to this

Catalogue', Southey! have I 'added *your name*'. You are *lost* to *me*, because you are lost to Virtue. (163)

The gist of Coleridge's argument here is straightforward: he has not lost a friend in losing Southey's companionship, for Southey would have to be virtuous in order to be called a friend. More relevant in this context is how actual and existing friendships are described: friends have 'high esteem' and 'unextinguished Tenderness' for Coleridge, while he displays 'affection' and 'Reverence' towards them. These two terminological couples may be reduced – even if such a reduction necessarily entails a certain violence of simplification – to one. For tenderness and affection would seem to be almost synonymous, while – perhaps a little less obviously – esteem and reverence might be deemed equivalent.

Thus friendship would consist of a both bond of intimacy (affection, tenderness or ardour) and a more ethically tinted bond. The latter bond would combine dissymmetry (the esteem is 'high', that is, it entails a certain element of subjection with regard to the other) with a religious inheritance ('reverence' obviously has such connotations). The latter might even bear a hint of a threat or a potentially violent power in it, if one grants any importance to the resources of etymology: the word 'reverence' stems from the Latin verb 'verere', which means both to fear and to respect, and is the origin of the English adjective 'wary'. Friendship, for Coleridge, would thus be a complex relation: it would not only consist of the affection that he, for instance, felt for Mary Evans – it would also entail wariness and an ethical, perhaps even religious, sense of awe.[12]

Lest it be thought that Coleridge here is befuddling the simple task of describing a very quotidian and unexceptional phenomenon through the introduction of such terminology, I would like to underline the fact that he is not in quest of the ordinary. He is not engaged in an empirical generalisation based upon several individual instances of friendship in everyday life, but rather in search of an exceptional and non-existent community. This he shares with Kant's strikingly similar definition of friendship, a definition which explicitly states that it is dealing with a perfected (and hence not necessarily existing) state: '*Friendship* (considered in its perfection) is the union of two persons through equal mutual love and respect.'[13] This projective ideality is the reason why Coleridge's early friendships for Mary Evans and Southey are deemed to be beyond what is 'common'. It is also the reason why he approaches the term with no small amount of trepidation in several letters, insisting for instance to John Thelwall that 'I do not *esteem*, or LOVE Southey, as I must esteem & love the man whom I dared call by the holy name of FRIEND!' (294).

According to this last quotation, friendship is not only sacred, but it also allows itself to be summarised by two characteristics: esteem and love. This would seem to be another variation of the bifurcated definition we already have encountered. It is repeated almost verbatim one and half years later, on 15 September 1798, when he writes to Poole: 'Of many friends, whom I love and esteem, my head & heart have ever chosen you as the Friend – as the one being, in whom is involved the full & whole meaning of that sacred Title' (415). Here it would seem that Coleridge's understanding of friendship is placed in conformity with the dichotomy of the faculties of thought and feeling: 'head & heart'. More intriguingly, and again in proximity to Kant, is the recurrence of another dichotomy in Coleridge's understanding of friendship: the opposition between the sublime and the beautiful constitutes something of a hidden subtext for how he conceptualises his relationship to his elder brother, George.

George's position as a preacher, and his more circumspect and settled lifestyle, make him an edifying, if limited, role model for his more wayward brother. George is quite explicitly imbued with paternal authority, as an early letter of 1793 expresses in Latin: 'Vale, mi frater – frater animo et voluntate erga me plane paternâ' (56).[14] Later, George's successful efforts to free Coleridge from his military obligations (incurred by enlisting in the 15th Light Dragoons) contribute to bring this paternal undercurrent in their relationship even more to the fore. A note of supplication and almost hysterical prostration enters the younger brother's guilt-stricken letters:

> Shall I confess to you my weakness, my more than Brother! I am afraid to meet you –. When I call to mind the toil and wearisomeness of your avocations, and think how you sacrifice your amusements, and your health – when I recollect your habitual and self-forgetting Economy, how generously severe – my soul sickens at it's [sic] own guilt – A thousand Reflections crowd on my Mind – they are almost too much for me. Yet you, my Brother, would comfort me – not reproach me – and extend the hand of forgiveness to one, whose purposes are virtuous tho' infirm, and whose energies vigorous, tho' desultory. – Indeed I long to see you, altho' I cannot help dreading it. (74)

A paradoxical conjunction of opposite emotions is made explicit in how the final sentences combine affection and dread. The liminal suspense alluded to with regard to the crowding of thoughts that 'are almost too much for me' points in the same direction: both these traits are typical of the sublime. It would seem that George Coleridge is being projected as something very similar to a sublime object here, his sublimity both taking the form of the cause of a mathematical sublime (in the numerical excess of thoughts) and a dynamical cause (as a dreaded force which simultaneously indicates a benevolent source).

Coleridge shows some interest in Edmund Burke's distinction between the beautiful and the sublime at this time. He introduces it on one occasion into a discussion of typography,[15] and also (more conventionally) when he deems the beautiful surroundings of Shrewsbury inferior to the sublime ruggedness of the scenery at Nether Stowey. The sublime experience of nature is also broached in a discussion, in October 1797, with the fellow poet and radical John Thelwall, whose indiscriminate admiration for nature is countered by Coleridge's hankering for the sublime: 'My mind feels as if it ached to behold & know something *great* – something *one & indivisible* – and it is only in the faith of this that rocks or waterfalls, mountains or caverns give me the sense of sublimity or majesty!' (349).

Burke linked the authority of fathers with sublimity, and with the following emotions awakened by Cato: 'we have much to admire, much to reverence, and perhaps something to fear; we respect him, but we respect him at a distance.'[16] This emotion is contrasted with how the beautiful manifests itself in sociality. According to Burke, one can see the beautiful in the love of a mother, and the emotions awakened by Caesar, who 'makes us familiar with him; we love him, and he leads us whither he pleases'.[17] The defining traits of Coleridge's understanding of friendship, namely love and esteem, thus can be seen as integrating the traits of both the beautiful and the sublime into the basic social relation. If we now move from Coleridge's early letters to those of his early poems that are commonly called 'conversation poems', we will find the same opposition at work in the latter.

Parerga: Demarcating the conversational genre

The conversation poem has an oddly obscure inception. For one thing, there is considerable uncertainty about when it saw the light of day. According to the influential opinion of G. M. Harper, the first instance of this genre was written by Coleridge on 20 August 1795, and was named 'The Eolian Harp' – or 'Effusion XXV' as the poem was originally dubbed.[18] But Coleridge does not himself use the term until 1798, in the *Lyrical Ballads*, and then as a subtitle to another, and later, poem, namely 'The Nightingale'. Even then he uses the term 'Conversational poem', and does not amend it to the more familiar appellation ('conversation poem') until nineteen years later, in connection with the publication of the *Sibylline Leaves*.

This is the only use Coleridge makes of the term: he never calls 'The Eolian Harp', or any poem other than 'The Nightingale' for that matter, by this name. So if one were to veer to the uttermost extreme of biographical punctiliousness, one might even hazard that the conversation poem was born in 1798 and that it had no issue after that date. A more inclusive approach is, however, warranted by the fact that Coleridge collected a total of seven poems (including the two aforementioned ones) under the heading of 'Meditative Poems in Blank Verse'. Since then, several editors and commentators on his work have opted to designate some of his poems as 'conversation poems', but the members of that group has varied. The basic nucleus arguably consists of 'The Eolian Harp', 'Reflections on having left a Place of Retirement', 'This Lime-Tree Bower My Prison', 'Frost at Midnight', 'Fears in Solitude', 'The Nightingale' and 'To William Wordsworth'.[19] Apart from these, various other of Coleridge's poems have been included in the group, including 'Lines written in the Album at Elbingerode, in the Hartz Forest',[20] 'Dejection: An Ode',[21] 'To the Rev. George Coleridge'[22] and 'To a Friend'.[23]

As one would expect, the content of such a list depends upon a preliminary definition of the conversation poems. The delimitation of a genre can never be made on exclusively internal grounds.[24] Although one might hesitate to concur with the mature Coleridge in affirming that every method must begin with an *idea*, his critique of a directionless empiricism is nevertheless valid.[25] In order to collect every instance of the conversation poem, the critic must already have previously identified its specific characteristics. There is a strong tendency amongst critics of the conversation poems towards including poems written in five-foot blank verse only. But this premise can be overridden if a poem is deemed exceedingly suitable on the basis of thematic considerations. If one follows G. M. Harper in stressing that these are Coleridge's 'Poems of Friendship', the poems addressed to George Coleridge and a 'Friend' (Charles Lamb) will of necessity commend themselves.

I will include these two poems in the basic group, in *my* preliminary and delimiting gesture, and see what the conversation poems say about themselves – in both their verse and their parergonal remarks and subtitles. If the archetypal conversation poem could speak to me directly – like a friend, as it were – and tell me what it is, what would it say? What would for instance 'To a Friend' say? This is the earliest of all the suggested conversation poems, and makes for an interesting firstborn of the conversational brood – mostly, perhaps, because of its self-conscious thematisation of its own aberrant, even slightly monstrous nature. It is subtitled 'Together with an unfinished poem', due to the fact that it was presented to Charles Lamb together with an unfinished draft of 'Religious Musings'. The latter poem is a lofty and pretentious effort, a specimen of Coleridge's more ambitious and epic mode, which is mocked in the opening lines of 'To a Friend':

> Thus far my scanty brain hath built the rhyme
> Elaborate and swelling: yet the heart
> Not owns it. (ll. 1–3)[26]

From the very beginning, then, the conversational poem answers to a need to cater for the demands of the 'heart'. In doing so, it will avoid the grandiloquence of the epic manner, opposing that manner's tendency to indulgently pile up (cf. 'built') too luxurious edifices with humbler and more homely abodes. The humility of the conversational poem is thus born from a lack in the epic edifices, a lack that is addressed in the next lines of this poem:

> From thy spirit-breathing powers
> I ask not now, my friend! the aiding verse,
> Tedious to thee, and from thy anxious thought
> Of dissonant mood. (ll. 3–6)

Lamb is too disturbed by the sickness of his sister to supply what Coleridge's 'Religious Musings' need, and that is a collaborative contribution that would provide it with 'aiding verse'. Thus Coleridge's first conversational poem is born from the need to provide aid to poetry. From the conventional poem's lack, and its inability to help itself, a new genre is born – and yet it is not a genre that saves conventional poetry from its state of want, for 'To a Friend' does not itself rectify the lack inherent in 'Religious Musings'.

A state of penury is observed, but not amended. Yet the poet is not completely impassive, for in initiating the conversational genre, 'To a Friend' opens up a new space of intimacy and proximity. It opens up a space for poetry that is close to that of private letters: a space that *the heart will own*. If it does not aid poetry by any direct, innovative contribution to its existing genres, it nevertheless aids by example: it sets itself up as a differing precedent, worthy of imitation. The conversation poem is typically, for Coleridge, a *parergon*: a supplement coming to the aid of the main work.[27]

In a manner similar to how 'To a Friend' supplements 'Religious Musings', 'To William Wordsworth' is explicitly written as a response to a reading of Wordsworth's *Prelude*. Furthermore, as is indicated by its subtitle ('With some Poems'), 'To the Rev. George Coleridge' is supplementary, in the form of a dedication, to Coleridge's entire volume of *Poems* of 1797. If I may personalise these dynamics of genre in Coleridge's own terms, and allow form and content to inform one another, there is a sense in which the conversation poem presents itself as the *friend* of poetry. It is close to traditional poetry, yet it insists upon its own integrity and authority as worthy of esteem. 'Love me', it seems to say to poetry, 'but keep your respect: for I am to be your affectionate preceptor.'

Only by being distant can the conversational poem teach poetry closeness. Coleridge repeatedly comes back to this distance from traditional poetry. 'Reflections on Leaving a Place of Retirement' originally has the subtitle 'A Poem which affects not to be poetry'. Taken in its perhaps most strikingly immediate sense, this subtitle would seem to suggest that the pretension of the conversational genre to preserve its alterity from conventional poetry would be precisely that: a *pretension* rather than a reality. The conversation poem would affect or pretend to be something else than poetry: it would play up to a similitude of otherness, feigning an aberration it cannot essentially maintain. Yet even if it is only a feigned friend of the normal poem, there is still the possibility that the friendship might flourish to the point of actually becoming authentic. In an early letter to George, Coleridge indeed claims that his pretending to have a fraternal affection for his brothers James and Edward might create a real feeling: 'I will assume the semblance of Affection – perhaps, by persevering in appearing, I at last shall learn to be, a Brother' (53).

The conversation poem, then, affects not to be a poem, on the basis of its claim to inwardness. Even as it affects to creep closer to the inner crevices of the heart, it risks being plunged into indelicacy and loathsome, humiliating obscurity. When he sends the original of 'The Nightingale' to Wordsworth, Coleridge scribbles down some frivolous introductory lines, humorously denigrating his own work:

> In stale blank verse a subject stale
> I send *per post* my *Nightingale*;
> And like an honest bard, dear Wordsworth,
> You'll tell me what you think my Bird's worth.[28]

The same passage goes on to proclaim indecorously that 'There's something falls off' at the nightingale's 'bottom'. As the only one of Coleridge's poems which is expressly designated as conversational, 'The Nightingale' is thus implicitly belittled. Significantly, Coleridge also dishes out derogatory treatment to some other poems of the genre. In a manuscript he comments on 'Fears in Solitude', another of the conversation poems, in the following manner: 'NB. The above is perhaps not Poetry, – but rather a sort of middle thing between Poetry and Oratory – *sermoni propriora*. Some parts are, I am conscious, too tame even for animated prose.'[29]

Even if the conversation poem is close to the heart, or maybe precisely because of this, it risks being too tame. Paradoxically, the conversation poem's recourse to the very seat of life, to the language of the heart, risks robbing it of all liveliness. Again there is a glimpse of Coleridge's dilemma: how can one wholeheartedly pursue the quick of life, when life at its centre burns up in a cataclysmic fire? The conversation poem defers, or camouflages, this approach to nothingness by virtue of a turn towards religion. Rather than affirming a negation or annihilation of poetry, in an utter tameness or indifference that is both supra-poetical and supra-prosaic, Coleridge suggests that there is a 'middle thing between Poetry and Oratory'. The phrase 'sermoni propriora' is identical with the motto for 'To the Rev. George Coleridge', a mistranslation from Horace which Coleridge takes as meaning 'properer for a sermon'.

The reference to the sermon is, of course, not accidental. By this time, Coleridge has had some experience as a priest, and has only narrowly (thanks to the Wedgwoods) escaped becoming a Unitarian minister. He also describes his plan to move to Nether Stowey, in a letter from November 1796, in terms that try to reconcile his seclusion with the duties of a priest:

> You think my scheme *monastic rather than Christian.* Can he be deemed monastic who is married, and employed in rearing his children? – who *personally* preaches the truth to his friends and neighbours, and who endeavours to instruct tho' Absent by the Press? ... Shall I not be an Agriculturalist, an Husband, a Father, and a *Priest* after the order of *Peace*? an *hireless* Priest? (255)

Coleridge's position, according to this letter, is not that of a Unitarian priest spreading the Word from the pulpit. Nor is it that of a Godwinian spreading of the dominion of truth in 'the conversation of two persons' or 'in small and friendly circles' where every man 'will commune with his neighbour'.[30] Rather, it is a compromise between these two positions, which comes close to Schleiermacher's vision of a mediator, or priest, whose vocation is exclusively a 'private affair'.[31]

The activities of the 'hireless' priest would not be exclusively personal, though: not only would he *'personally'* preach to friends and neighbours, he would also preach publicly by way of literature. The conversation poem would, ideally, answer to both these exigencies, combining the appeal to the friend with the instruction of the absent stranger. This is what the *exerga* of the conversation poems suggest as a middle way, a route projected and planned for navigating away from both the Scylla of the conventional platitudes of poetry's exhaustion, as well as the Charybdis of the utterly tame and indifferent lifelessness of mere idle conversation. Only through a reading of the poems, though, can the success of this route be judged.

Between prayer and conversation

If the conversation poems permit Coleridge to fuse the roles of family man, neighbour, and preacher, it is because all these roles are vectors whose virtual point of intersection is the *topos* of friendship. The friend is familial, neighbourly and sacred. Friendship resolves the near and the distant, the particular and the general, in a manner anticipatory of Coleridge's later theory of the symbol, and yet also points beyond the solution of this dichotomy to an impossible third, i.e., its projected and foundational synthesis in the divine.

I have already shown how Coleridge's conception of friendship combines intimacy with distance. The same structure is evident in the conversation poems. The most obvious and explicit instance is probably the description of Coleridge's feelings for his brother in 'To the Rev. George Coleridge'. After referring to George as 'my earliest Friend' (l. 43), the poem goes on to depict the nature of that friendship:

> He who counts alone
> The beatings of the solitary heart,
> That Being knows, how I have lov'd thee ever,
> Lov'd as a brother, as a son rever'd thee! (ll. 48–51)

Friendship thus combines fraternal affection with the esteem one feels for a father. It represents a synthesis of both the hierarchical and mutual dimensions of the family. The presence of God (i.e. 'He who counts alone ...') also alerts one that this structure is not self-sufficient, but is borne by an ulterior and absent authority. George's authority is not absolute. Earlier in the poem he is addressed as 'Thee, who didst watch my boyhood and my youth' (l. 44). Yet the purview of his caring vision is obviously not that of God's eye, which has unique access to the innermost workings of the heart.

In Coleridge's conception of friendship any friend may take over this limited authority by proxy. In 'The Eolian Harp' it is his wife, Sara Coleridge, who is invested with it, as her 'more serious eye a mild reproof / Darts' (ll. 49–50), recalling him from pantheistic speculation to the straight and narrow of Christian orthodoxy. When the friend's authority becomes too prodigious, as in 'To William Wordsworth' where Wordsworth is called both a 'Friend' and a 'Teacher' in the very first line, the conversational genre approaches that of confession. In a sense, one can say that one of Francis Bacon's three 'fruits' of friendship, the cathartic establishing of 'peace in the affections' through the divulgence of self,[32] is given a new role by Coleridge. It is not merely a convenience of friendship for Coleridge; rather it is a *right*, an inalienable prerogative, of friends to demand the revealing of innermost secrets from one another. In the first of his five autobiographical letters to Thomas Poole, Coleridge explicitly states that 'what I am depends on what I have been; and you, MY BEST FRIEND! have a right to the narration.'[33] This narration will, he hopes, make his friend 'behold with no unforgiving or impatient eye' the weaknesses of his character. Thus the adjudicating authority of the friend is invested with an almost divine ability to judge and forgive the entirety of an existence.

This strain of confessional autobiography is, perhaps, particularly strong in the poems to Wordsworth and George Coleridge. The absolute responsibility to the friend makes even confession problematic, though. In the poem to George there is the retraction of the final lines, where not the life of Coleridge but the poetical utterance itself is deemed as possibly in need of forgiveness. The confession to Wordsworth is not retracted in the same manner. It is more stridently negated, by the following interruption:

> That way no more! and ill beseems it me,
> Who came a welcomer in herald's guise,
> Singing of Glory, and Futurity,
> To wander back on such unhealthful road,

> Plucking the poisons of self-harm! And ill
> Such intertwine beseems triumphal wreaths
> Strew'd before thy advancing! (ll. 76–82)

Here autobiography is interrupted not only due to its potentially detrimental effects, but also because the poem's major exigency is an encomium of the friend, not self-depiction. Coleridge's responsibility to Wordsworth must ultimately leave all thought of self behind.

One thus approaches something of a radical limit in Coleridge's understanding of friendship. A pure state of dependency – of unbounded respect – is broached later on in the poem, where Wordsworth is addressed in adulatory terms: 'O Friend! my comforter and guide! / Strong in thyself, and powerful to give strength!' (ll. 102–3). The image of Wordsworth proffered here is close to Cicero's conception of the ideal friend as one who has 'qualities that relieve him of dependence upon others'.[34] Yet although Coleridge's notion of friendship constantly draws upon such Greco-Roman precedents, he also consistently goes beyond them. He differs from Cicero, in this instance, in that the self-dependency of the friend in question is so pronounced, that there can be no pure fusion. Whereas the Roman, in accordance with Aristotle, claims that the 'significance of friendship is that it unites human hearts',[35] Coleridge opens for a potentially far more asymmetrical relationship. In the poem to Wordsworth, the author of *The Prelude* is implicitly cast as a father (though the rhetoric is far less insistent than in the poem to George), and Coleridge as his child:

> In silence listening, like a devout child,
> My soul lay passive, by thy various strain
> Driven as in surges (ll. 95–7)

Coleridge's childlike passivity before the poetry of his friend is also evident in the manner in which 'To William Wordsworth' pays tribute to *The Prelude*. For much of the first half of the poem is devoted to a simple résumé, of sorts, of Wordsworth's 'long sustainéd Song' (l. 104) – a manner of showing respect which approaches the echolalia of a child.[36]

In Coleridge's relation to Wordsworth in this poem, two interpretations of friend's passivity are partially overlaid. The first involves a form of divinity. Wordsworth's grand poem is called 'a sacred Roll' (l. 55) and 'a song divine' (l. 46), and the poet's pure independence and unadulterated power to give assistance, invest him with a quasi-religious status. The second interpretation is the aforementioned relation between child and parent. Here Coleridge's conception of friendship is linked to the whole Rousseauist and idealist tradition concerning the project of pedagogy and *Bildung*. Pedagogy seems to be inherent in all friendship for Coleridge, affecting all acts of sympathy. This is true, for instance, of his act of identification with Lamb in 'This Lime-Tree Bower My Prison', but it is particularly conspicuous in relations where the age or authority of the persons concerned is unevenly balanced.

If one returns to the poem 'To William Wordsworth', it is worth noting that, although Wordsworth is granted the epithet 'Teacher of the Good' in the opening line, his parental authority does not grant him any sure means of teaching. Pedagogy has its problems. Even early in the poem the close reader might notice considerable reservations as to the scope of Wordsworth's gift:

> Of the foundations and the building up
> Of a Human Spirit thou hast dared to tell
> What may be told, to the understanding mind
> Revealable; and what within the mind
> By vital breathings secret as the soul
> Of vernal growth, oft quickens in the heart
> Thought all too deep for words! (ll. 5–11)

What has Wordsworth done here, in telling 'Of a Human Spirit'? The verb 'dared' would seem to indicate that the telling of it has been risky – perhaps even with a hint of murky transgression akin to Alcibiades' revealing of the Eleusinian Mysteries. Yet it would seem that not all has been revealed, especially if the contents of that revelation – 'What *may* be told' – is interpreted as being limited. Wordsworth may have committed a transgression of some sort, but the mystery has not been fully disclosed. By such a reading, the qualification 'to the understanding mind / Revealable' would indicate that *The Prelude* is limited to the faculty of the understanding, and does not reach the hidden depths of the faculty of reason.

By the indeterminate manner in which it continues after the semicolon in line 8, the syntax achieves an almost Wordsworthian complexity. Are the 'vital breathings secret' which lie 'within the mind' something which Wordsworth has revealed *in addition* to the revelations which are strictly of the understanding, or are they subject to the same limitation? Has Wordsworth told all that can be told, including all that is pertinent *both* to the understanding and to reason? Or has he written of 'the foundations and the building up / Of a Human Spirit', as well as the hidden and vital inner workings, but only insofar as both are amenable to being filtered through the understanding?

Coleridge may or may not be adding a little salt to his praise of Wordsworth. Coleridge's later critique of much contemporary thought, may be anticipated here: he may be accusing Wordsworth of grasping reason through the understanding, and not on its own premises.[37] But here none of the belligerent stridency of the later critiques is evident. Perhaps this absence is explicable by the *necessity* of Wordsworth's indirect access to the deepest truths. After all, if the 'vital breathings' indeed really *are* 'secret', there cannot be immediate access to them. Such an interpretation finds support later on in the poem, paradoxically in a passage where Coleridge seems to be saying the opposite:

> thy work
> Makes audible a linkéd lay of Truth,
> Of Truth profound a sweet continuous lay,
> Not learnt, but native, her own natural notes! (ll. 57–60)

Truth is made manifest in Wordsworth's poem, but it manifests itself with a reserve, like an open and explicit secret. For it cannot be learnt. Even when it gives itself to intercourse through a 'lay' such as *The Prelude*, there can be no *knowledge* of it. Wordsworth is a natural and he is a teacher, but he cannot teach nature to others. Thus the friend cannot give what makes him or her esteemed to another friend: that power is not communicable.

Coleridge looks more explicitly, and more consciously perhaps, into the pedagogical relation in another of the conversation poems, 'Frost at Midnight'. Like 'To William Wordsworth', this is another poem dealing with secrets. The very first lines claim that 'The Frost performs its secret ministry, / Unhelped by any wind' (ll. 1–2). The frost, later emblematic of the entirety of nature, performs a ministry: it is a mediator (like a Christian minister) of divinity. But this communication of divinity is hidden from any direct view, secret from those who have not gained access to its mysterious ways. As the poem later makes clear, all of nature – however barren or unprepossessing it may seem – is

> Of that eternal language, which thy God
> Utters, who from eternity doth teach
> Himself in all, and all things in himself. (ll. 60–2)

A semiotics of nature is to be discovered, whereby Coleridge's son Hartley can be taught by the greatest teacher of them all, namely God. But Coleridge himself must first function as a preparatory teacher, teaching Hartley the alphabet and grammar of God's language, so that God may speak directly to Hartley.

How does one learn this secret language? How does it work? An important premise is Hartley's becoming native to a natural environment. If the boy may 'wander like a breeze / By lakes and sandy shores' (ll. 54–5), living and taking his leisure in nature, he might avoid the fate of Coleridge himself, who was 'reared / In the great city, pent 'mid cloisters dim' (ll. 51–2). The pedagogical programme to be undergone by Coleridge's son is also central to the ending of 'The Nightingale', where the speaker deems 'it wise / To make him Nature's play-mate' (ll. 96–7). In the latter poem, the father wishes for the child 'that with the night / He may associate joy' (ll. 108–9) in a manner akin to that of 'Frost at Midnight', where it is not all times of day, but 'all seasons' that 'shall be sweet to thee' (l. 65).

In learning the uniform benevolence of nature – whether day or night, summer or winter – the child has a potential for redemption. It has an uncorrupted innocence that the more mature father lacks. For this reason, the child can reverse the pedagogical structure – a reversal implied in Wordsworth's poem 'My heart leaps up', where it is famously stated that 'The Child is father of the Man'[38] – and become a spiritual guide for the adult. Thus in 'The Nightingale' the son instructs the adults to listen to the bird's song:

> he would place his hand beside his ear
> His little hand, the small forefinger up,
> And bid us listen! (ll. 94–6)

But in the same poem it is stated that he 'Mars all things with his imitative lisp' (l. 93). In the latter example his mimetic proficiency, so essential to all pedagogical appropriation, functions more like a blemish on the natural harmony than as a fulfilling of it. Without apt regulation, the mimetic drive risks destroying all harmony. The same detrimental childishness is present in 'Frost at Midnight', but there it is the father who incorporates it. Coleridge's own interpreting of a 'thin blue flame' (l. 13) which flutters on the grate of his fire, as something alive and akin to himself, is described in the following terms:

> Methinks, its motion in this hush of nature
> Gives it dim sympathies with me who live,
> Making it a companionable form,
> Whose puny flaps and freaks the idling Spirit
> By its own moods interprets, every where
> Echo or mirror seeking of itself,
> And makes a toy of Thought. (ll. 17–23)[39]

Although this act of detrimental copying is pronouncedly active, whereas Hartley's 'imitative lisp' is more passive, the same kind of childishness or immaturity is alluded to in the reference to the 'toy of Thought'. True imitation is not playfulness, or the 'aimless activity' of childhood, which Coleridge was later to distinguish from the 'ripened and deliberate judgment' of a mature individual.[40]

If the most important and sublime undertaking of man, according to a later formulation of Coleridge's, is to 'form the human mind anew after the DIVINE IMAGE',[41] this demands that one knows how to separate divinity from the surrounding dross of life. But neither 'Frost at Midnight' nor 'The

Nightingale' tells one precisely how to distinguish between good and bad mimesis, between divine and profane imitations – or, to use terms from Coleridge's later critical work, between 'imitation' and 'copying'.[42] In effect, the border between these two mimetic modes is undecidable, and the crit-ical gesture of distinguishing between the mimesis of the friend and the mimesis of the foe must ultimately be haphazard and chanced. The beneficence of nature may be real, as the frost may provide good ministry, but that ministry is *secret* for essential reasons, and even Coleridge is no adept at its language.

Just as the irresponsible toying of speculative thought cannot be safely distinguished from true pedagogy from the divine teacher, the stolid satiety of a self-satisfied staying at home cannot be distinguished from the settled rootedness which is Coleridge's ideal of domesticity. Here one approaches another dimension of the conversation poems. They project an ideal of living at home, pre-dating Wordsworth's similar vision in *Home at Grasmere*. This settled living at home is posited as the *result* of good ped-agogy – it is the *telos* of the mimetic process, the self-sufficient maturity that follows upon dependent infancy and adolescence. Thus George Coleridge, 'having passed / His youth and early manhood in the stir / And turmoil of the world, retreats at length' ('To the Rev. George Coleridge', ll. 1–3). Now fully matured, he retires to the place of authority that he pre-viously was dependent upon himself – he retires

> To the same dwelling where his father dwelt;
> And haply views his tottering little ones
> Embrace those agéd knees and climb that lap,
> On which first kneeling his own infancy
> Lisp'd its brief prayer. (ll. 5–9)

After climbing 'Life's upland road' (l. 11), he has now been drawn to 'one centre' (l. 13). The centred and safe existence of the elder brother is con-trasted with Coleridge's own fate, which is to have 'roam'd through life / Still most a stranger' (ll. 40–1). The latter wanderer has 'chance-started friendships' (l. 20); that is, his friendships follow no settled plan, nor are they rooted in one fixed abode.

The dichotomy of rootedness versus wandering informs the poem addressed 'To the Rev. George Coleridge', but it is a dichotomy that is iron-ically undercut by another, earlier conversation poem. For 'Reflections on Having Left a Place of Retirement' envisages precisely the *trap* inherent in a too rooted and secluded life. The speaker of this poem dismisses, after first extolling, the idyll of living in 'a Blessèd Place' (l. 17). Such an existence is interpreted as guilty of a pre-emptive staging of what can only rightfully be a post-apocalyptic harmony. Until the millennium has arrived, one cannot give in to 'delicious solitude' (l. 58), but must rather 'fight the bloodless fight / Of Science, Freedom, and the Truth in Christ' (ll. 61–2).

Thus the solitude of a settled life both is and is not an ideal for the figure of the friend. The friend must both be independent *and* engaged, according to a contradictory double imperative which was one of the stumbling blocks that doomed Plato's attempt to define friendship in the early dialogue *Lysis*.[43] Coleridge is well aware of this problem, as he alludes to Poole's friendship in the following way: 'you will have served me *most* effectually, by placing me out of the necessity of being served.'[44] A friend is someone who is free – in accordance with the etymology of the word, stemming as it does from the Anglo-Saxon *freo*, 'not in bondage' – but this freedom risks ridding one of all need of friends. The goal or end of friendship is the state of being friendless.

Yet for Coleridge another kind of friendship defers that end. The same letter to Poole shows that the finishing of most friendships only prepares one for the eternal beginning of this different kind of friendship: 'indeed what can any body [do] for me? – They do nothing who do not teach me how to be independent of any except the Almighty Dispenser of Sickness & Health!'[45] This almighty dispenser can, of course, be named by a singular and unique appellation: God. If friendship cannot ever lead to pure solitude, it is because even the purest of solitudes is not self-sufficient: one is always dependent upon that very best of friends, upon God – since God is 'our universal Friend', as Coleridge puts it in a lecture of 1795.[46]

The pure dependency of this first friendship precludes any mutual, two-way conversation. In transcending 'the ethics of reciprocity' Paul Ricoeur has described as being typical of Aristotelian friendship, [47] the conversation poems continually open out onto the more fundamental address of prayer. Dialogue or conversation always needs a supplement. There is, for instance, the prayer that suddenly and surprisingly caps the poem 'To William Wordsworth'. The ending of the poem envisages a circle of harmonious relations, spreading from 'thou thyself [that] / Wert still before my eyes' (ll. 105–6) to the surrounding 'happy vision of belovéd faces' (l. 107). Yet even the happy band of friends cannot suffice to dislodge Coleridge's sense of anxiety, and when he rises after listening like a helpless infant, the absolute is beckoned through the address of prayer: 'And when I rose, I found myself in prayer' (l. 112).

The concluding line of 'To William Wordsworth' is not only remarkable for its arresting interruption of the horizon of conventional friendship. It is also significant for two other reasons. First, it is notable in alluding to the *passivity* of prayer. Coleridge 'found' himself in prayer. He did not seek prayer actively, or start praying according to some premeditated plan. Thus prayer does not figure here as an active reflection of God's power, internalised in man, as the work of the imagination will in the *Biographia Literaria*, but rather as a *passion*. The passion of prayer is akin to the respect inherent in friendship, rather than to its love. Prayer would be the verbal equivalent of pure respect.

Second, this quote is striking for its vagueness. Who did Coleridge pray to? What did he pray for? One does not know – for the simple reason that the poem does not tell one. Should one acknowledge what my argument already has seemed to take for granted: namely that Coleridge is praying to *God*, the friend of friends, in the default of any absolute assistance from his friend Wordsworth? Perhaps, yet one must bear in mind that Coleridge himself insists that prayer is no simple address to another person. If prayer is the absolute form of conversation, it is also the absolutely other of all conversation. In one of his annotations, Coleridge makes the point that 'we must not worship God as if *his* Ways were as *our* ways. We must not apply to him, neither as tho' God were the same with sensible Nature, or the sum total of the Objects of our bodily senses.'[48] God is no friend that can be sensed, nor is he the aggregate of the sensible. This transcendence of the ontic has radical ramifications for prayer: 'to speak aloud to God and by the sound and meaning of our words to suppose ourselves influencing him as we in this way influence our fellow men – this is a *delirious* Superstition.'[49] Followed to its extreme conclusion, this stance would really situate prayer beyond encomium, since the praise of an encomium almost always entails a determination of the addressee.[50]

If one extends one's purview beyond 'To William Wordsworth', the conversation poems as a group give ample evidence of the fact that addressing God is a unique act for Coleridge. The prevalent tone is set already in 'To a Friend'. At the end of that poem, Coleridge notes that any requests of God are superfluous, unlike what is the case in the context of intersubjectivity: 'Aught to *implore*' of God 'were impotence of mind' (l. 28). The activity of demand is made silent or muted, and therefore all Coleridge may show God is 'mute thoughts' (l. 29). In the absence of any viable way of asking anything of God, there are nevertheless gifts from God – thus opening up the praising *response* as the only proper manner of address in this context. Coleridge is 'Prepar'd … / Thanksgiving to pour forth with lifted heart, / And [to] praise Him' (ll. 30–2).

In a letter of this time, Coleridge makes a similar point concerning the act of requesting anything of God. Prayer is described as being a 'petition' which one should not expect to 'influence the immutable', and every prayer 'should indeed join to our petition [the words] – But thy will be done, Omniscient, All-loving, Immutable God!' (316). Any request should be accompanied by a counter-request, every demand countermanded in its very utterance. This is why the ending of 'The Eolian Harp' insists that only an encomium of God is proper, any other address being a transgression:

> For never guiltless may I speak of him,
> The Incomprehensible! save when with awe
> I praise him, and with Faith that inly *feels* (ll. 58–60)

Pure praise of God would not involve one in an economy of bartering, of giving and taking, and it would also involve a total responsiveness that would not fix the divine essence on the basis of the world or any of its attributes. This responsiveness entails an elliptical, almost completely negative approach, which is the harbinger of Coleridge's lifelong proximity to negative theology.

Still, despite the fact that only praise is 'guiltless', it is nevertheless true that Coleridge often transgresses such a prescription. Just as the pedagogical friend hovers on the border between pure self-sufficiency and the incomplete, the divine vacillates between being a mysterious and unknown origin of the gift, on the one hand, and a more approachable and personal being on the other. Coleridge oversteps his own restraint by sometimes listing the attributes of divinity, and God is almost made into a personal schoolteacher for Hartley in 'Frost at Midnight': being a 'Great universal Teacher', God 'shall mould / Thy spirit, and by giving make it ask' (ll. 63–4). The circular structure of question and response envisaged here, demonstrates how the appeal to God risks being subsumed into the conversational structure it previously seemed to transcend. 'Fears in Solitude' goes even further, by making an appeal for God to intervene on behalf of the British forces in their war with France.

Nevertheless, the divine resists the economic space of conversational communication. This is underlined by the poem 'To a Friend' when it notes that He is 'the Spirit that in secret sees' (l. 26). The space of the secret is the truth of friendship, and the seclusion of this space is predominantly figured in the conversational poems by the song of birds. Birdsong is an image of an utterance that is spontaneous and aneconomical, not subject to any bartering or principle of exchange. Thus in 'Reflections on Having Left a Place of Retirement', the 'inobtrusive song of Happiness' (l. 23) is compared to the 'viewless sky-lark's note' (l. 19). The skylark's withdrawal from the field of vision is emblematic of the heterogeneity of pure calling, alien to the economic desire of the 'wealthy son of Commerce ... Bristowa's citizen' (ll. 11–12) present in the same poem. Similarly, the skylark of 'Fears in Solitude' is also withdrawn from the compass of the eye, as it 'sings unseen / The minstrelsy that solitude loves best' (ll. 18–19). The very heart of friendship, these poems would seem to intimate, consists more in the silence of reclusiveness than the mutual expression of self.

In an epiphany, this divine minstrelsy would not be 'unseen' – it would be manifest to all, or at least to a chosen few. In 'The Nightingale', it is the 'gentle Maid / Who dwelleth in her hospitable home / Hard by the castle' (ll. 69–71) that is the recipient of the epiphany. She is granted a vision of *concordance*, given in two different versions. In the first version, it is a group of 'wakeful birds [that] / Have all burst forth in choral minstrelsy / As if some sudden gale had swept at once / A hundred airy harps!' (ll. 79–82). The second vision involves a nightingale, and how it is able to 'tune his wanton song' (l. 85) to the motion of the swinging twig it is perched upon. On the face of it, both these epiphanies would seem to be simple visions of natural harmony. They would represent nature's mirroring of friendship, something like an intellectual intuition of friendship, i.e. friendship's auto-presentation of its communal unity through the medium of nature. Yet such an interpretation is insufficient. In the case of the second of the two epiphanies noted, the motion of the twig is significantly described as being a 'swinging from the breeze' (l. 84). Thus both visions of harmony are emblems of an impossible concordance of the natural with the supernatural, the supersensible being metaphorically figured by the wind – a traditional metaphor for the spirit. The same structure is noticeable in the epiphany of 'This Lime-Tree Bower My Prison', where the simultaneous movement of a group of weeds – 'all at once (a most fantastic sight)' (l. 18) – is caused by the external means of a waterfall. The harmony between natural beings can only be attained by a mimesis of that which is beyond nature. This relation to heterogeneity is similar to the way in which conversation's truth is an address beyond conversation, and the ultimate friendship is a friendship with that which is beyond all friendship. In all these cases, relations to something external and more fundamental (corresponding to the principle of hierarchical totalisation) supplement relations of mutuality (corresponding to the organic principle of interdependence).

The epiphany is occasionally revealed to be a *fictional* occurrence in the conversation poems. The song of the nightingales only create a harmony which is '*As if* some sudden gale had swept at once / A hundred airy harps!'[51] Similarly, the vision of an ordered and harmonious world from the coign of vantage of a West Country hill, in another conversation poem, is explicitly only a matter of similitude: 'the whole World / *Seem'd imag'd* in its vast circumference.'[52] The fictional nature of such visions may perhaps provide a hint of why Coleridge wrote these poems, rather than simply carrying on a daily round of conversation and prayer. For only in poetry could the interpersonal appeal of friendship's conversation be simultaneously present and surpassed, and only in poetry could the fictional nature of the address directed towards the basis of such conversation be stressed and ever insistent.

We have seen that Coleridge's birds of epiphany are transitional figures, facilitating a relation to divinity. Yet are natural beings merely stand-ins for the supernatural? Do they merely function in a manner akin to the surrogate objects of the sublime? Coleridge's response to these questions acquires a different slant, if one listens to the other sounds than birdsong. Even if the poem entitled 'To a Young Ass, its Mother being Tethered Near it' does not satisfy all the conventional criteria generally considered essential to the genre of the conversation poem, its exclusion from the genre is not unquestionable. Is the fact that it is not written in blank verse sufficient to discount it, or is the question of friendship more important than such a formalistic criterion? Written in the same year as 'To a Friend' (1794), this is arguably another poem addressed to a friend, although on this occasion the friend is neither a person nor God, but an animal. The outrageousness of this scenario struck Coleridge's contemporaries: a satirical drawing by Gillray depicts the poet with an ass's ears, as if the mere allusion to this poem suffices to discredit its author or even to question his (human) reasonableness.[53] Reasonable or not, Coleridge's poem consistently addresses the young ass in familiar, even affectionate terms. From its family feelings for its mother, he construes a fictional entreaty: 'It seems to say, "And have I then one Friend?"' (l. 24). The poet's resoundingly affirmative response includes the ass in a utopian brotherhood:

> Innocent Foal! thou poor despised Forlorn!
> I hail thee Brother – spite of the fool's scorn!
> And fain would take thee with me, in the Dell
> Of Peace and mild Equality to dwell,
> Where Toil shall call the charmer Health his bride,
> And Laughter tickle Plenty's ribless side! (ll. 25–30)

If the 'dissonant harsh bray of joy' (l. 34) of an ass can prove to be 'more musically sweet' (l. 33) than the most soothing and melodious music, this is, one may infer, because it is the sound of life. As the final line of 'This Lime-Tree Bower My Prison' says, 'No sound is dissonant which tells of Life'. This possibility of extending the community of friends to the point of including all living beings is also evoked in a humorous letter to Southey at the time. Writing of his plans to take a wagon in order to meet Southey, Coleridge imagines the brotherhood he will enjoy on the way: 'Wrapped up in Hay – so warm! There are four or five Calves Inside – Passengers like myself – I shall fraternize with them!' (148). Even if this fraternity beyond the limits of humanity is only evoked in passing, as a joke, it nevertheless sketches the outer limit of Coleridge's ideal community. There is a temptation, or dream (dreams and jokes have important affinities, as Freud showed), to extend this community beyond all limits – and pantheism is linked to such an impulse towards an unbounded and non-exclusive form of togetherness.

Animals such as the ass (or the calves) are, then, on the margins of the body politic implied by Coleridge's conception of friendship. They constitute an outer and extreme limit of this body, and share this liminal position with God and relations where friendship threatens to become pure affection (that is, love) or pure respect. At all these points of extremity Coleridgean friendship is adventurous and inclusive, yet is also troubled by its external limit. If the conversation poems aim at a balance of intimacy and generality, as I extrapolated from the *exerga* where Coleridge comments on the genre, then this limit entails the permanent risk of ruining such a fine-tuned balance. One finds the same problem with regard to inclusion and exclusion that would later trouble (as it was shown in the previous chapter) his more systematic efforts to formulate the principles of organicism *per se*. One also finds similar problems with regard to the constitution of the *centre* of the community of friendship, as is evident in his theoretical work on organicism which I confronted in the previous chapter. Coleridge cannot decide whether he should favour a purely formal, heterogeneous centre – such as the abstract 'God' beyond encomium, or the respected friend who is elevated to the point of being threatening – or if friendship should instead be characterised by interdependence and accessibility in its centre.

The nature of the ideal social community elucidated in the early letters and conversation poems thus in many respects anticipates Coleridge's later conception of organic unity – even if the latter is often more abstract and precise, as well as more susceptible to transformation and diversified application. Indeed, John Beer has shown that there is plenty of evidence of that Coleridge was approaching organicist tenets even at this early stage.[54] In my sketch of his understanding of friendship, one can see an early form of the fundamental tension, or polarity, between opposite forces which he will later characterise as essential to organisms. Coleridgean friendship is pitted between the extremities of respect and affection, and only in the balancing of the two does one find the singularity of friendship. Yet at the limit of respect, one can also see an anticipation of how Coleridge would later claim to be able to sublate oppositions in the religious domain. In the next chapter, I will show how Wordsworth's most ambitious application of organicism shows a similar link with religious concerns.

6
On the Threshold: Wordsworth's Architectonics of the Absolute

In medias res: Philosophy, architecture and *The Recluse*

It is time to enter the temple. In the middle of Wordsworth's large, narrative poem *The Excursion*, which again was to stand at the middle of his even more encompassing poem called *The Recluse*, one reads: 'As chanced, the portals of the sacred Pile / Stood open; and we entered' (V, 138–9).[1] Chance is kind to the figures of the Solitary, the Wanderer and the Poet, and they can stride straight into the church. There is no pausing at the threshold, no description of the façade, not even a fascination for the tympanum: the church is simply open, 'and we entered'. As in much of Wordsworth's poetry, the swift and matter-of-fact nature of this entrance is beguilingly direct. Yet it *is* an entrance, there is a threshold to pass, in the form of a portal, and both the passage and the border leave their trace in the text, even if it is only through a most innocuous and brief mention.

The passage takes place roughly halfway through Wordsworth's planned grand poem *The Recluse*, a text which was to be the answer to Coleridge's prayers for an absolute literary-philosophical work. This poem Wordsworth himself compares, in a passage I shall return to later, to a cathedral. Hence one might hazard that even if the entry into the 'sacred Pile' leads only into a lowly parish church rather than a magnificent cathedral,[2] it should grant access to something like a minor replica of the cathedral of the major poem. Here, if anywhere, it might be truly said that 'a step / Between the Portals of the shadowy rocks / Leaves far behind the vanities of life.'[3] If Wordsworth's edifice were to realise such a step beyond, it would represent the perfect place to end this journey through the variegated systematics and texts of German idealism and English romanticism. At last one would be present before the thing itself, the completed edifice of the absolute work which was projected by Schelling, Friedrich Schlegel and Coleridge, as a realisation of Lessing's call for a new gospel. Indeed Wordsworth's church ought to be that place, but it cannot. Why? Because the scandal of the threshold trips one up, or even demands its own obeisance.

Instead of striding confidently across the threshold, ignoring its innocuous frame and resistance, I would like to pay my respects to the question of threshold itself.[4] I will camp in the entrance to the absolute. In what cannot claim to be more than a preliminary topography, or topology, of Wordsworth's architectonics of the absolute, I will cross back and forth over the threshold of *The Excursion*. Mainly, though, I will hurry through the precincts of many of Wordsworth's later short poems, exploring their neglected nooks and crannies. All the while, the threshold will be my thing – the threshold, more precisely, of a sacred manifestation of *architecture*. As we have seen, the art of architecture is frequently evoked at the very heart of idealism. Even if Kant's text on the 'Architectonic of Pure Reason' quickly drops anchor in the much-frequented harbour of organicism, it nevertheless sets off from the architectural. If one is to identify the solid foundations of the first science, the cornerstone or *archē* of knowledge, as well as its *technical* principles of construction, what can be more natural than to invoke architecture? Fichte makes the same gesture:

> Science may be imagined as a building whose main object is soundness. The foundation is sound, and thus once the foundation has been laid this main purpose would be accomplished. But one cannot live in a mere foundation, which by itself provides protection against neither the wilful attack of the enemy nor the unwilled attacks of the weather; so one adds side walls and a roof above them. Every part of the building is attached to the foundation and to the other parts, and in this way the entire building becomes sound. ... Upon what then do we propose to base the foundation of our scientific structure? The first principles of our systems should and must be certain in advance.[5]

Despite philosophy's pretensions of being completely *a priori*, the inevitable metaphors of 'building solid foundations', 'grounding science' and the like, take their toll and result in extended conceits such as the above. Philosophy cannot, it seems, completely leave the premises of architecture behind. It tries to get out of the building, lifting itself to a higher vantage point (such as Zarathustra's mountains), but there is no way out, it gets stuck in the middle of the thing: *in medias res*.

In the beginning, architecture would lay the first stone. In an age which has seen the discourses of literature, sociology, linguistics, anthropology and history, among others, all lay claim to be the transcendental precondition (in some or another fashion) for the activity of philosophy, such a proposition is not as absurd as it may sound.[6] Yet if architecture is to undertake the prodigious task of establishing itself as a first science, it will have to defend those grounds. It too will have to protect itself, like Fichte's philosophical building, from enemies and inclement weather. It too will have to justify itself. This is a difficult act, and it is hard to see where such justification can come from – if not from without.

My justification for scrutinising architecture lies in Wordsworth's prose introduction to *The Excursion*, in what constitutes the introductory threshold of the text, so to speak, rather than its centre in book five. In that introduction, Wordsworth tries to formulate the relation between *The Prelude* and the more encompassing project of *The Recluse*:

> The preparatory poem [i.e. *The Prelude*] is biographical, and conducts the history of the Author's mind to the point where he was emboldened to hope that his faculties were sufficiently matured for entering upon the arduous labour which he had proposed to himself; and the two Works have the same kind of relation to each other, if he may so express himself, as the ante-chapel has to the body of a gothic church. Continuing this allusion, he may be permitted to add, that his minor Pieces, which have been long before the Public, when they shall be properly arranged, will be found by the attentive Reader to have such connexion with the main Work as may give them claim to be likened to the little cells, oratories, and sepulchral recesses, ordinarily included in those edifices.[7]

How compulsive this metaphor is for Wordsworth can be gleaned from the fact that Dora Wordsworth refers to her father's poem *The Prelude*, a full eighteen years after the publication of *The Excursion*, as 'a long Poem written thirty years back and which is not to be published during his life – The Growth of his own Mind – the Ante-chapel as he calls it to The Recluse'.[8]

In an invaluable study, the sole existing attempt at a comprehensive interpretation of *The Recluse*, Kenneth Johnston takes Wordsworth's metaphor at its word. He presents a relatively comprehensive overview of all the poems meant for *The Recluse*, and even illustrates their place in the finished whole by placing them within a schematic drawing of a church. If there is any fundamental objection to be raised against Johnston's handling of this passage, it is with regard to his interpretation of its organicism, which is rather loosely and uncritically applied. Both the cathedral and other of Wordsworth's less prevalent metaphors for the whole of *The Recluse* are summarised as being 'organic images'.[9] Dramatic consequences follow from this. Since the work as a whole is an organism, so is every poem included within its compass, including *The Prelude*. Of the latter, one is told that '"all" of *The Prelude* can be read in any of its books. While it is theoretically possible that any part of an organic whole may contain the whole, holographically, this feature is more marked in *The Prelude* than in any of the major canonical poems among which it stands.'[10] Johnston is in good romantic and idealist company when he uses organicism so flexibly, that all the fundamental problems underlying it are completely evaded. In a strict application of organicism, though, the idea of a coherent whole risks falling apart – for instance, into a dichotomy of form and content, or into an expressionless and nonsensical self-identity that is indistinguishable from nothingness, or into an infinite proliferation of independently existing fragments.

In effect, Johnston's reading actually sketches the last of these scenarios. For he tries to show how *The Prelude*, which was meant to be only a *part* of the whole, swallows up the entirety of *The Recluse* and in effect becomes identical to the temple it was only meant to precede as an ante-chapel.[11] The threshold, one might say, is the temple itself. But Johnston does not pursue this distension of the part far enough. According to its logic, not only every work contained in *The Recluse*, or every book in *The Prelude*, would have to contain the whole – no, every minuscule part of the whole would have to include the entirety of the edifice in itself. Every single sentence, even, would have to contain the essence of all other sentences, as well as the law of the passage or connection between them. Even these words would have to suffice: 'As chanced, the portals of the sacred Pile / Stood open; and we entered.'

Gothic structure and history

Thus the consequences would be enormous, were one really to read *The Recluse* as an organic work. But did Wordsworth really mean one to do so? What did he mean when he compared the poem to a gothic cathedral; and is this really an organic metaphor? Coleridge had certainly expected an organic interlinking of poems. *The Prelude* was, he wrote, 'as the ground plot and roots, out of which *The Recluse* was to have sprung up as the tree, as far as [there was] the same sap in both, I expected them, doubtless, to have formed one complete whole.'[12] But even while writing this description, in 1815, Coleridge proclaimed his disappointment with *The Excursion*, and used the past tense when he declared: 'I looked forward to *The Recluse* as the *first* and *only* true Phil. [*sic*] Poem in existence.'[13]

Thus Coleridge converts Wordsworth's cathedral to an organism – to a tree. But Wordsworth's own metaphor nevertheless remains that of a gothic cathedral and nowhere does he state that it could just as well be any organic structure *per se*. Thus the question arises: why is there this attraction, for Wordsworth, to the metaphor of the cathedral? Why does he evoke *architecture*, and why is it an expressly *religious* form of architecture of a particular style or era (the gothic)? Furthermore, what resonance do these metaphors have in his writings? By describing the entirety of his work as part of a church complex, Wordsworth has, in effect, made the motif of the church into something more than an internal element of his poetry: it is, paradoxically, both an interior ornament (like a sceptre or a priest's habit, within a church building), and an external means of entry (like a portal or a key) which has to be used before one can enter his poetry.

Before one could even start submitting the separate poems of Wordsworth's career to close reading, then, one would have to account for this gothic cathedral. It would function like the idea of Kant's organic science, granting an overview and order to the field it encompasses. I shall therefore try again to enter Wordsworth's sacred pile, following this lead.

First of all, I want to utilise the key of the structural side of the problem, already broached by Johnston: is it correct to read Wordsworth's metaphor as indicating that one is dealing with an organic structure? Gothic architecture is distinguished stylistically by rib-vaults, pointed arches, external buttressing, as well as various other features. Recent commentators have been reluctant to claim that there is any deep and unifying logic underlying these characteristics. When interpretation nevertheless is forwarded, the general consensus is that the cathedrals are symbols of the Celestial City of the saved, namely, the city of God.[14] But there have been few attempts to articulate the principle of organisation behind that symbol; that is, exactly *how* the cathedral and divine city are constructed in a similar fashion. The most notable (and controversial) attempts to formulate such a logic in recent years have fastened onto mathematical proportion or scholastic logic, rather than organic form, as constituting the deep logic of the cathedrals.[15]

There is, however, some agreement as to how *space* is handled differently in gothic architecture, as compared to the preceding Romanesque style. In Abbot Suger's influential rebuilding of the choir of St Denis around 1140, a characteristic change is taking place:

> The general plan was traditional but the difference in St. Denis is that the architect dispensed with divisions between the chapels, and there is, in effect, some ambiguity whether these form a row of chapels or a second ambulatory.[16]

Interior divisions and boundaries are elided or minimised, resulting in an increased homogenisation or unification of space. In other words: *'gothic' signifies the suppression of the boundary.* In some cases, this tendency is taken so far by gothic architects that they actually omit transepts from the ground plan – thus suppressing the traditional, and highly emblematic, cruciform shape of the church – in order to streamline the space of the nave and choir into one long, unbroken passage.[17]

A form of spatial organicism is evident in the more notable romantic elucidations of the gothic style. Goethe's early raptures over the cathedral of Strasbourg in 'On German Building' (1773) make the soon to be influential point that it is characteristic of gothic to unify all the parts in a whole. The gothic architect is responsible for the vital and configuring act of synthesis:

'He is the first from whose soul all the parts come forward in one eternal, unified whole.'[18] Goethe's views constitute a basis for Friedrich Schlegel's more sophisticated and articulated response to gothic architecture in his travel letters of 1806 (letters that later were re-edited and republished under the title of 'Fundamentals of Gothic Building'). In close proximity to the organicist theories of art presented by his brother, August Wilhelm Schlegel, and by Schelling, Friedrich Schlegel sees the gothic cathedral as a construction wherein the divine city is imitated by way of a plethora of natural, organic forms.[19] Even if gothic architecture as a whole subordinates all decoration to vertical elevation, Schlegel nevertheless locates a tension between the lofty height and the luxurious ornamentation. Together, these two constitute a 'dual striving for an infinite fullness and for the highest attainable height'.[20] Elsewhere, he calls this characteristic of 'the human mind's equal proclivity to strive for the highest and the smallest'.[21] Although these are sketchy comments made in passing, it is possible to see in them a reapplication of Schlegel's organicist tension between a (vertical) hierarchical totalisation and a (lateral) interrelationship between the parts.

One can find traces of a similar tension in Wordsworth's writings on gothic cathedrals. Wordsworth is surprisingly interested in cathedrals in general, given that he often is quickly summarised as (or implicitly dismissed for) being a nature poet. In the early verse there is an interest in religious ruins which, although a very traditional *topos* inherited from the eighteenth century, never actually abates. The reference in the prose introduction to *The Excursion* is linked to the widespread Gothic Revival in England at the time, and within a few years the building of gothic churches becomes something of a fad in England. The religious revival sparked by the threat of the new French radicalism, leads to a vigorous building programme, for which gothic is the most favoured architectural style.[22]

Wordsworth takes a small but active part in this movement, by campaigning for new and better churches. Thus 'Ode: 1815' celebrates English triumphs over France with speculation as to where and how a possible new church, as a commemoration and place of burial for the deceased war heroes, ought to be built. The late sonnet 'When Severn's sweeping Flood had overthrown' similarly argues for the building of a new church in Cardiff. He also seems to have been smitten with some of the anti-classicist rhetoric of the time, reacting strongly, for instance, against the erection of a full-size replica of the Parthenon in Edinburgh. A poem titled 'The Modern Athens' derides the ancient deity of that temple (Pallas), by describing her as 'an outlandish Goddess the just scorn / Of thy staunch gothic Patron, grave St. Giles' (ll. 10–11). Here a local gothic heritage – both in architecture and in faith – is deemed superior to imported classicism.

Beyond this, there is a link here to how Wordsworth wants to rebuild in his own poetry the fundamentals of the harmonious cosmos that he claims remains unchanged throughout, despite, for instance, his own early and passing flirtation with Godwinian scepticism. However much he discovers that 'the building stood, as if sustained / By its own spirit',[23] he nevertheless feels the exigency of erecting and reconstructing that sanctuary in *The Recluse*. The poem is to be an 'ideal cathedral', which, like Viollet-le-Duc's later attempts at synthesis of the gothic, is to transcend its undeniably particular and eclectic empirical manifestation.[24] Even if the result is Wordsworth's own work of art, he denies it any autonomous existence (whether subjective or aesthetic). The following sonnet may be read as describing, in anticipation, the act of writing the poem:

> In my mind's eye a Temple, like a cloud
> Slowly surmounting some invidious hill,
> Rose out of darkness: the bright Work stood still;
> And might of its own beauty have been proud,
> But it was fashioned and to God was vowed
> By Virtues that diffused, in every part,
> Spirit divine through forms of human art:
> Faith had her arch – her arch, when winds blow loud,
> Into the safety of consciousness thrilled;
> And Love her towers of dread foundation laid
> Under the grave of things; Hope had her spire
> Star-high, and pointing still to something higher;
> Trembling I gazed, but heard a voice – it said,
> 'Hell-gates are powerless Phantoms when *we* build.'[25]

The particularly Christian resonance of Wordsworth's architectural metaphor, a resonance which is very insistent in this sonnet, may be interpreted as indicating a clearer subjection of Wordsworth's own *magnum opus* to the Bible and to Christian dogma than was previously the case. Coleridge's tendency to blur the line between secular and religious poetry is now circumvented – at least implicitly – by Wordsworth's reverence for the Christian heritage. It is a heritage that he finds to be increasingly embattled and threatened by extinction. His own work is, in many ways, a work of compensation for the sins of his age (including, arguably, those of the French Revolution):

> Communities are lost, and Empires die,
> And things of holy use unhallowed lie;
> They perish; – but the Intellect can raise,
> From airy words alone, a Pile that ne'er decays.[26]

Wordsworth's absolute poem aims to represent a complete internalisation of past community and lost churches, through a process of mourning which would keep the lost objects safe and sound in a kind of imaginative sanctuary.

The immensity of this task can be inferred by Wordsworth's response, in connection with his overseas tour of 1820, to the still uncompleted cathedral of Cologne. According to Wordsworth's sonnet, the finishing of this edifice seems to be beyond the means of any human builder. Only God – or angels – can save us:

> O for the help of Angels to complete
> This Temple – Angels governed by a plan
> Thus far pursued (how gloriously!) by Man,
> Studious that HE might not disdain the seat
> Who dwells in heaven! But that aspiring heat
> Hath failed; and now, ye Powers! whose gorgeous wings
> And splendid aspect yon emblazonings
> But faintly picture, 'twere an office meet
> For you, on these unfinished shafts to try
> The midnight virtues of your harmony: –
> This vast design might tempt you to repeat
> Strains that call forth upon empyreal ground
> Immortal Fabrics, rising to the sound
> Of penetrating harps and voices sweet!

This poem can be read as a wry, indirect comment on *The Recluse*, already anticipating how the latter 'edifice' will forever remain incomplete. At the same time, it is evident that Wordsworth does not see the cathedral as an isolated, autonomous structure. The cathedral is dependent on a hetero-geneous, divine foundation: it is both built to the glory of God, and in con-scious repetition of the divine (or at least angelic) act of creation. The sonnet also contains an allusion to the gothic cathedral's excessive height (it is pictured as 'rising' to the angelic song) and to the 'harmony' (in line 10) of divine creation. One finds roughly similar traits being evoked in 'Ode: 1815', where the projected cathedral is said to combine two different virtues: 'there meet / Dependence infinite, proportion just' (ll. 54–5). In this meeting, one can glimpse something similar to Schlegel's twin virtues of internal beauty and externally striving verticality. Inhabiting an impossi-ble crossroads, the cathedral combines and negotiates between the auton-omy of the aesthetic and the transcendence of the divine.

Wordsworth's poetry is consistently sensitive to the sublimity of the height of cathedrals. This is linked to the divine foundations of the church:

> Watching, with upward eye, the tall tower grow
> And mount, at every step, with living wiles
> Instinct – to rouse the heart and lead the will
> By a bright ladder to the world above.[27]

The tower of the cathedral is here comprehended within a dynamics of organicism, as its tendency to 'grow / And mount' before the gradually entering spectator is an expression of increasing closeness to the heterogeneous foundation of the church-organism. Ultimately, this power of ascending the skies seems to overshadow any sense of internal, spatial harmony, in Wordsworth's depictions of cathedrals and churches. This is one reason why there is so much recourse to ruins: however much the ground plan of a church may be destroyed by wear and tear, there often remains a spire or a rising silhouette. Indeed, that very feature may be all the more conspicuous when the lower levels of the church are damaged. The internal harmony of churches almost becomes damaging to their ability – especially characteristic of the gothic style – to evoke grandeur through elevation.

It is not insignificant that the tower is the first visible part of the church visited in book five of *The Excursion*, when the wandering company arrives at the valley. It is also the last they see of the church: 'far off, / And yet conspicuous, stood the old Church-tower' (IX, 574–5). All of the bulk of the edifice is on the verge of being swallowed up by this one feature, until the whole is reduced to being nothing than a transparent sign of the sublime. From this perspective, the gothic cathedral would be nothing but the passageway to the beyond.[28] A complete dissolving of its structure is usually resisted, however, by the bulk of the thing. Wordsworth is attracted to the heavy mass and imponderability of the cathedral, as this is one of the traits that most immediately link it with the immutability of the divine. Hence he describes cathedrals as being 'everlasting Piles',[29] and one is told that 'They dreamt not of a perishable home / Who could thus build.'[30]

Precisely this aspect of endurance is stressed with regard to the church of *The Excursion*. I will now return – having indulged in my own excursion across the varied terrain of Wordsworth's architectural poetry – to book V of that poem, finally entering into the church in the company of the Solitary, the Poet and the Wanderer. Once inside the church portals, the reader is provided with a surprisingly chaotic and fleeting look. Even if the interior inspires 'temperate awe / and natural reverence' (V, 142–3), it neither seems particularly exalted, nor provokes a particularly striking exercise in *ekphrasis* on Wordsworth's part. The actual interior, with its 'nave and aisle' (V, 154) and 'capacious pew / Of sculptured oak' (V, 164–5), seems homely in accordance with the rustic valley in which the church is located. Nevertheless it is a solid structure, combining the effects of elevation and apparent timelessness:

> Not raised in nice proportions was the pile,
> But large and massy, for duration built;
> With pillars crowded, and the roof upheld
> By naked rafters intricately crossed,
> Like leafless underboughs, in some thick wood,
> All withered by the depth of shade above. (V, 144–9)

The absence of 'nice proportions' alludes to the fact that solidity is more important than symmetry here. Wordsworth's description of the interior is basically devoted to matters of temporality and focuses on the commemorative 'vain distinctions, marks of earthly state / By immemorial privilege allowed' (V, 157–8). The only notable exception is the singular deployment of the tree metaphor. Wordsworth is hardly being original when he compares this gothic cathedral to trees; this is one of the ever-recurring clichés of the literature of the gothic. But this particular simile is, all the same, striking in how it stresses that the dark, inscrutable workmanship of the edifice operates to the depletion of the lower levels of the church-tree: the boughs below the top are both 'leafless' and 'withered'. Hence there is not only elevation, but also an effect of subservience and domination – almost violence – in the structure of the whole. In this trope one catches a glimpse of the complicated workings of the *nature* of architecture (as well as the politics of architecture, and the politics of nature) that ultimately folds Wordsworth's temple to its outside, and converts its threshold to a rotatable fulcrum at the centre of several interlinking grounds.

Outside: The garden and the graveyard

We have seen that Wordsworth's cathedral is never an autonomous structure. It is always incomplete, begging divine intervention and acknowledging dependence. It shows the tension of the warring principles of organicism, since this hierarchical dimension coexists with a more collateral dimension of mutually interdependent parts. Ultimately, the edifice is folded towards an unlimited exterior through this tension: the exterior delimitation of the organism falls away or, more frequently, becomes a virtual and problematical boundary, once its interior is shown to be devoid of autonomy. The absolute cathedral yields to the grounds beyond, as is demonstrated, as a matter of fact, by the progress of *The Excursion*. For, surprisingly perhaps, this poem does not dwell for long on the inside of the church. The visitors behave like impatient tourists, making only a brief stop before they again go outside:

> The pale Recluse
> Withdrew; and straight we followed, – to a spot
> Where sun and shade were intermixed; for there
> A broad oak, stretching forth its leafy arms
> From an adjoining pasture, overhung
> Small space of that green churchyard with a light
> And pleasant awning. (V, 224–30)

The sacred temple thus becomes almost indistinguishable from a momentary halt of a tourist outing. Rather than granting a settled and atemporal abode, it essentially – at its very heart – becomes traversed by the distracted and passing steps of an *excursion*. Yet this is no simple eradication of the sacred: tourism is in the *proximity* of the temple, remaining on the threshold. One might notice that the protection granted by the stretching tree, the 'broad oak', of this churchyard is very similar to that which was previously granted by the branching roof inside the church. The inside is thus dispersed into the outside, rather than simply obliterated.

What follows in the next few books of the poem is indeed in many ways an external repetition of what was a central motif inside the temple. For the Pastor's subsequent narratives are mostly commemorative speeches, retelling the lives of the deceased, just as the interior of the church was dominated by sepulchral stones telling

> The ordinary chronicle of birth,
> Office, alliance, and promotion – all
> Ending in dust; of upright magistrates,
> Grave doctors strenuous for the mother-church,
> And uncorrupted senators, alike
> To king and people true. (V, 173–8)

Those that are the subjects of the Pastor's narrative are, however, less prominent persons. To a certain degree, this is a gesture of levelling: according to a tradition which includes Gray's churchyard elegy, the lowly and the humble are shown to be just as edifying as the wealthy and the influential. However elevated, for instance, 'the noblest relics, proudest dust, / That Westminster, for Britain's glory, holds / Within the bosom of her awful pile' (VI, 263–5) might be, nothing can change the fact that commemoration 'is due to all' (VI, 267). If the church folds out to its exterior, embracing a spacious graveyard, this is because it is in its essence an open space, welcoming the poor and needy just as much as the more privileged.

The churchyard represents a threshold on the border between architecture and landscape, art and nature, the living and the dead. However much the cathedral, as a metaphor, has a tendency to swallow up its surroundings within itself, Wordsworth is very aware that a church does not exist in a vacuum. Even though the church bestows new meaning upon its surroundings, the pre-existence of a natural soil amenable to building is a prerequisite. Nowhere is the edifice's dependency upon nature more evident than in the *Ecclesiastical Sonnets*, where Wordsworth's preparatory letter explains that the entire series of sonnets owns its existence to the search for a fitting location for a church planned by a friend.[31] The conclusion to that search, as well as future hopes for this particular church, is set forth in sonnets 39–41 of the third, and final, part of the series. A

vision of a harmonious communal activity between man and nature is
presented:

> Be this the chosen site; the virgin sod,
> Moistened from age to age by dewy eve,
> Shall disappear, and grateful earth receive
> The corner-stone from hands that build to God.[32]

Even if the sod disappears, the earth receives gratefully: in the nexus of
these two operations one can glimpse something of Wordsworth's double
bind with regard to nature. On the one hand, art and architecture must
subject nature, even to the point of wiping out its surface manifestations.
Thus 'the lonely Sexton's spade / Shall wound the tender sod',[33] in preparing a surface for the first building blocks. On the other hand, art cannot be
anything more than a gift to grateful nature, an act of retribution surrendering back what is rightfully nature's own. If this act is properly carried
out, nature will embrace the church just like 'the fresh air of incense-
breathing morn / Shall embrace' the crucifix of Wordsworth's planned
church.[34] The first movement is only permissible if it ultimately is in
accordance with the second, but this accord of violence and retribution is
hard to fathom. Where is the boundary where architecture would
ultimately leave the grounds of nature?

Here the whole problematic of Wordsworth's transcendental or sacred
architecture intersects tangibly with that of the home or abode. The two
relations are parallel: the relationship between the church and the surrounding graveyard and nature, on the one hand, mirrors that between the
dwelling-place and nature, on the other. This parallel is no accident: in
many ways, Wordsworth's vision of a grand 'gothic cathedral' is the sequel
to his earlier one of the harmonious microcosm of the home. When *Home
at Grasmere* fails to embody that earlier ideal, the stage is set for the more
public and transcendental forms of habitation exemplified by edifices such
as Cologne cathedral and the rectory at Grasmere. The use of the church in
The Tuft of Primroses, where it is described as 'the spot of sacred ground, the
home / To which all change conducts the thought',[35] is an important part of
this transition. Together with *The White Doe of Rylstone*, *The Tuft of
Primroses* arguably represents the clearest and earliest marker of how the
home is superseded by the church as a central metaphor in Wordsworth's
poetry.

In any case, the challenge in the erecting of the church-home is to build
upon, and never leave the precinct of, nature. Only then can the building
avoid being counted among 'Art's abused inventions'.[36] In situating a
church in natural surroundings, Wordsworth's poetry is also intimately
linked at this juncture with the entire eighteenth-century interest in landscape gardening. Some of these gardens had indeed gothic temples (often

expressing an implicit opposition to the more usual Palladian and classical buildings) in their midst.[37] The English garden represented an attempt to do precisely what Wordsworth's cathedral must do: namely, artistically transform nature, without actually ever leaving the realm of the 'natural'.

Of course, it is often hard, in principle, to differentiate the workings of this kind of engineering from the more overtly constructed phenomenon of *la belle nature* in the French garden. A demystification of an only apparent naturalness seems to be in order, and such a gesture is the predictable staple when a modern, sceptical reader confronts such gardens. Any symbolic expressivity is quickly dismissed, or exposed, in favour of purely analogical, emblematic relations.[38] One finds ample evidence of such demystification in Wordsworth's texts, despite their attempts to present the harmonious unification of architecture and nature. For instance, the cottage of a prosperous widower in *The Excursion* proves, at closer inspection, to be feinting its miraculously natural appearance:

> Ye might think
> That it had sprung self-raised from earth, or grown
> Out of the living rock, to be adorned
> By nature only; but, if thither led,
> Ye would discover, then, a studious work
> Of many fancies, prompting many hands. (VI, 1143–8)

But art does not only imitate nature in Wordsworth's poetry. For the process is often reversed, and in the long-term development of his imagery nature becomes more and more of a temple. As true civilisation is never fully removed from its natural roots in his writings, the opposite is also true – insofar as nature is sacred, it always approaches the state of being a temple:

> thee would I conduct
> Through woods and spacious forests, – to behold
> There, how the Original of human art,
> Heaven-prompted Nature, measures and erects
> Her temples, fearless for the stately work,
> Though waves, to every breeze, its high-arched roof,
> And storms the pillars rock.[39]

Within this divinely informed architecture of the non-human, the traditional Christian metaphor of God being the architect of cosmic order is reapplied. Insofar as human beings construct sublime buildings, these are at best imitations of 'the eternal Architect'.[40] The latter is always elevated above human architects, so any similarity in the results of the two cannot bridge the fundamental gap between them. Nevertheless, only a tangential touching of the two practices is needed for Wordsworth to link them in a simile. Hence Staffa's cave is described as a spot 'where the almighty hand / That made the worlds, the sovereign Architect, / Has deigned to work as if with human art!'[41]

The many picturesque ruins scattered through Wordsworth's texts, both early and late, find their rationale in this view of nature. Since nature is 'the Original of human art', it is also the end and final destination of the latter: the source is also the aim, according to an Aristotelian notion of organic development. Hence a sonnet apostrophising Roslin chapel, the latter now reduced to a state of ruin where the 'wind is now thy organist',[42] celebrates the gradual subsumption of religious architecture into the encompassing harmony of nature:

> From what bank
> Came those live herbs? by what hand were they sown
> Where dew falls not, where rain-drops seem unknown?
> Yet in the Temple they a friendly niche
> Share with their sculptured fellows, that, green-grown,
> Copy their beauty more and more, and preach,
> Though mute, of all things blending into one.[43]

Here Wordsworth has reached agreement, through his singular line of reasoning, with the leading exponent of the picturesque, William Gilpin: 'A ruin is a sacred thing.'[44] Here, if anywhere, the great blending reconciliation of art with nature, and of architecture with the earth, takes place. Wordsworth's poetry usually goes to great pains to subdue all sinister resonance in such descriptions of ruins, often presenting nature's work as a soothing embalming and preservation of what otherwise would go utterly to waste. This is true of Furness Abbey, where the historical destruction of the monument is described as in terms of 'havoc' and 'rash undoing' (l. 1),[45] while nature's subsequent reclaiming of the ruins is the 'counter-work' (l. 4) of a 'soothing spirit' (l. 3). This spirit is embodied in how the ivy clasps the abbey's ruin, which Wordsworth interprets as an act that aims 'Fall to prevent or [to] beautify decay' (l. 6).

To prevent destruction is, however, something else than to prettify it,[46] and ultimately Wordsworth's view on the interrelationship between nature and human architecture is not without its tensions. This is evident by comparing the 'counter-work' of nature evident at Furness Abbey with the very different effects adumbrated in 'Among the Ruins of a Convent in the Apennines'. In the latter poem, nature once more shapes, and blends with, the ruins of a religious edifice, but this time there is no consoling issue. The ruins

> Do but more touchingly recall
> Man's headstrong violence and Time's fleetness,

> Making the precincts ye adorn
> Appear to sight still more forlorn. (ll. 15–18)

Although Wordsworth's note on this poem seems to ascribe such effects to a passing phase, where nature's beautifying work hasn't yet 'matured' to the state it has attained, for instance, at Furness Abbey,[47] the immediately contrary effect of this ruin shows that nature does not only have a benevolent side. Another poem, written around the same time, stages an almost Manichean struggle between nature and mankind. Even if a human may seem the slave of nature, after death mankind will gain 'glory without end'. A more gruesome fate awaits unfortunate nature, personified as a worm, which – the poem states with some barely subdued relish – 'sinks into a hopeless grave'.[48] Apparently nature is not only the epitome of permanence: Wordsworth's timeless nature coexists, in the poems, with the more traditional figure of ephemerality. Nature thus works both with and against time.

Through the bifurcating functions of embalming and dissolving the corpse, nature plays the role of being both the grounds for the churchyard and its destructive, potentially invading exterior. Between these two functions there runs an obtuse threshold which insinuates itself into the very centre of the graveyard. Paradoxically, this lack of any clear demarcation is made into a cause for celebration by Wordsworth. Precisely because the outside is inside, it can always be dissimulated. If death and destructive nature have always already crossed the threshold, this ultimately means one can ignore their presence. Such is the logic underlying the striking sonnet on 'A Parsonage in Oxfordshire', which begins with the following lines:

> Where holy ground begins, unhallowed ends,
> Is marked by no distinguishable line;
> The turf unites, the pathways intertwine;
> And, wheresoe'er the stealing footstep tends,
> Garden, and that Domain where kindred, friends,
> And neighbours rest together, here confound
> Their several features, mingled like the sound
> Of many waters, or as evening blends
> With shady night. (ll. 1–9)

A number of widely disparate positions are quickly relayed in this poem. The first line seems to draw a strict division between the interior and exterior of the sacred grounds, only for the next line to completely suppress that division. From a seemingly watertight dichotomy, one arguably moves on to the point where life-in-death and death-in-life nightmarishly mirror each other as indistinguishable, interlocked and warring twins. The third line then dramatically alters the course of the poem for good, eliding this state of indistinctness into the placid unity of an English garden. Before long, death itself is completely subsumed by the natural landscape, and the graveyard's more destructive potential is softened to the point of its being described as 'that Domain' where close ones can 'rest together'. Only the slight suggestion of a transgression in the adjective 'stealing', in line 4, remains as a trace of the act of stealth committed in transforming the state of disharmonious confusion into one of harmonious fusion. In the final lines of the poem, the transcendence of destructive nature is made complete by reference to the 'glimpses of eternity, / To saints accorded in their mortal hour' (ll. 13–14).

The complete melding between the divine, the landscape garden and the graveyard, thus functions as a relay where, one by one, boundaries are crossed. The natural landscape of the English garden is not, however, nature itself. For here, too, there is a threshold to be passed. Wordsworth showed a keen interest in this limit, especially when he was actively involved in planning Lady Beaumont's garden at Coleorton. A poem written in connection with this work, 'A Flower Garden at Coleorton Hall, Leicestershire', contains an explicit reference to this threshold. Here one is faced with a very different scenario from the one encountered in the sonnet on 'A Parsonage in Oxfordshire'. In the latter poem, the problem of the threshold was raised and then dissimulated in a quasi-Hegelian, step-by-step process of dialectical subsumption. In the poem on the garden at Coleorton Hall this process is repeated – but this time around there is an open acknowledgement of the element of deceit underlying the *schöne Schein*. A peaceful enclave has been created, where nature's flowers need not fear the outside forces of destruction. Indeed the whole is so perfectly at rest within itself, that there does not even seem to exist an outside:

> Yet, where the guardian fence is wound,
> So subtly are our eyes beguiled,
> We see not nor suspect a bound,
> No more than in some forest wild;
> The sight is free as air – or crost
> Only by art in nature lost. (ll. 25–30)

This is no pure *hortus conclusus*: Wordsworth's ideal garden is something more akin to, or even anticipating, the modern conception of the open work of art.[49] There is no clear distinction between the inside and the outside, as the garden-work seamlessly blends with the free and 'wild' nature surrounding it. As a matter of fact, though, this blending is openly admitted to be a construction. The threshold has simply been levelled, as the fence is hidden rather than abolished:

> Apt emblem (for reproof of pride)
> This delicate Enclosure shows

> Of modest kindness, that would hide
> The firm protection she bestows;
> Of manners, like its viewless fence,
> Ensuring peace to innocence. (ll. 43–8)

The whole garden turns out to be an emblem, a sign for its planner's 'modest kindness' and 'manners'. At the same time, it is not *only* an emblem, since it also takes place on the threshold to the wild nature beyond.

The politics of ruin and the places of poetry

All of Wordsworth's poems share such an impurity. They take place on the uneasy borderline between being allegorically emblematic (where the ultimate projected referent is transcendental) and interacting with the passing and incidental facts of history. To a certain degree, this can be called *the* threshold of his cathedral-organism, the limit upon which all the thematic acts of delimitation, passage, and confusions of borders, are played out. All the churches, ruins and buildings embraced by Wordsworth's later verse are, on the one hand, emblems for the transcendental mansion eulogised as early as in the Simplon Pass episode of *The Prelude*:

> The invisible world, [there] doth greatness make abode,
> There harbours; whether we be old or young,
> Our destiny, our being's heart and home,
> Is with infinitude and only there.[50]

After *Home at Grasmere* fails to fully realise that heavenly abode in the figure of Dove Cottage, any impressive architectural structure encountered by Wordsworth can potentially be called upon to be a makeshift embodiment of the invisible home. On the other hand, Wordsworth increasingly becomes an incidental or topical poet (partly, perhaps, out of despair for never actually completing the 'gothic cathedral' of *The Recluse*), attempting to celebrate and fix passing experience. The latter tendency is central to his many late tour poems, where a series of effusions commemorate the history and geography of various places encountered on the road.

The long, rambling poem titled 'Stanzas Suggested in a Steamboat off Saint Bees' Heads, on the Coast of Cumberland', assimilated into the late collection *Poems Composed or Suggested During a Tour, in the Summer of 1833*, is a good exponent of how this threshold disseverates Wordsworth's temple from within. Occasioned by the ruins of St Bees, a former Benedictine priory converted into a theological college not long before Wordsworth's visit, this poem is something of a typical set piece. Its picturesque description and brief historical narrative make it a 'poetical postcard' of sorts. Yet the poem also has more ambitious designs. The final stanza makes explicit a wide-reaching resistance to 'the Genius of our Age' to whom 'Matter and Spirit are as one Machine' and to whom, furthermore, religious concerns are irrelevant.[51]

The religious practices of the medieval monks, who are significantly called 'these Recluses',[52] are said to be animated by something else than the idolatry of purely formal prowess that is the hallmark of Wordsworth's own utilitarian age. Rather than being a mere formalism, the practice of the monks has a vital kernel to it. It is the survival of this kernel that is celebrated: 'once more the local Heart revives, / The inextinguishable Spirit strives' (ll. 149–50). The poem thus builds upon the standard romantic dichotomy between a spiritually informed organism and an empty mechanism devoid of any organising instance. The organically vital ages of the past leave their most perceptible image of unity in the architecture of the church of St Bees:

> Nor be it e'er forgotten how by skill
> Of cloistered Architects, free their souls to fill
> With the love of God, throughout the land were raised
> Churches, on whose symbolic beauty gazed
> Peasant and mail-clad Chief with pious awe;
> As at this day men seeing what they saw,
> Or the bare wreck of faith's solemnities,
> Aspire to more than earthly destinies;
> Witness yon Pile that greets us from St Bees. (ll. 118–26)

Thus a ruin is all that remains of the church in the age of the machine. But even a 'bare wreck' or ruin of the past splendour of the church suffices to keep the memory of the lost faith alive. Hence it is not merely a *memento mori*, marking the spot of extinct pieties, but a sign potentially prophetic of a future revival.

Does such an interpretation fully comprehend what is referred to here as the church's 'symbolic beauty'? It is hard to say, since the poem does not clarify what the significance of that symbolism might be. Here the beginning of the ensuing stanza may be of some help:

> Yet more; around those Churches, gathered Towns
> Safe from the feudal Castle's haughty frowns;
> Peaceful abodes, where Justice might uphold
> Her scales with even hand, and culture mould
> The heart to pity, train the mind in care
> For rules of life, sound as the Time could bear. (ll. 127–32)

The church thus yields 'more' than the aspiring for 'more than earthly destinies'. It both negates the quotidian present and affirms it. In affirming it, both ethical rectitude (having to do with pity and the 'rules of life') and political liberation are made possible. In granting the city a centre, the medieval church grants access to a state beyond the iniquities of feudalism.[53] The hinge between these two stanzas is signalled by an obscure 'Yet more'. Do these two words signal an excess of the political and ethical functions of the medieval church, as compared to that of its 'symbolic beauty' and historical promise of a religious renaissance? Or are all these aspects collected together within the walls of the edifice? Wordsworth's text does not tell one to choose and to separate these functions, but neither does it convincingly unify what is 'more than earthly' with what is 'more' than that again. It is as if an invisible choirscreen internally divides Wordsworth's sacred pile, leaving it functionally unified *and* wrecked into several parts at one and the same time. It both functions like a hierarchical organism and a set of interdependent, but potentially independent, parts. In dismissing the unified machine of utilitarianism, where all values – and all edifices – are purportedly levelled down to the same level of materialism and economy, Wordsworth's organicism exposes his text to a much more complicated interlinking of differing spheres. This is one of organicism's recurrent perils: in rejecting the banal unity of the mechanical and also attempting to escape from antagonistic dualities, it engages in a complex interlinking of different elements which ultimately is beyond its own capabilities.

It becomes apparent how this complexity also has effects on Wordsworth's figuration of his own role as a poet, if one turns to how his poetry treats the connection between the church and song. Surprisingly perhaps, Wordsworth's poetry can never fully identify with such moments where 'With one consent the people rejoice, / Filling the church with a lofty voice!'[54] One would expect this to be the precise spot, in the vast architectonics of the absolute which envelops much of his later poetry, where the voice of his poetry might find a home. It would be the logical expansion and domestication of the related quasi-personal manifestations of social togetherness evident in both Coleridge's conversation poems and Wordsworth's early poetry,[55] into a vision of a fully collected and universalised sociality. But the figure of the poet – whether imaged by a dramatisation of Wordsworth himself, or by way of other characters – remains for the most part on the threshold, or even outside it, seemingly banished from the celebrations he himself heralds.

This idiosyncrasy is evident in an odd passage early on in *The White Doe of Rylstone*, which describes the gathering of the congregation within the church walls of Bolton Priory. Just after the congregation has sung its first song, the local priest is set to take over the proceedings. Yet at this point the poem eerily veers outside, to nature and the emblematically charged natural creature of the doe:

> A moment ends the fervent din,
> And all is hushed, within and without;

> For though the priest, more tranquilly,
> Recites the holy liturgy,
> The only voice which you can hear
> Is the river murmuring near.
> – When soft! – the dusky trees between,
> ...
> Comes gliding in serene and slow,
> Soft and silent as a dream,
> A solitary Doe![56]

If 'you' refers to the poet, then it would seem that he really has no ears for anything other than nature. But since the previous lines describe the church and the congregation's song, these lines seem to hint at a hidden *agon*. This is the implicit struggle between Wordsworth's archetypal figure of the poet and that of the priest. Here the problem concerning the embodiment of the centre of the organic structure (evident in Schlegel and Kant's differing conceptions of the role of a political ruler, as well as Coleridge's strictures on papacy) finds a new articulation. Does the poet or the priest take charge of proceedings at the centre of Wordsworth's sacred edifice? Significantly, it is only when the priest begins to recite that the poet shuts up his ears and crosses to the outside of the church. It is not stated whether outside nature actually can grant anything different than 'the holy liturgy', but nature would at least seem to be a domain upon which the poet has a singular proprietary claim.

Another, but related, inflection is given to this poetical counter-work by the events of *The Excursion*. We have already seen how the company of *The Excursion* leave the interior of the local church, choosing to saunter outside in the grounds of the graveyard rather than pay obeisance within. Towards the end of the poem, the Pastor finally gives vent to a collective thanksgiving:

> Whence but from Thee, the true and only God,
> And from the faith derived through Him who bled
> Upon the cross, this marvellous advance
> Of good from evil; as if one extreme
> Were left, the other gained. (IX, 720–4)

The simplistic and dogmatic conventionality of this homage is undeniable. Yet its occasion is peculiar: the Pastor and his company have by now walked far from the church. Their gathering takes place in the open air of nature. Only from this distance does the Pastor self-consciously evoke the site of the church and its congregation, as if mentioning it can somehow recompense for its absence:

> – O ye, who come
> To kneel devoutly in yon reverend Pile,

Called to such office by the peaceful sound
Of sabbath bells; and ye, who sleep in earth,
All cares forgotten, round its hallowed walls!
For you, in presence of this little band
Gathered together on the green hill-side,
Your Pastor is emboldened to prefer
Vocal thanksgivings to the eternal King. (IX, 724–32)

Perhaps one can speak of an incomplete internalisation of nature in passages such as this. The church is meant to be the spiritualised and elevated manifestation of nature (symbolised, for instance, by the tree-like roof we encountered earlier), but this process is never fully worked through in Wordsworth's poetry. In what psychoanalysis would call a regressive fixation, it is as if he – or the Pastor – has organised the service and collected the congregation within the church's walls, only to remain outside himself. The church-organism's outer limit, its door, is left just barely open, and the poet-priest spends the entirety of the service calling for the *ecclesia*, ushering in all the latecomers (such as a stray doe) from the fields outside. Although Wordsworth does not, like Margaret in *The Ruined Cottage*, wander so far astray in this effort so as to neglect his own habitation, the temptation and the danger of such an uncontrolled and eccentric course is nevertheless present.

Poetry should, then, be the shared song of a community gathered within the transcendental frame of an absolute architectonic. Nevertheless, poetry resists inclusion within those divine walls, and becomes a counter-work unfolding on the outside of the gathering of the divine tract. This causes a skewed relation between church and poetry, and between place and language, in Wordsworth's later poems. Disengaging myself briefly from those poems, in order to fashion something akin to an overview of their varied terrain, I will now show how the metaphor of a grand gothic church changes its significance, all according to how one approaches this relation. The church is in itself located on a threshold of three different positions bordering upon each other, none of which can convincingly stand on its own.

First, Wordsworth's gothic cathedral can be seen as being *merely* a poetical figure. As a simile, it is part of a rhetorical arsenal, linking with other tropes which it uneasily borders onto (such as home, house, churchyard, garden, mind, and mother). Poetry, in short, is always essentially exiled from the church, and yet comprehends it within its own language.

Second, there is a subtly differing view: as an architectural figure, Wordsworth's trope can be read as having a unique status. For it is a metatrope, figuring the very mechanism of tropology. Typically, a reading following de Man's normal trajectories could unfold from this position, contending that Wordsworth's church does not designate being itself, or an actual entity such as a church, but (*pace* Heidegger) language as the very house of being.[57] Thus there is no outside-of-the-church, and Wordsworth's poetic resistance can be dismissed as a facile and passing sentimentalism.

But just as the metaphysical subject always betrays its weakness in needing a mirroring other in order to grasp itself (even in the intellectual intuition), language's grasping of itself via the external mediation of space and habitation can be taken as a sign of dependency. It is in effect an indication of the impossibility of poetry, rhetoric, or indeed any form of language to be conceived of as autonomous. Thus, third, one might claim that a sense of place is a necessary ground even for the unfolding of poetry. Wordsworth's poetry is *also* an attempt to manifest that unnameable precondition, a tract or trace prior to all law courts, academies, and all other buildings: 'the *trace* that is not yet language or speech or writing or sign or even something "proper to mankind".'[58] Outside any actual church, the 'nature' of Wordsworth's poetry might be taken as a term pointing towards this primal place – however insufficient and time-worn such a term might be.

Thus Wordsworth's distance from the ideal communal song is an overdetermined affair. It is also a *political* affair. Insofar as his poetry tries to comprehend the space of the church, it is not merely (as the saying goes) building castles in Spain; rather it is engaged in the very struggle and history of institutions. Thus poetry cannot but propound an ideology, both suffering and modifying the institutions it is wrapped up in. In this respect, Wordsworth's and Coleridge's radicalism of the 1790s is significant as early evidence of a breach from mainstream, institutionalised Christianity so large that they can never completely embrace, or be embraced by, the fold of the Anglican Church. When Wordsworth returns to the Lake District, it is as a partial stranger, desiring his own particular vision of a local 'pure Commonwealth' presided over by a chapel.[59] His idealisations of medieval and Elizabethan church communities are *inter alia* symptoms of a persistent alienation from the institutionalised church of his own day. But not only a distance from Christianity may lie behind the Lake Poet's distance from realised vocal thanksgiving: an uncomfortable proximity may also be involved. There is some evidence that he sees his own poetry as *prophetic* of the new gospel, rather than as its actual manifestation, as in the famous words directed to Coleridge towards the end of *The Prelude*:

> Prophets of Nature, we to them will speak
> A lasting inspiration, sanctified
> By reason and by truth; what we have loved
> Others will love, and we may teach them how. (XIII, 442–5)

Part of the reason for Wordsworth assuming no more than a prophetic stance here, lies in his related, ever-growing humility before the Bible. If Christian temples 'take / Form, spirit and character from holy writ',[60] so too does the cathedral of *The Recluse*, however magnificent it may turn out to be. Nevertheless, one should not conceal the considerable amount of *slanting* involved in how the later Wordsworth erects the Christian edifices of his poetry, evident, for instance, in how he approaches problems concerning ritual and mourning. Despite an increasing desire to embrace the conventional Protestantism of his age, a noticeable amount of deviation cannot be discounted.

We have seen how the devotion to nature threatens to make the green-grown ruins of churches more fitting emblems of the divine for Wordsworth, than more orthodox imitations of the Celestial City. More generally, we have seen how his architecture of the absolute shares with organicism a befuddlement about the threshold. In the clash between heterogeneous and autonomous conceptions of the church (represented, for instance, by the opposition between gothic transcendence and classical symmetry), his church suffers a version of the related aporia between the organic principles of hierarchical totalisation and interdependence. Romanticism is, among other things, a name for these problems shared by organicism and Wordsworth's grand gothic cathedral. It is also a name for the search for the solution of such problems, a search one should be wary of reducing to an exclusively historical, political, literary, aesthetic, philosophical or religious phenomenon. For the utopia or atopia of absolute architecture would engage, unify and transcend all such domains. In transcending the religious, it would, of course, even transcend the cathedral. Perhaps Wordsworth suggests as much, when he – early on in *The Excursion* – describes a vision encompassing 'temple, palace, citadel and huge / Fantastic pomp of structure without name'.[61] Can one hope for such a 'fantastic' apparition to come and solve the problems of organicism? Or is such a building merely the stuff of addling dreams? To find out whether recent theorists have come any closer to constructing it, I will now turn to more recent, post-romantic explorations and critiques of organicism.

Part III
Modern Theory

7
Balance and Extremity: A Comparison of Richards and Bataille

Richards and the tragedy of organicism

A sense of the disparate reception of organicism in the twentieth century can be gleaned by comparing the early writings of I. A. Richards with those of Georges Bataille. In what follows, I will present their response to the organicist heritage in the 1920s and early 1930s. This seemingly incongruous coupling will demonstrate an important crossroads in the development of thought on organicism. From this junction, one way leads towards more moderate and simple structures, and to the ignoring of inherent problems of organicism. The other way is embroiled in the extremities and aporias inherited from Coleridge and his contemporaries, and in the process leads to the abandonment of the possibility of structural closure. While my reading of Richards will show that the notion of the closed totality of the work can only perilously put its trust in organicism, the following interpretation of Bataille's early texts will show how a modern, subversive understanding of the body is born from radical elements of the heritage of organicism.

I will begin with the man who has been called 'the most representative critic in the English-speaking world in this century'.[1] As one of the most distinguished commentators upon, and revivers of, Coleridge's theory of literature, Richards represents a seminal link between romanticism and modern theory. His importance in the history of modern criticism stems mainly from his being an important formative influence on Anglo-American New Criticism through, amongst other things, his conception of the literary work of art as an organic whole. Richards' fervid faith in organicism, which at one point leads him to claim 'that the so-called metaphor that treats a poem as organic is not a metaphor, but a literal description',[2] cannot be said to be ever present in the work of the later New Critics.[3] Nevertheless, a critical reading of the organicism which dominates Richards' most influential work, with particular emphasis on *Principles of*

Literary Criticism, will throw light on some fundamental issues concerning New Criticism's conception of textual wholes.

Early on in *Principles of Literary Criticism*, Richards states his 'desire to link even the commonplaces of criticism to a systematic exposition of psychology'.[4] This linking is connected with his general aim to counter the influence of the 'art for art's sake' movement by rooting literature more solidly in human experience – the latter experience being defined on the basis of an interpretation of the old Aristotelian adage that 'man is a social creature' (49). Richards unequivocally identifies the end of man as being sociality, a sociality not understood primarily as a function of institutions or collective rituals, but rather in terms of intersubjective communication. Mankind's need to communicate is, Richards admits, 'second in import- ance to physiological necessities', but by an unexplained sleight-of-hand he nevertheless claims that the former need is 'more directly necessary' to our 'well-being' (49).

When one pursues the question of structure in Richards' thought, one is faced with a huge, sprawling field of inquiry. Explication of his conception of structure has to straddle several areas – theories of meaning, understanding and literature, as well as of the mind – since all of these areas are presented in related ways. As in the case of Coleridge and Friedrich Schlegel, a general organicism is applied to a wide variety of concerns, which includes that of literature. The human essence, sociality itself, is particularly well served by literature. Richards' entire understanding of literature takes off from this anthropological and utilitarian premise, which is buoyed up by an understanding of experience as a complex and potentially systematic manifold.

Experience is understood as primarily concerning bodies, as Richards' materialism entails the choice of the neurological body as the essence of human identity. The ordering principle of the systematisation of bodies is organicism, while the particular elements that are to be ordered are defined as individual, psychological impulses. It is hard to find any description of organic systematisation, in the early texts, that is not couched in terms that are at least tinged by an element of psychology. Since Richards is an unabashedly normative critic, this entails that the best structure is always the best life, and vice versa.

The essence of a good mind, and a good poem, one is repeatedly told, is a *healthy* structure. Poetry, as Richards puts it in a later text, 'is our exemplar – for that kind of mutual and just control of part by part which is health'.[5] In general, health entails balance and a minimisation of sacrifice: 'States of mind in general are valuable in the degree in which they tend to reduce waste and frustration' (59). Even if he grants a modicum of relativity to this thesis, by pointing out that 'no one systematisation can claim a supreme position' and admitting 'Men are naturally different' (60), Richards nevertheless remains firm on this issue. He is allegedly stating a general truth when he claims that most 'human attitudes are wasteful, some to a shocking degree', and that the 'mind which is, so far as can be seen, least wasteful, we take as a norm or standard' (198). The aim of his system is to provide 'a system of measurement by which we can compare not only different experiences belonging to the same personality but different personalities' (288). In other words, deviations from the ideal personality are – in theory, at least – to be objectively quantified, categorised and ranked. Richards admits, though, that sadly one does 'not yet know how to make the measurements required' (288).

Richards' theory aligns the Confucian ideal of a balanced life of equilibrium and harmony with the ancient Greek predilection for *sophrosune* or moderation, and links them to a Darwinian emphasis on self-preservation. The use of literature is to assist one in achieving such an ideal balance. Those who oppose such an economy – for instance, those that claim 'that highly valuable hours must be paid for afterwards', that is, that no progress occurs without sacrifice – are dismissed as generally being 'those who have the least refined views of value' (59). An accumulative model of experience is chosen to the detriment of any possibility of conversion or heterogeneous experience whatsoever, partly as a side-effect of Richards' reaction against the Paterian cultivation of 'momentary *consciousness*' rather than the 'permanent modifications in the structure of the mind' (132). The close connection between Richards' preference for certain personality types and his understanding of the working of the mind is summed up in the following passage:

> Every systematisation in the degree to which it is stable involves a degree of sacrifice, but for some the price to be paid in opportunities foregone is greater than for others. By the extent of the loss, the range of impulses thwarted or starved, and their degree of importance, the merit of a systematisation is judged. That organisation which is least wasteful of human possibilities is, in short, the best. ... The debauchee and the victim of conscience alike have achieved organisations whose price in sacrifice is excessive. ... Upon grounds of prudence alone they have been injudicious, and they may be condemned without appeal to peculiarly 'ethical' standards. (52–3)

This, unfortunately, comes across like a neurological version of Judgement Day. Richards' theory finds its elect in 'those fortunate people who have achieved an ordered life'. These people have developed an extra organ or instance which launches them beyond 'the crude moralities of Puritans and perverts' (37). They are fortunate enough to have 'developed clearing-houses by which the varying claims of different impulses are adjusted' (53). Richards does not pursue this peculiar notion elsewhere,[6] but it represents a rare attempt to try to articulate how a faculty of organisation, roughly equivalent to the romantic conception of the imagination, can operate within a neurological model of the mind. It is also a distant, bureaucratic relative of Wordsworth's internalised gothic church.

These 'clearing-houses' point towards Richards' structural dilemma, which in one manner or another will upset all of his attempts to formulate the principles of a coherent structure. This dilemma seldom provokes an overt crisis in Richards' thought, however, thanks to his penchant, noted by Hotopf, for a '"something along these lines" way of saying things, which one suspects sometimes allows him to avoid to come to grips with the hard problems'.[7] The problem is this: Richards needs a structural system ruled by an economic principle of equivalence and reciprocity of all its elements. At the same time, order can only be achieved through some form of externally applied control. Although he is a utilitarian, Richards is no Adam Smith of the impulses: without systematic control one is left with 'a state of chaos' where 'important and trivial impulses alike are frustrated' (59). As a materialist, he would like to avoid constructing that control on the basis of any non-material law; hence he must materialise the imagination. The upshot is this mythical creature or 'clearing-house' miraculously built out of the sticks and stones of mere impulses.

By transforming the imagination into a material entity, Richards is taking a risk, for such a stance converts the imagination into an element *within* the very field it is supposed to regulate. The risk of something like Plato's 'third man' scenario occurring is obvious: the mutual relation between the imagination-element and the other elements would require other elements, of a higher order, to regulate their relations. Thus one would get an infinite generation of higher-order instances, precisely the scenario we have seen celebrated by Friedrich Schlegel in his conception of organicism as leading to an infinite process of self-reflection.

The problem of infinite reflection made its impact on idealism because of the absence of an intellectual intuition. Without a secure, heterogeneous and absolute foundation for the subject–object dichotomy, that proliferous dichotomy made its way into all thought and all matter. Fittingly, it is in his study on *Coleridge on Imagination* that Richards tries to face this classical idealist problem, entitling his third chapter 'The Coalescence of Subject and Object'. But nothing more than a roughly Kantian position is offered – a position which is the grounds for the idealist aporia rather than its solution – whereby the abstract standing apart of subject and object is circumvented by having the subject already having determined any possible grounds for the appearance of the object. There is no clash, one might say, between the two, since the subject always already has violated and enslaved the object:

In the simplest seeming 'datum' a constructing, forming activity from the mind has entered. And the perceiving and the forming are the same. The subject (the self) has gone into what it perceives, and what it perceives is, in this sense, itself. So the object becomes the subject and the subject the object.[8]

In this last sentence the reciprocity between subject and object is only fictional. The formal, subjective instance determines and directs the material outside to the point where externality almost dissolves entirely: 'the self ... perceives ... itself'. Richards is in good romantic company, not only with Coleridge but also with Coleridge's German predecessors here, as what is presented as being an all-inclusive and balanced system is actually a strictly unbalanced and hierarchical one.

The hierarchical slant of Richards' thought is, in general, tilted towards a humanist notion of a common communicative rationality. A shared subjectivity rules and dominates all objectivity, and – as for Emerson – the poet is, *par excellence*, 'the master of experience'.[9] The same hierarchical slant inevitably colours all parts of Richards' thought. Thus his theory of meaning, as it is presented in *Practical Criticism*, involves a balancing of four different kinds or functions of meaning, all of which seem to be equally vital elements of one system (encompassing both the structure of art and acts of refined understanding). Thought, feeling, tone and intention are all mutually modifying and interrelated:

> Innumerable cross influences and complications between these four kinds of meaning are possible and frequently present, in what may appear a quite simple remark. A perfect understanding would involve not only an accurate direction of thought, a correct evocation of feeling, an exact apprehension of tone and a precise recognition of intention, but further it would set these contributory meanings in their right order and proportion to one another, and seize – though not in terms of explicit thought – their interdependence upon one another, their sequences and interrelations.[10]

This formulation conceals a profound imbalance, which is at loggerheads with the 'interdependence' of these different kinds of meaning. Richards' basically subjectivist slant discloses itself when he, a little later on in *Practical Criticism*, adds a qualification: one particular kind of meaning, namely intention, 'controls the relations among themselves of the other three functions'.[11] In *Coleridge on Imagination*, the heterogeneity of intention is such that it is not even listed together with sense, feeling and tone as one of the 'parts' of meaning.[12]

The particular problem of intention illustrates the odd position of the hierarchical, structural centre: a centre is both among, above and totally outside the elements it is supposed to control. Richards has later been criticised for including the very principle controlling meaning among other uses or functions of meaning,[13] but it must be stressed that this is a typical gesture of his: to try – somewhat half-heartedly – to include a formative instance on the same level as the elements it collocates. The resulting variation with regard to systematicity, on occasion ruled by a hierarchical principle and on occasion by the interdependency of its elements, is perhaps Richards' most important inheritance from post-Kantian thought. He departs from the romantic and idealist precedent, though, in avoiding a logic of fusion in his structures. If Coleridge prefers a pure unity over a union of elements, Richards wants only union, that is, an ordering of elements from the elevated instances of a systematic hierarchy. All overtones of mysticism and the orgiastic are banished. Since this strategy is accompanied by the Kantian strategy of deferring systematic satisfaction by making it contingent upon never-ending progress, Richards' thought can keep clear of the heterogeneity and inherent paradoxes of an intangible centre. Rather than confronting the paradox of the centre, he adds a caveat: one does 'not know enough yet about the precedences, hierarchies, the modes of systematisation, actual and possible, in that unimaginable organisation, the mind, to say what order in any case actually exists' (50).

Instead of volatilising the centre of Richards' system, heterogeneity and paradox unsettle its borderlines. At those borderlines, the implicit conflict we have observed between a vertically organised, hierarchical structure and a horizontal and interdependent one, where all means are also ends, can be said to finally come to a head. As a result, another of organicism's persistent aporias lives on. Like Coleridge before him, Richards has no consistent stance on whether a well-organised structure must entail *exclusion* or not. Coleridge is cited as the authority for a view of artistic creation as the work of the whole mind. This total experience, Richards writes, involves 'all the impulses, conscious or unconscious, relevant to it, without suppressions or restrictions' (189). Thus Richards ignores Coleridge's dithering on this question, which I have shown earlier, by presenting art as a straightforwardly all-inclusive experience. Richards builds upon this idea in his theory of tragedy, describing this genre as the apex and quintessence of literature:

> It is essential to recognise that in the full tragic experience there is no suppression. The mind does not shy away from anything, it does not protect itself with any illusion, it stands uncomforted, unintimidated, alone and self-reliant. ... Suppressions and sublimations alike are devices by which we endeavour to avoid issues which might bewilder us. (246)

The rather surprising equation of suppression and sublimation, in the final sentence, can be taken as an indication of how Richards diverges from Freud. Although he is very conscious of the tenets of psychoanalysis, Richards neglects the psychoanalytical feature of splitting the mind into *separate* systems with borders of resistance. To be sure, he does on occasion evoke the dizzying multiplicity of 'an immense hierarchy of systems of tendencies poised in the most delicate stability' (125) when trying to substantiate his image of the human organism. By and large, though, the complexities of transference and inner resistances, which such a multiplicity would necessitate, are never seriously envisaged. The result is a much more seamless structure, which in Richards' early texts draws upon C. S. Sherrington's neuropsychology, and which gains uniformity only at the price of forfeiting specificity. No consistent notion of various degrees of resistance survives, since everything that is external to the psyche is taken to be easily convertible, with a little effort and refinement, into something internal.

One can find a trace of the violence of appropriation in another of Richards' definitions of tragedy: 'Tragedy is perhaps the most general, all-accepting, all-ordering experience known. It can take anything into its organisation, modifying it so that it finds a place' (247). External impressions may, evidently, have to be modified in order to find 'a place' – it is possible to read this phrase as indicating that some impressions do not find *their* apposite and predestined place, but 'a' place, that is, any place that will give a semblance of order. A similar hint of violence or friction occurs in one of Richards' definitions of poetry. He wants to describe how the meanings of individual words are modified by the context of a poem, in effect defining very much the basis for the practice of close reading:

> Is the pull exerted by the context (and in these cases the whole of the rest of the poem is the context) sufficient to overcome what may be described as the normal separate feeling of the questionable word? Can this pull bring it in, as an item either in accordance or in due contrast to the rest? Or does the word resist, stay outside, or wrench the rest of the poem into crudity or confusion? To triumph over the resistances of words may sometimes be considered the measure of a poet's power (Shakespeare being the obvious example), but more often it is the measure of his discretion ...[14]

Any simple distinction between exclusion and inclusion becomes too vague here. Words may be brought in by the pull of context, or they may stay outside, or they may disfigure the poem. More importantly, the gravitational 'pull' of the context may be accomplished both as violent 'triumph' over their 'resistances', as well as a discrete and seemingly painless act of inclusion. In the tension between these two last figures of the work of context, one can glimpse two different theories of poetry – two different interpretations of context at the heart of Richards' understanding of contextual reading. In fact, Richards embraces both theories. Poetry is *both* a discrete act of including all, an act projected onto an idealised image of tragedy, *and* a violent act that excludes all superfluous or unassimilable baggage. In the latter theory, the poet is still the romantic figure that organises the diverse elements of experience, but this is only on the basis of an act of sacrifice:

> Impulses which commonly interfere with one another and are conflicting, independent, and mutually distractive, in him combine into

a stable poise. He selects, of course, but the range of suppression which is necessary for him is diminished, and for this very reason such suppressions as he makes are more rigorously carried out. Hence the curious local callousness of the artist which so often strikes the observer. (243)

Thus a complete befuddlement is evident in Richards' handling on the question of external delimitation: one has no sure rule of whether art includes all experience or whether it, to the contrary, rigorously sacrifices an outside. Here the latent conflict between a hierarchical model and the model of interdependence surfaces. In the former, the poet is the equivalent of a tyrannical dictator in charge of the highest orders, or – as Emerson phrased it – 'the poet is not any permissive potentate, but is emperor in his own right'.[15] In the latter, the poet is more like a self-effacing diplomat.[16]

This theoretical disarray displays itself further in a lack of distinction. Richards admits that one 'can only conjecture dimly what difference holds between a balance and reconciliation of impulses and a mere rivalry or conflict' (251). This criterion is lacking because 'we do not yet know enough about the central nervous system' (ibid.). This is Richards' tragedy, the hyper-tragedy surpassing and debilitating his own definition of the specific literary genre of tragedy. It leads directly to what is perhaps the most singular turn taken by this particular appropriation of organicism. Richards inherits all the structural problems encountered by Coleridge and his predecessors, dimly perceives the presence of these problems and then entrusts their solution to future science, the latter being a panacea for all structural incoherence. If 'Coleridge's thought has not even yet come into its own',[17] all will nevertheless be clear and consistent in due time. Richards repeatedly locates that deferred moment of epiphany in the not too distant future, when the science of neurology will give one an objective description of the structure of the mind. He insists that 'it is as certain as anything can be that in time psychology will overhaul most of our ideas about ourselves, and will give us a very detailed account of our mental activities'.[18] The father of New Criticism presents himself, as it were, as a prophet for a future enlightenment, where 'Custom, Convention and Superstition, the underlying basis of morality' will no longer leave the physical structure of the mind 'veiled and disguised' as he admits it still is in his own day (56).

The persistent absence of the scientific enlightenment of the mind vitiates Richards' entire scheme of evaluation, as he lacks any means of systematically articulating a hierarchy of concerns. He wants an account of the mind as 'an organic hierarchy of interests' to provide the basis of differentiating 'between Good and Evil',[19] but without this foundation all his judgements – such as his early contention (later withdrawn) that Yeats, unlike the best English poets, writes minor poetry – are only evidence of his jumping the gun.[20] In a sense, the projected consummation of a perfected science of the mind is what will give his thought its justification. Yet his own subjectivism rules out the possibility of such a consummation: there really is no such thing, according to Richards' own thought, as a pure, non-metaphorical description. Converting what he later qualifies as 'would-be' systems into true systems, science – an impossible and endlessly deferred science – bears the onus of saving Richards' academic activity from being that most dreaded of all things: a waste of time.[21]

Bataille, the mobile body and sacrifice

Like Richards, Georges Bataille consciously responds to a state of crisis. Both write in the shadow of the crisis of civilisation that first was diagnosed by Nietzsche and then was intensified by the experience of World War I. Richards identifies the crisis as a general one, influencing the most quotidian of habits: 'We may suspect that today the demand for violence [of emotion] reflects some poverty, through inhibition, in everyday emotional life.'[22] He also laments that human development of increased order may be in the process of being hampered by 'too lax and volatile a bond between our interests (a frivolousness that is perhaps due to the draining off of energy elsewhere) so that no formations firm enough to build upon result'.[23]

Whereas Richards complains at the hidden drain of energy specific to his times, Bataille finds a profound significance in it. And while the English critic wants to pacify and cure the modern demand for violence through educational control, Bataille wants to engage it – or at least placate it – through a modern repetition of ancient ritual. The latter sees level-headedness as an accomplice of 'capitalist exploitation' rather than as a transcendental and ahistorical value.[24] Whereas Richards wants to improve and refine what he calls 'everyday emotional life', and endorses a modified Benthamite position (wherein the satisfaction of impulses replaces happiness as the aim of utility), Bataille wants to keep the everyday in touch with its neglected, sacred other on the far side of utility. Nevertheless, Bataille shares with Richards a desire for heightened communication, as well as a penchant for organic or biological models accompanied by an anti-idealist rhetoric.

That anti-idealist rhetoric leads the early Bataille to focus on the *body* as the fulcrum of human significance. While Richards dissolves the body into underlying impulses, Bataille sticks to a more classical form of organicism by privileging the organ. The titles of some of his essays of the 1920s illustrate this tendency: among those texts are 'The Solar Anus', 'Eye', 'The Pineal Eye', 'The Big Toe', 'Mouth', as well as 'Sacrificial Mutilation and the Severed Ear of Vincent Van Gogh'. Bataille is more radical than Richards in his suspicion of less stringent forms of materialism: 'Most materialists, even though they may have wanted to do away with all spiritual entities, ended up positing an order of things whose hierarchical relations mark it as specifically idealist.'[25] Hierarchy *per se* is suspicious for Bataille, whereas Richards posits it as a structural necessity and a prerequisite for a systematically organised whole.

Bataille's early position is often more in line with the notion of an originary state of the polymorphously perverse, explored by Freud.[26] In his complex texts, one of the most central themes is that of a radical bodily unrest that is set into motion. One is faced with a mobility in which no single organ achieves hegemony, least of all the head or brain: 'Man has escaped from his head just as the condemned man has escaped from his prison.'[27] According to this radicalised, acephalic fetishism, the anus is no stand-in for the phallus, nor is the eye or head simply a sublimating replacement for the sexual function. Still, organic unsettlement occurs only despite a more unified and strictly hierarchical model. The attraction of the abject so characteristic of Bataille is only comprehensible as a violation of a taboo, that is, through the reversion of an already established hierarchy. The gradual elevation of the human figure, which grants the *head* a central place, is central to the understanding of humanity that he wants to counter. Regressions to animality and anality come together in Bataille's fascination with apes and 'the obscene blossoming of their bald, haloed anuses, bursting like boils'.[28]

The obscene backside of an ape does not, however, constitute an unquestioned fundament for Bataille's early thought. As Denis Hollier has pointed out, this is a materialism concerned with what does not last.[29] As makeshift or parodic instantiations of the absolute, Bataille's organs achieve only a strictly *provisional* rule: here there is an agreement with Schlegel's organic politics. In 'The Solar Anus', where Bataille states that 'each thing seen is the parody of another',[30] the circulation between provisional centres extends even beyond the body:

> And if the origin of things is not like the ground of the planet that seems to be the base, but like the circular movement that the planet describes around a mobile center, then a car, a clock, or a sewing machine could equally be accepted as the generative principle.[31]

Ultimately, though, such an interdependence of all things will not suffice, however seductive this vision of distended and deregulated bodily mobility has been for some of Bataille's followers. This is due to the hierarchical pull of Bataille's thought, a pull that seeks sovereignty rather than the objectified servitude of being dependent upon means-end relations, and will not make do with the mere slippage from term to term. His goal is, as he will put it in a later autobiographical note, to 'comprehend the totality of possibility, or to put it more precisely, to reject, untiringly, any possibility exclusive of others'. He wishes to attain 'a sovereign existence, free of all limitations of interest'.[32] This position is not far removed from that granted by Richards to the poet who attains the pinnacle of all experience: the poet, according to Richards, attains 'a fullness of being, the sense of all possibilities before one'.[33] But Bataille does not allow any permanence or solidity to such a state, as its liberty of possibilities is itself an impossibility. Slippage is reproduced in the very sovereign act that would enclose the multiplicity of slipping possibilities.

At this juncture Bataille typically has recourse to sacrifice and poetry, as well as non-productive eroticism: these could be entitled *symbolic forms* for the ground of being, had it not been for the fact that the abyssal ground, which they relate to, eludes all presentation. This last qualification is what essentially preserves Bataille from repeating the Hegelian journey from dismemberment (*Zerrissenheit*) to absolute wisdom. Nevertheless, mere particularity is to be transcended. In fact, it is precisely particularity in the form of *reciprocity* – that essential principle of organicism – that has to be transcended by a hierarchical and encompassing gesture. In death, Bataille writes, 'the shadow of the divine person, laden with love, disappears – not exactly as vain appearance, but as *dependence on a denied world that is founded on the reciprocal dependence* [la dépendance réciproque] *of its parts.'*[34] The interdependent elements of the universe are to be transcended through an act of sacrifice – the interrelated organs of the body of the universe are to be centred and illuminated in a cataclysm of lightning and violence.

In short, the part is to be sacrificed for the whole. Individuation is to be replaced by the undifferentiated continuity of the absolute. Bataille thus takes over another idealist and romantic *topos*, that of the sacrifice, and the understanding that the quick of life can be salvaged only from the extremity of death. In his writings, sacrifice acquires values closely related to, at times even overlapping with, those of the intellectual intuition and the sublime. Indeed Schlegel's version of the sublime – which we encountered in chapter 3, and where the sublime surrogate object was marked by disappearance in its very being – was itself hard to distinguish from sacrifice.

Here Bataille's focusing on single organs acquires an additional complication. For the passing cathexis of one single organ does not simply indicate that that organ is privileged as being a provisional centre of a system of relations; it also implies that the organ in question is being singled out as a sacrificial object. This becomes especially clear in Bataille's article on 'Sacrificial Mutilation and the Severed Ear of Vincent Van Gogh', a text ostensibly provoked by a newspaper article concerning an embroidery designer who cut off his finger. Van Gogh's sacrifice of an ear is, he claims, 'the sign of the irreducible heterogeneity of the lacerated (and unrestrained) elements of Van Gogh's personality'.[35] Self-transcendence is the goal of his gesture of self-mutilation, in the form of 'the necessity of throwing oneself or something of oneself *out of oneself*'. This is a 'mechanism that

in certain cases can have no other end than death'.[36] In order to gain
ascendance, then, the organ singled out must be brutally expulsed from the
system of the body – it must, as Bataille often puts it, be transferred from
the sphere of homogeneity to that of heterogeneity.

In confronting the heterogeneous, which he ties to an economy of waste
rather than preservation, Bataille touches the limits of organicism. In close
proximity to Freud, whose death drive amongst other things expressed the
nostalgic return route for the organic back to the inorganic, he explores the
inherent paradox of the centre of the organism that so plagued romanticism. The acme of a structure is also its lowest point, and the most elevated
is a source of the greatest fall. In his early texts, Bataille frequently figures
this paradox through the image of the sun:

> The sun, from the human point of view (in other words, as it is con-
> fused with the notion of noon) is the most *elevated* conception. ... If on
> the other hand one obstinately focuses on it, a certain madness is
> implied, and the notion changes meaning because it is no longer pro-
> duction that appears in light, but refuse or combustion ... . All this
> leads one to say that the summit of elevation is in practice confounded
> with a sudden fall of unheard-of violence. The myth of Icarus is particu-
> larly expressive from this point of view: it clearly splits the sun in two –
> the one that was shining at the moment of Icarus's elevation, and the
> one that melted the wax, causing failure and a screaming fall when
> Icarus got too close.[37]

As an emblem of the centre of the cosmic organism, the sun is both an
instance of elevation and abjection.

This same structure repeats itself, if one moves from Bataille's mythical
cosmology to his understanding of human society.[38] Bataille's most extensive early discussion of what later was to become the opposition
between limited and general economies in *The Accursed Share* takes place in
an essay on 'The Psychological Structure of Fascism'.[39] In this text he constantly changes registers, interlinking psychological and social structures.
In both the mind and society, Bataille shows the same mechanisms at
work, and in the process he gives a lucid summary of his own early thought
upon structure. He explores and spells out the heterogeneity within organicism which I have pursued throughout this study, and in effect anticipates
and delineates some of the main tendencies of poststructuralist thought,
long before the advent of French structuralism.

The most significant trait of society's superstructure is, according to
Bataille, its homogeneity. Homogeneous society, he writes,

> is productive society, namely, useful society. Every useless element is
> excluded, not from all of society, but from its *homogeneous* part. In this

part, each element must be useful to another without the *homogeneous* activity ever being able to attain the form of activity *valid in itself.* (138)

The homogeneous structure is thus characterised by a means–end structure, one of purposeful utility. Its homogeneity resides in the pervasiveness of this trait, that is, in how it is equally distributed within. Furthermore, homogeneous society is marked by the 'calculable equivalent of the different products of collective activity' (138).

This homogeneous structure needs some end or goal for its useful activity: it is like a torso without essential and life-giving organs. Such an orientation guaranteeing hierarchical totality cannot come from within. Bataille does not, like Richards, dissemble this problem by opting for compromise and coming up with an ad hoc postulate of the creation of 'clearing houses': instead, he presents it in all its incommensurability. As useful elements, all homogeneous members of the structure need an external foundation for their existence. This is where the heterogeneous sphere makes its impact, for it has 'being *for itself*' and is not reducible to a means (cf. 147). This role of teleological grounding is only one of the two differing functions of heterogeneity. For heterogeneity is both a characteristic of the hierarchical co-ordinating function *and* the excluded parts at the margins of homogeneous society. On the one hand, the heterogeneous and imperial power poses itself 'as the principle for the association of innumerable elements' (148). On the other, the 'very term *heterogeneous* indicates that it concerns elements that are impossible to assimilate' (140). In this latter respect, the psychological mechanism that inflicts censorship on unconscious desires – explored by Freud, *par excellence*, with regard to dreams – is evidence of a more large-scale law.[40]

As an excessive or extreme principle in the functioning of social structures, heterogeneous elements would thus seem to be confined to either rags or riches – to repression or sublimation. Either they are banished from homogeneity, or they structure it. Bataille does however indicate that there is a third option. Since heterogeneity can enter homogeneous structure – indeed, is necessary for providing the latter structure with external organisation – it need not be excluded. There is always exclusion, in one or another form, for Bataille – here his *agonistic* universe differs from Richards' – but any element may be granted a temporary and provisional inclusion. Yet once a heterogeneous element is included, it may be repulsed again: 'in certain circumstances, any object of repulsion can become an object of attraction and vice versa' (142). An assimilated heterogeneity that subsequently is repulsed need not be completely banished from the structure. Presumably this is the explanation for the existence of what Bataille calls heterogeneous elements' constant tendency towards 'a split-off structure' [*une structure tranchée*] (140), as well as their capability of acting as 'free-floating imperative forces' [*les forces impératives libres*] (146).[41]

A will-o'-the-wisp: The politics of ambivalence

In general, 'The Psychological Structure of Fascism' can be read as indicative of Bataille's reworking of organicism. By pitting the organic principles of interrelationship and hierarchy against one another, he has in effect given the explanation for why – given the premises of organicism – there can be no such thing as an autonomous structure. Basically, the gesture of the early Bataille is to embrace organicism in the very same gesture as he unworks it. This unworking – the *désœuvrement* that Blanchot would later articulate more stringently – is achieved by setting organicism's romantic mission to work. Organicism is the desire for the solution of the dichotomy of form and matter, the dream of a perfect interfusion of these antagonists – or of a compromise formation which allows them both their roles in a hierarchically articulated whole. Bataille sets that desire to work, but does so only endlessly to postpone its completion. For there is always a remainder, as he holds on to a 'base materialism' which resists all subjugation to form or spirit.[42]

The price to be paid for the acknowledgement of this remainder is self-contradiction: since science itself is assimilative and homogeneous, according to Bataille, speech can only beckon from afar towards the heterogeneous. Such a remainder is, of course, seldom thematised in Richards – and therefore performative self-contradiction is less insistent in his case. Instead, Richards affirms a seamless organic whole, a seamlessness that is also the ideal of his own discourse.[43] Whereas Bataille advocates the limit-experience which pursues and engages the extremity in its irreducible marginality, Richards sees no other possibility than assimilation without risk. The latter has, in general, no serious objection to the organic dream of a fully articulated and autonomous totality. There are exceptions, though, some of which I already have pursued. A particularly striking exception is provided by Richards' account of *feeling*, which seems to admit the possibility of there being such a thing as an unassimilable entity:

> If we compare our powers of analysing sense and feeling we shall recognise at once that feeling, in contrast with sense, is a will-o'-the-wisp. ... For a feeling even more than an idea or an image tends to vanish as we turn our introspective attention upon it. We have to catch it by the tip of its tail as it decamps. Furthermore, even when we are partially successful in catching it, we do not yet know how to analyse it.[44]

This obscure, nocturnal animal dubbed 'feeling', which strangely seems to resist the murder inherent in its dissection, is nevertheless only a deceptive appearance: an ignis fatuus. If one does not *yet* know how to analyse it, given time and the progress of science, one will soon. Such is Richards' faith.

That faith can be summarised as follows: Communication is always poss-ible. Linked to this belief is a politics that the early Richards never devel-ops. If form is 'sedimented content', as Adorno claims, Richards never mines the political ores of his forms.[45] Bataille, on the other hand, does not hesitate to dirty his hands with such political sediments. 'The Psychological Structure of Fascism' explicitly presents itself as a strategic intervention into the volatile political situation of his time, an intervention strongly marked by a consciousness of the historical precedent of the French Revolution and its aftermath. It is a complex intervention that adjusts itself to the shifting political configurations of the time and embraces radically exclusive alternatives. On the one hand, Bataille does not shy away from a radically egalitarian dream of a community where we find *all* members of the people acting as masters.[46] On the other hand, a more authoritarian bent is evident in his need to affirm 'the reality of values, the resulting inequality of men, and acknowledge the organic character of society' [*la réalité des valeurs, l'inégalité humaine qui en résulte et reconnaître le caractère organique de la société*].[47]

Bataille is neither a conventional communist nor anything remotely close to an identifiable fascist, during this period. Yet these two ideologies are primary co-ordinates of his thought and the objects of its scrutiny. Bataille's problem is that he identifies both Leftist and Rightist interven-tions as heterogeneous, and does not come up with any way of substan-tially differentiating the two. He does make a distinction when he identifies the choice between them as being between 'subversive or imperative solu-tions' respectively (158). There is also a related opposition between com-munism's 'formless uprising ... "for the men in revolt"' (144) and fascism's constituting 'as *authority*, an agency directed *against* men' (143). Nevertheless, both remain anti-bourgeois forms of 'organic' insurrection,[48] and may necessarily – given that inequality is unavoidable in organic society – result in hierarchical structures. As their common origin is a form-less continuity prior to all distinction – an 'undifferentiated *heterogeneity*' (152) as Bataille calls it – there is a fundamental equivalence. Indeed, Bataille goes further: communism and fascism are 'two segments that share a common opposition to a general dissociation of *homogeneous* society' and 'this explains the numerous connections between them and even a kind of profound complicity' (159).

Insofar as all society lacks a heterogeneous foundation, and insofar as that foundation cannot be incarnated in the state or in bureaucratic and technocratic machinery, it has no inherent need to embrace any specific kind of extraneous intervention. Democracy, according to this view, is impotent, while fascism and communism are both equally potent in solving its quandary and lack of sacredness. Generally speaking, Bataille's thought here may be said to illustrate a large-scale law. Any politics that takes its exigency from a transcendental value beyond all dichotomies and all objectivity will run the risk of a similar undecidability, or indifference, with regard to the more orthodox configurations. This is true of Coleridge,[49] and one may even detect traces of it in Richards. This tendency is submerged in the latter, though, as the political consequences and applications of his organicism only surface through metaphors and analogies.[50] Nevertheless, just as Schlegel and Novalis presented monarchy and democracy as equally feasible instantiations of organicism, the following passage from *Coleridge on Imagination* embraces opposite extremes:

> the structure or *constitution* of poetic meanings may vary from extreme federalism ... to the strictest centrality – from a case ... where the meanings of the separate words are almost completely autonomous (and their grouping is for a purpose that does not concern them) to the case ... where the several units of meaning surrender almost all of their local independence in a common cooperative purpose.[51]

Thus Richards and Bataille share an embracing of opposites: both imply – Richards metaphorically, Bataille more expressly – radically disparate visions of collectivity. For both, organicism can entail both a radical, differential *dispersion* of power, as well as a radical *concentration* of it. Two possible consequences, or hypotheses, can be educed from this ambivalence. On the one hand, it can be read as a symptom of how organicism (as a presumably impersonal, structural law) is essentially alien to questions concerning concrete political collectivity, which would imply that its imposition on the political realm is necessarily filtered through the strategic intervention of ideology – or indeed constitutes the essence of ideology. On the other hand, the same ambivalence could also be interpreted as implying that organicism touches upon the general but heterogeneous foundation of the political, as the general trait of all politics.[52] In the latter case, organicism would be the common name of all politics (and hence not identifiable with any single one). The consequences and limits of organicism when it is applied to modern politics will be one of the themes explored in the next two chapters.

8
The Connections of Significance: Gadamer and the Vitality of Understanding

Modern hermeneutics has contributed a powerful meditation on how existence is embroiled in historicity and language. Hans-Georg Gadamer is widely recognised as one of its most accessible and influential proponents, in his attempt to surpass conceptually the fundamental limitations he believes to have been introduced by a dualistic, Cartesian world-view and the dominance of the mind-set of the natural sciences. The rationalistic isolation of the thinking subject has had disastrous consequences, Gadamer claims, and his grand opus *Truth and Method* represents a tripartite attack on its dominion. Not only in the fundamentals of philosophical ontology, which is the main provenance of Gadamer's enquiry, but also within the theory of art and the methodology of the human sciences, this work attempts to provide a new and non-Cartesian footing. Inevitably, it has weighty ancestors – among other things, Gadamer is engaged in a continuation, albeit a transformative one, of romanticism. At the same time, he manifests considerable resistance to the romantic heritage, as is evident in his problematical relationship to figures such as G. W. F. Hegel, Friedrich Schleiermacher and Wilhelm Dilthey in particular.

This resistance is, among other things, a resistance to organicism. *Truth and Method* is replete with references to the organic metaphors and methodologies of Gadamer's forebears, but his relative proximity to their practice is offset by a measure of reserve. In this respect, one would expect that Heidegger's important distinction between understanding beings and organic beings would represent a weighty precedent. One of the most decisive distinctions made in *Being and Time* was between the temporality of organic and truly mortal beings. Whereas organic structures have the completion and ending of their lives inscribed as a teleological goal, the temporality of *Dasein* entails that the end – though necessary – has an accidental quality about it.[1]

Gadamer has acknowledged that he is 'indebted for the decisive matters' of his thought to Heidegger.[2] Heidegger's critique of the scientific '*Ge-stell*' which imposes a technical and instrumental view upon existence, his search for a primary being-in-the-world, his rooting of the experience of art in the sacred: all these features, and many more, have had a strong influence upon Gadamer. But this influence is limited by the manner in which Gadamer circumvents Heidegger's notion of 'Being towards death'. For the former has always primarily interpreted finitude in terms of delimitation – in terms of being determined and enclosed by a potentially widening horizon – rather than as mortality.[3] The expanding of a subjective sphere within the flexible bounds of a temporary delimitation is, as we have seen, a feature of romantic organicism – for instance, in Coleridge's notion of friendship as a gradual widening of 'home-born Feeling'. Gadamer's acute proximity to such thought is amplified by the fact that he believes any Heideggerian distinction between a heterogeneous or sacred temporality (related to 'Being towards death') and an everyday temporality must be overridden by the basic continuity of human experience. As a result, Gadamer represses the manner in which Heideggerian temporality resists organic schemas (cf. 121–2).

Even if Gadamer tries, according to standard hermeneutical practice, to comprehend human understanding on the basis of the model of text interpretation, his very understanding of textuality most frequently rests upon another model: that of an organism. This is an unacknowledged model, for organicism is not one of the traditional concepts given a new, legitimising elucidation in *Truth and Method*. Nevertheless, although it confronts this question only in a roundabout fashion, Gadamer's hermeneutics might be said to display an impressive awareness of the aporias of organicism – of the pitfalls inherent in the utilisation of organicism as an approach. To a certain degree, Gadamer's own work represents what one might be tempted to call a *renovated organicism*, as he attempts to preserve its aspects of holism and vitalism, even in the act of discarding its more unmanageable and subversive effects. As I will show, though, Gadamer cannot fully extricate himself from the problems that plagued romantic organicism.

Gadamer's ambivalent reception of organicism is particularly evident in his discussions of the thought of Dilthey. As Gadamer has pointed out in retrospect, insofar 'as it dealt with the theory of the human sciences ... my own endeavor was closely linked to Dilthey's philosophical development of the heritage of German Romanticism'.[4] Dilthey's critique of the positivist transposition of the methodology of the natural sciences over to the human sciences is recognised as important, but also as ultimately insufficient. An inner, authentic experience – an *Erlebnis* – presents itself as an organic means of synthesis, and on its basis Dilthey develops 'a concept of life that restricts the mechanistic model' [*ein Lebensbegriff der das mechanistische Modell einschränkt*] (65–6 [71]). While Coleridge saw organicism as a defining feature of any general method whatsoever, for Dilthey it is demoted from its universal, romantic aspirations, in order to become the exclusive methodological premise for the human sciences. Experience, as

Dilthey understands it, is created on the basis of a significant connection, a 'structural whole of the life of the soul' [*Strukturzusammenhang des Seelenlebens*],[5] and the task of the *Geisteswissenschaften* is to grasp this interior configuring of experience into a meaningful whole.

Although he is engaged in a similar differentiation between the provenances of the human and natural sciences, Gadamer opposes this theory on two points, based on the claim that Dilthey's holism ultimately falls apart at the seams. First, he holds that Dilthey's stress on passing, inner experience leads to a fragmentation of the historical field. Through a radicalisation of the values of interiority and intensity, the grand whole of experience risks unveiling itself as discontinuity – as what Walter Pater famously (but probably unknown to Dilthey) called 'that continual vanishing away, that strange, perpetual weaving and unweaving of ourselves'.[6] This splintering of experience, the origin of which is attributed to Leibnizian monadology, is presented by Gadamer as being an unmitigated evil: 'Basing aesthetics on experience leads to an absolute series of points [*absoluten Punktualität*], which annihilates the unity of the work of art, the identity of the artist with himself, and the identity of the person understanding or enjoying the work of art' (95 [101]). We have already observed how this inner fragmentation of organicism was a general topic in romanticism, utilised by Friedrich Schlegel and denigrated by Coleridge. In Gadamer's view, the disintegration resulting from Dilthey's concept of experience is to be avoided by anchoring hermeneutics firmly in a more general context. Although generally vague on what kind of context this is, the author of *Truth and Method* does not resist identifying it in Hegelian terms as the collective entities of 'family, society, and state' (276).

Gadamer's brand of hermeneutics thus tries to escape from the aporia of organicism. But it does so at a price: inevitably, to give up on the immediacy of organicism – its complete fusion of form and content, activity and passivity, subject and object – leads to the construction of a highly regulated alternative. That alternative is an articulated, hierarchical model. By dismissing what he calls 'the false romanticism of immediacy' [*die falsche Romantisierung der Unmittelbarkeit*] (400 [404]), Gadamer leaves himself exposed to other problems. Arguably, radical organicism always represents a desire for immediacy and complete unity that is, strictly speaking, impossible. Fleeing from the spectre of nothingness observed in such immediacy, more mediated forms of holism (whether or not they identify themselves as 'organic') must take recourse in compromise. Yet such compromise inevitably tends towards the hierarchies and dualisms that organicism was meant to be the cure for in the first place. In this respect, it is significant that the second point on which Gadamer faults Dilthey's organicism is its tendency to split into a dualism. He sees Dilthey as being uneasily perched on the borderline between positivism and romantic idealism, unable to construct a feasible and lasting sublation of the two.[7] Dilthey is said to suffer from an 'unresolved Cartesianism' (237) that pits thought against life. Gadamer opposes this by embracing a Hegelian position of the inherent unity of life and reflection. As was also the case for I. A. Richards, thought and life are equated: 'historical research is carried along by the historical movement of life itself' (284). A more seamless structure than Dilthey's is thus desired, but it is a structure that preserves a connection with the vitality of the latter's organicism. This persistent recourse to the tradition of vitalism, a remnant of romanticism that survived in sundry forms throughout the nineteenth century, consistently causes Gadamer's thought to diverge from Heidegger's.

Gadamer briefly touches upon this problem in *Truth and Method*, trying to minimise the difference between Heidegger and his own self-professed anthropological approach. He does so through an appeal to the *Letter on Humanism* rather than *Being and Time*:

> If we really want to break out of the spell of idealistic speculation, then we must obviously not conceive the mode of being of 'life' [*die Seinsart des 'Lebens'*] in terms of self-consciousness. When Heidegger set about revising the transcendental self-conception of *Being and Time*, it followed that he would have to come to grips afresh with the problem of *life*. Thus in his letter on humanism he spoke of the great gulf between man and animal. It is quite clear that Heidegger's own transcendental grounding of fundamental ontology in the analytic of Dasein did not yet permit a positive account of the mode of being of life. (263 [268])

Any rigorous reading of the *Letter* would have to admit, however, that Heidegger's sparse remarks on this issue never grant the notion of life any fundamental validity. The philosophy of life does not measure up to the manner in which *Dasein* is engaged with Being by way of language: 'man is not only a living creature [*ein Lebewesen*] who possesses language along with other capacities. Rather, language is the house of Being in which man ek-sists by dwelling, in that he belongs to the truth of Being, guarding it.'[8] Presupposing the structures of 'life' entails, from Heidegger's vantage point, a foreclosure of a truly ontological questioning.

Thus on this matter Gadamer is closer to the romantics than he is to Heidegger. But does this entail that his thought is locked within the structural thought, and inherent dualisms, of romantic organicism? Like the latter, Gadamer is in pursuit of a transcendence of an abstract dichotomy of subject and object. In the question that concerned Dilthey – the investigation into the methodology of the human sciences, which dominates part two of *Truth and Method* – this is to come about through Gadamer's critique of the positivist claim to objectivity characteristic of nineteenth century historicism. Here, too, Gadamer explicitly signals his allegiance to a tradition stemming from the romantics: the historian is not a scientist experimenting with independent physical matter, he insists, but rather a being thrown into the field – the field of temporality – which he is trying to describe. The historian is always in an unfinished dialogue with the past, a dialogue which takes the form of projective interpretations of the whole alternating with detailed analysis of the parts.

This alternation between parts and whole constitutes the famous hermeneutical circle. Although its familiarity might invest it with almost apodictic self-evidence – Gadamer insists that it 'will be obvious to every interpreter who knows what he is about' (266) – it is itself an intra-historical construction. As Gadamer points out, the genealogy of the hermeneutic circle stretches far back, even beyond the impressive precedents of Heidegger and Schleiermacher:

> This circular relationship between the whole and the parts is not new. It was already known to classical rhetoric, which compares perfect speech with the organic body, with the relationship between head and limbs. Luther and his successors transferred this image, familiar from classical rhetoric, to the process of the understanding; and they developed the universal principle of textual interpretation that all the details of a text were to be understood from the contextus and from the scopus, the unified sense at which the whole aims. (175)

Even if Gadamer, following Heidegger, displaces the ultimate validity of this circle from the realm of method to that of ontology, he nevertheless embraces its workings. From this one can infer that hermeneutics preserves the schematics of organicism at its very heart, even if it is wary of its potentially errant consequences. For the circle between whole and part is another version of the interdependent relationship between the head and the body.

The space between the interpreter and interpreted is the particular field upon which the hermeneutic body or skin is stretched out, and the two instances involved in the act of historical understanding are the two extreme poles that it is hitched upon. As in romantic organicism, it is indeed a case of polarity: 'Hermeneutic work is based on a polarity of familiarity and strangeness' (295). Between these two extremities, which are the hermeneutical equivalents of the poles of affection and respect upon which Coleridgean friendship was based, Gadamer strives to attain a certain equilibrium. The interpreter necessarily configures his understanding on the basis of his own historical situation, yet at the same time he is responsive to the context and facticity of the historical text. A balanced duality is the ideal of this process, where past and present ideally relate to each other as interdependent entities in a dynamic exchange.

Yet Gadamer's account of this balance veers from one extreme to another, in what often seems a case of wanting to have one's cake and eat it, too. At one extreme, an almost complete voluntarism is the result of his

Hegelian leanings. Paraphrasing Hegel on the concept of life, in an attempt to link life and thought more closely than Dilthey managed, Gadamer describes an act of assimilative appropriation which encounters no resistance:

> What is alive preserves itself by drawing into itself everything that is outside of it. Everything that is alive nourishes itself on what is alien to it. The fundamental fact of being alive is assimilation. Differentiation, then, is at the same time non-differentiation. The alien is appropriated. (253)

Given that a thinking being is a living being, and that there is no essential disparity between these two activities, the act of understanding would seem to be essentially the same thing as, say, a Neanderthal devouring an animal. Cogitation is the equivalent of sacrificing the other. They are both living acts of appropriation in the name of self-preservation and cannot be essentially differentiated if hermeneutical understanding is to escape being dismissed as a sublimating result of more essential life-processes.

The potential rapaciousness of the resulting image of understanding – where self-understanding rather than any true encounter with the 'alien' is the ultimate aim – leads Gadamer to pursue other correcting extremes. In the third and final section of *Truth and Method*, the potential rapaciousness of life will be offset by the introduction of Aristotelian ethics. In the second section, it is subverted by a stress upon context. By stressing the effect of the delimiting situation and hermeneutical horizon upon all understanding beings, Gadamer roots the subject in objectivity. Hence the task of hermeneutics is *also* to reverse Hegel, to 'retrace the path of Hegel's phenomenology of mind until we discover in all that is subjective the substantiality that determines it' (302).

This tug-of-war between substantiality and subjectivity, between the weight of the past and the invention of the present, is the source of the dramatic tension of Gadamer's *Truth and Method*. It is the locus of its vacillations, reversals and passing affiliations.[9] The term *Horizontverschmelzung* (usually translated as 'fusion of horizons'), used to describe the interaction resulting from an encounter with the past, has as one of its historical ancestors Fichte's thesis of a *Verschmelzung* of subject and object. Is Gadamer's use of this term evidence of more than lip service being paid to a long-lost 'romantic' dream of immediacy? Certainly some of the formulations of fusion in *Truth and Method* hark back to romantic scenarios. Just as the romantics dreamt of messianically opening their readers' eyes to the interconnectedness of a great cosmic totality, for instance, Gadamer would like to unlock the doors of perception and grant everyone entry to 'the one great horizon that moves from within and that, beyond the frontiers of the present, embraces the historical depths of our self-consciousness' (304).

Can modern hermeneutics fulfil such a promise? And can it do so while avoiding the pitfalls of its predecessors, avoiding the internal seams and unresolved dichotomies that troubled Dilthey and romantic organicism? As long as hermeneutics takes place in the struggle and negotiation between the past and future, such an escape is hard to envisage. For as long as the interstices of time is its habitation – '*The true locus of hermeneutics is this in-between'* [In diesem Zwischen ist der wahre Ort der Hermeneutik] (295 [300]) – the gap between horizons, and the arbitrariness of the process of mediation between them, is inevitable. Despite his pretensions to relative immediacy, Gadamer's rhetoric of fusion does not bear sustained scrutiny.

The gap is unavoidable. This becomes evident through the multiplicity and incommensurability of the approaches with which hermeneutics tries to close it. Trying to find *the* significant connection, Gadamer has recourse to a number of models in order to account for the process of hermeneutical understanding. He negotiates between favoured approaches such as bodily assimilation, festive ritual, imitation of Christ, emanation, reading, writing, legal text interpretation, classicist prescription and ethical practice, trying to weld a universal model of understanding in the more general crucible of hermeneutical reflection. Readers only familiar with Gadamer's methodological critique often overlook the resulting complexity. Indeed, the plot is different in each of the three parts of *Truth and Method*, even if they are meant to be ever widening explications of the same phenomenon. We have already observed the subjectivist slant which comes from the stress upon biological appropriation, and which stems from Gadamer's attack on the overly objectivist cast of nineteenth-century historicism in Part II. In the explication of the ontology of the work of art, which constitutes the first part of the book, there is again no real fusion – but this time the emphasis mainly goes in the opposite direction.

In that first part of *Truth and Method*, an audience's response to a work of art is mainly described in terms of a surrendering of one's individual initiative to its collective event. Such a response is the equivalent of 'true participation' [*wirkliche Teilnahme*]' that is, it is 'not something active but something passive' [*kein Tun, sondern ein Erleiden*] (124–5 [130]). The aesthetic reduction and isolation of the work of art is presented as a modern chimera which must be countered by a more traditional, sacred conception of the artistic event. Particularly the modern stress upon the relative independence and creativity of the interpreter – exemplified by the theories of Paul Valéry and André Malraux – must be circumvented.[10] Rather than responding to a call for radical dislocation, Gadamer thus believes that the reception of a work of art must primarily consist in a participation in the originary happening of that work. Interpretation of a work of art is, in this sense, an experience of yielding to community rather than a solitary performance.

Gadamer utilises several different models in order to express this sense of community. He ties the reception of the work of art to a notion of play, which is deemed to be 'a natural process' [*ein Naturvorgang*], in accordance with the explicitly cited precedent of Friedrich Schlegel (105 [111]). Like an organic being, play is characterised by 'energeia which has its telos within itself' (113). In addition to this notion of natural play, Gadamer also evokes a Kierkegaardian concept of 'contemporaneity' in order to express how reception overlaps with original production, and finds such contemporaneity especially evident in religious ritual (128). This leads to the paradigm most consistently privileged by Gadamer: art is to be grasped via the model of the togetherness of a 'religious rite' [*Kulthandlung*] (116 [121]). Whereas romanticism – in the cases of Friedrich Schlegel and Coleridge – saw the equation of the literary with the sacred as an impossible but pressing exigency, for Gadamer it is simply the precondition for any true understanding of literature and art in general.

Even if a religious rite grants a sense of togetherness, though, one might object that it always unfolds on the basis of distinctions and exclusions. A similar distinction unfolds within Gadamer's cultic interpretation of art. In order to avoid a completely unbalanced structure, Gadamer stresses that the reception is a productive image (*Bild*) rather than a mere derivative copy (*Abbild*). The work of art is partly dependent upon its reproductions and interpretations for its afterlife, but that dependency is less than the inverse dependency of the reception upon the work itself. The explicit model for this process is that of Neoplatonic emanation:

> That the picture [i.e. the reproduction] has its own reality means the reverse for what is pictured [*das Urbild*], namely that it comes to presentation in the representation. It presents itself there. It does not follow that it is dependent upon this particular presentation in order to appear. It can also present itself as what it is in other ways. But if it presents itself in this way, this is no longer any incidental event but belongs to its own being. ... By being presented it experiences, as it were, an *increase in being* [*gleichsam einen* Zuwachs an Sein]. The content of the picture itself is ontologically defined as an emanation of the original [*Das Eigengehalt des Bildes ist ontologisch als Emanation des Urbildes bestimmt*]. (140 [145])

Gadamer's theory of interpretative reproduction entails, as he says, granting a positive status to the reproduction. It is not a simple copy or the result of any form of transparent mimeticism. A modicum of interdependence between original and reproduction, between *Urbild* and *Bild*, is introduced by this Neoplatonic construction. Indeed, a similar aim was the origin of the romantic differentiation between 'imitation' and 'copy'. Nevertheless, Gadamer must acknowledge that the original is *not* dependent upon any particular reproduction. Not surprisingly, given that the Neoplatonic notion of emanation was developed as an aspect of organicism,[11] there is the equivalent of an unevenly articulated organism here. The centre of the structure is granted the status of being an absolute end compared to the relative ends of all the other members, in a relationship that is by no means symmetrical.

Gadamer applies the same logic of emanation in the third and final section of *Truth and Method*, which – as the fruition of the preparatory excursions into the theories of art and science – most directly addresses the *ontological* dimension of hermeneutics. There, emanation is employed in order to show how language functions as a positive instance of mediation, in its characteristic of granting a connection between the world and the mind. Just as the Son was a divine emanation of the Father, according to St Thomas, the word is 'simultaneous' with the original 'forming (formatio) of the intellect' (424).

On the whole, Gadamer's understanding of the interwoven nature of language and the world is more interdependent than his understanding of the relation between an original work of art and its reproductive interpretation. There is a strong sense of reciprocity between the distinct, but potentially interwoven, spheres of language and world. He stresses the universal structure of language and has later strongly emphasised that it is 'an intrinsically limitless element which carries everything within it – not merely the cultural heritage transmitted through language, but *everything* pure and simple'.[12] In *Truth and Method*, though, an odd note of irony or doubt is struck when language is described as being '"absolute"' (450) – *in quotation marks*. The hermeneutic resistance to the absolutist temptations of idealism reaches its hardest challenge on this point.

If one looks closely, there are limits even to language. Being a humanist, Gadamer restricts access to this absolute by denying that animals have recourse to any real linguistic capability. Animality is part of life, but not of language, and hence human language must be thought of as 'a special and unique life process' [*ein besonderer und einzigartiger Lebensvorgang*] (446 [450]). Thus language is both a universal *and* a particular form of life and one of the borderline problems of Coleridge's pantisocratic community of friends – the animal on the threshold of collectivity – raises what one might call, recalling not only Coleridge's ass but also Nietzsche's, a potentially deafening *hee-haw* challenging philosophy to envision wider and more encompassing forms of universality and community.

Gadamer glosses over this issue, as he also glosses over the potential conflicts within the general horizon-forming instance of language. For language is itself no univocal phenomenon, and it takes a particular interpretation to fit it into Gadamer's understanding of hermeneutics as a transindividual experience of historicity. This is evident in the manner of his complex correlation of the different media of language, a correlation that is construed by way of a teleological dialectic rather than his more typical strategy of balancing extremes. Although the basic situation of verbal dialogue is the model for the alternation of questions and answers at the heart of the hermeneutic circle, speech is only at one end of the linguistic spectrum for Gadamer. On its own, it becomes a too private medium: only by being balanced by the temporary mediation of written language (which on its own is too abstract and removed from life) can the desired medium of the hermeneutic situation be achieved. Only through writing does language gain 'its true ideality' [*ihre wahre Geistigkeit*] (391 [394]), but this ideality is only a necessary and temporary negation. Navigating from its all too private and psychological inception (in speech), via its too anonymous self-alienation (in writing), the hermeneutic event or odyssey is completed when it reaches the final harbour of a third stage: a return to the context of living, spoken language. Augmented by the odyssey into the alien territory of writing, speech is the ideal *telos* and concretion of the historical experience of language.

Thus the event of historicity is the equivalent of an organic growth process, where the meaning of the utterance comes into its own through writing – through being exposed to an exterior. History itself is understood as a way of opening up to the generality of this exterior, as Gadamer also conceives of historical distance as a necessary and cathartic process which allows the work to flower into its truth. Contemporary readers will have great problems understanding a text, since 'what a thing has to say, its intrinsic content, first appears only after it is divorced from the fleeting circumstances that gave rise to it' (298). Gadamer explicitly relates the characteristic of detachment or external delimitation to the traditional conception of an *ergon*, that is, of a work in the original Greek conception that stands at the head of the whole tradition of organicism.[13] Without such a transcendence of the moment, the dross of life – the accidents of life that Gadamer, at this juncture, has no more time for than Hegel had – cannot be discarded. The strange flower of art can truly unfurl only through the interweaving of the understandings of different ages, as well as the different media of language.

The symbiotic undertones of this thought could lead one to believe that, had *Truth and Method* been written a century and a half earlier, it might been called *The Metamorphosis of Plants*. For obviously there are important organic underpinnings here which derive, in part, from the heritage of romanticism. This feature has come even more to the fore in Gadamer's later texts. For instance, in the essay 'Science as an Instrument of Enlightenment', he deems a mechanistic worldview to be inferior to what is presented as its only alternative: 'the biological model of a self-regulated organism'.[14] In the essays collected in *The Enigma of Health*, Gadamer stresses the need for humanity to 'sustain a relation of harmony with nature'.[15] He claims that this harmony can be approached if we ask ourselves what the fundamental equilibrium, holism and non-objective essence of 'the living body ... can teach us about how we are to deal with our whole cultural apparatus and all its various instrumental possibilities'.[16] Furthermore, the significant connection between Gadamer's conception of the work of art as an *ergon* and the more general theory of organicism is made overt in his ambitious essay on 'The Relevance of the Beautiful', where he aligns himself with the tradition to which 'art has always appeared in close proximity to life in the fundamental sense of organic structure' [*Die Erscheinung der Kunst hat ... immer eine große Nähe zur Grundbestimmung des Lebens, welches die Struktur des 'organischen' hat*].[17]

Despite such affiliations, Gadamer's project is, of course, not simply identical to that of, say, Coleridge. Even if there is proximity between Gadamer and the romantic tradition, there can be no true *Verschmelzung* between the horizons of hermeneutics and romantic organicism. On the one hand, this non-identity is the result of Gadamer's paradoxical inheritance of a typical modern (and indeed also romantic) desire, the desire to escape and explain the errors of the past. On the other, *Truth and Method* constitutes a labyrinthine and rich interweaving of texts, which engages a large number of different models to throw light upon understanding: some of these models, such as the juridical application of texts of law, do not *immediately* imply organic connections. Yet one might note that even Gadamer's foray into the environs of jurisprudence – in the chapter on 'The exemplary significance of legal hermeneutics' – is guided by the holistic aim of unifying work and context and creating a closer connection between comprehension, interpretation, and application. A more widely encompassing reading than can be pursued here – one that would, for instance, clarify the status and extent of the latent organicism in Gadamer's extensive borrowings from Aristotle – would be needed in order to fully address this question.

Nevertheless, I have shown that Gadamer's holistic approach does not fully transcend the problems that beset romantic organicism. His vitalism consistently leads him to embrace romantic systematics, even if his organic underpinnings often need to be made explicit by a critical reading. If Gadamer's critique of Dilthey was based on the premise that a new, non-dualistic unity of experience – immune to the aporias of organicism – was attainable, this reading surely shows otherwise.

9
On the Double: Blanchot, Derrida and the Step Beyond

Work at the breaking point: Blanchot and Heidegger

Is there an end to organicism? What is the extent of its dominion? While the romanticism of thinkers such as Coleridge and Friedrich Schlegel is characterised by an attempt to expand the jurisdiction of the figure of organicism to all areas of thought and writing, much modern thought has the opposite aim. The restriction – or even downright rejection – of the organism is what is sought. In this chapter I want to scrutinise this alternative strategy, by way of two different readings: the first will focus upon Maurice Blanchot's early theory of the work of art, and the second will look into Jacques Derrida's later resistance to organicism and the Western metaphysical tradition. In both, I will be scrutinising – and questioning – the radical nature of a movement that tries to set aside organicism in order to replace it with the alternative, ontotypological figure of the text.

Violently, precipitately, this chapter will try to deliver these goods *on the double*. The two readings will disclose what is in many ways a complex and erring path; one that I hope to demonstrate entails neither a simple progression away from organicism nor a straightforward return to its foundations. This alternative path has the same point of departure as Hans-Georg Gadamer: namely, the Heideggerian philosophy of historicity. But by virtue of a more radical insistence upon mortality (as opposed to finitude primarily interpreted merely as horizon-enclosed limitedness) it has to be situated further away from the beaten track of romanticism. From another vantage point, though, this more radical interpretation of mortality and death is made in terms of a relation to immediacy, or the aporia of immediacy, and this characteristic bends the trajectory of this erring path closer to that of romantic organicism. As I will soon show, Blanchot and Derrida are never very far from romantic problems, and one might be tempted to see organicism as a kind of *doppelgänger* to their endeavours, even if their proximity to romantic organicism reaches its apogee only in, and according to, the strange logic of dreams.

Should one dream of immediacy? We have seen that even if a hermeneutic philosopher such as Gadamer is heavily involved in questions handed down by romantic organicism, he nevertheless denounces the romantic fascination for immediacy. Instead, like Richards, he displays a strong predilection for Aristotelian virtues of balance and practical reason. This is in accordance with a strong humanist bias, which sees in immediacy the unacceptable potential for a destructive, orgiastic subversion of human rationality. Hermeneutics also denounces immediacy as the pernicious sign of an impatience that seeks gratification quickly, on the double, rather than through patient submission to the long haul of interpretation.

Nevertheless, what one might call the 'heritage of immediacy' constitutes a Mephistophelian temptation that has not been completely eradicated from modern thought. For Bataille, the fact that 'every animal is *in the world like water in water*'[1] does not mean that this form of immediacy is without relevance to the human condition: instead it subverts and solicits human quasi-autonomy from afar, as the impossible but necessary precondition of transgression. Bataille thus orients human subjectivity towards its heterogeneous ground, in a manner reminiscent of these lines of Coleridge's:

> Resembles life what once was deem'd of light,
> Too ample in itself for human sight?
> An absolute self – an element ungrounded –
> All that we see, all colours of all shade
> By encroach of darkness made? –
> Is very life by consciousness unbounded?
> And all the thoughts, pains, joys of mortal breath,
> A war-embrace of wrestling life and death?[2]

Blanchot is perhaps the modern thinker who has most persistently addressed the 'war-embrace' of life and death, and its relation to immediacy and literature. He has done so without shirking the obscurity of that which is 'Too ample in itself for human sight.' In what follows, I want to focus on his unique approach to these problems, particularly in *The Space of Literature* (1955), an approach which takes its bearings from the intersection between Heidegger's understanding of the work of art and his conception of 'Being towards death'.[3] For Heidegger, the connection between these two themes – between art and mortality – is implicit rather than spelled out. Both art and 'Being towards death' remove one from the sphere of the everyday, where the world presents itself in the form of objects available to one's use as equipment, but Heidegger does not make explicit what link there is between these two experiences.

In his famous treatise on *The Origin of the Work of Art* (1935), Heidegger grapples with 'the riddle of art'.[4] Art is a riddle because it has a separate existence and ontology from objective things and utilitarian pieces of equipment. As Heidegger dismisses the traditional form–matter distinction as being derived from equipment, the conceptual formulation of what art is becomes an imposing challenge. This is evident, for instance, in the fact that he preserves the term 'work' even if he criticises its Greek forefather – the *ergon* – for implying a metaphysics of form and matter. In order to explain his own conception of the work, Heidegger replaces the dichotomy of form and matter with a complicated relation between 'world' and 'earth'. Although his use of these two terms is sketchy and provisional, one significant feature is that they both evoke the larger context within which the work of art takes place. The work transcends any pure aesthetic immanence in the way it thus instantiates a microcosm within its macrocosm (to use inappropriate and traditional terms that are not Heidegger's own). A more singular tendency is evident in the particular interpretation Heidegger gives of the two terms, by relating them to his revival of the Greek concept of truth (*aletheia*) in the form of revealing: earth is tied to the movement of concealing within closure, while world is the movement that brings into the open and reveals. Although earth's characteristic of sheltering is reminiscent of ancient determinations of Mother Nature, a different note is struck by the fact that earth resists, to a certain extent, the exertions of the world.

Nevertheless, Heidegger sees earth and world as combining to form a whole in the work of art. His treatise struggles to articulate – without making use of the Hegelian dialectic – that this does not entail any peaceful or static relationship. In the process, he goes further than the most romantic uses of dynamism and development (evident in organic theories of polarity) in his attempt to avoid a placid, classicist aesthetics, by stressing the necessity of a conflict between the two.[5] However far Heidegger goes in insisting on the irreducible nature of this conflict, it is nevertheless comprehended by the unifying ground and boundary of the work, which he derives from the work's status of being created. Since it is created, the work has a unifying design, or 'rift':

> This rift carries the opponents into the source of their unity by virtue of their common ground. It is a basic design, an outline sketch, that draws the basic features of the rise of the lighting of beings. This rift does not let the opponents break apart; it brings the opposition of measure and boundary into their common outline.[6]

This design brings their opposition into one singular figure or *Gestalt*, and, as such, this figure is 'the structure in whose shape the rift composes and shapes itself' [*das Gefüge, als welches der Riß sich fügt*].[7] It structures their duality within a whole.

Apart from the ontological dimension implied by opening art up to the event of being, touched upon but not pursued at length in *The Origin of the*

Work of Art, Heidegger's stress upon the strife between earth and world may be seen as his most crucial contribution to the modern movement from an organicist aesthetics of the work to the textual paradigm. But if one turns to Blanchot, it becomes evident that the latter takes an even more radical step, bringing us to the brink of the new conception of the text. Blanchot is also important in that he integrates this conflict with the understanding of mortality presented in *Being and Time*.

Blanchot's radicalisation of the Heideggerian *Streit* may best be approached by way of how he links art to the experience (or absence of experience) of death. Like Heidegger in *Being and Time*, he resists any framing of death in organic teleology. Blanchot finds fault with Rainer Maria Rilke, for instance, for framing death in precisely such organicist terms:

> When one considers the images that serve to sustain Rilke's thought (death 'ripens' in our very heart; it is the 'fruit,' the sweet, obscure fruit, or else a fruit still 'green,' without sweetness, which we, 'leaves and bark,' must bear and nourish), one sees clearly that he seeks to make of our end something other than an accident which would arrive from outside to terminate us hastily.[8]

In dismissing such an appeal to images of 'vegetable or organic maturation' (125), Blanchot severs any link between death and the goal-oriented development of one's possibilities. Death is a radical impossibility, an alien intervention into human life, and not a resource to be conquered or confronted. Organic teleology is not out of place in describing how mankind projects its possibilities and negates nature, in its everyday concerns, but it does not articulate its relation to death.[9]

While Gadamer collapses Heidegger's distinction between the everyday and 'Being towards death' into one, project-oriented conception of time, Blanchot insists upon the difference between the two. Insofar as there is a bridge between one's everyday self and the part of one's being that is engaged and set aside in death, it is a tenuous one that can be illuminated, according to Blanchot, in the relationship between the will to commit suicide and the disastrous outcome of such a will. He claims that suicide is

> an absolute right, the only one which is not the corollary of a duty, and yet it is a right which no real power reinforces. It would seem to arch like a delicate and endless bridge which at the decisive moment is cut and becomes as unreal as a dream, over which nevertheless it is necessary really to pass. (105)

This is, in effect, Blanchot's ironical rephrasing of Kant's granting the aesthetic the role of being a bridge between the sensible and the supersensible. Like an act of suicide, art must hover between life and death, the everyday and dissimulated Being. But the bridge it thereby facilitates is no resource or possession that can be accounted for: it is both endless and 'unreal as a dream'.

This bridge is a figure of the suspended relation between work and its beyond, a relation that is constitutive of both death and literature. The confluence of the latter two activities is emblematically represented by the mythical figure of Orpheus, whose descent into Hades 'links the "poetic" to an immeasurable demand that we disappear' (156). From his understanding of mortality, Blanchot constructs a relation between opposites that subtly differs from Heidegger's opposition of earth and world. Blanchot's determination of these opposites varies within *The Space of Literature*: sometimes the distinction is between the quasi-mythical entities night and day, and sometimes it is a struggle between reader and writer. On another occasion he evokes 'the torn immediacy of irreconcilable and inseparable moments which we call measure and measurelessness, form and infinitude, resolution and indecision' (199). Such semantic instability is evidence of the extreme volatility of the artistic process as Blanchot sees it; a volatility that he believes pushes the relation beyond the bounds of mere polarity. Even if it may perhaps not be a matter of polarity, one can sense the workings of traditional organicism in the fact that Blanchot deems the relation between these opposites to be one of 'equals' and 'reciprocity' when it is instantiated in the struggle between reader and writer (227).

Yet equality and reciprocity are not the primary hallmarks of Blanchot's understanding of the work of art. He exacerbates the tension already evident in Heidegger's struggle between earth and world, and stresses that the work of art has a relation to an origin that is beyond itself. This self-transcendence is reminiscent of the manner in which the organic body, according to Blanchot's friend Bataille, is related to its heterogeneous foundation. In the work of art, the movement of measure and form is linked to an elemental depth. In this elemental depth, the work encounters its own unworking, and must 'surpass itself, be united with its origin and consecrated in impossibility' (174). Blanchot's complex rendering of this event situates the origin of the work beyond both the work itself *and* the everyday world that it negates. This origin is immediacy itself, outside of the form–content distinction, the absolute romantic *topos* that now is located at the heart of language. It is 'the place where the unmanipulable which language is escapes every division and is pure indeterminacy' (182). This indeterminate immediacy either ruins the work in a movement of sacrifice or is compromised and left behind by the work. Any simple balance or unity between the work and its origin is made impossible by a fundamental dualism that stems from the ineradicability of the threshold or bridge between the two realms.

As such, the elemental depth is at the furthermost remove from the active, everyday work of negation. Combined with the fact that it also is the potential destruction of the artistic quest for a unified totality, this is the justification for Blanchot's naming this movement *désœuvrement*. The fact that this term contains within itself not only a reference to idleness but also to the work (the *œuvre* that is negated) is an indication of how Blanchot suspends, but does not completely leave behind, organicism and the aesthetics of the work. Even if his early writings in many ways herald the coming of the decisive abandonment of the concept of the work, Blanchot does not simply cross that bridge. He celebrates both 'that the work is this leap and that it immobilizes itself mysteriously between the truth which does not belong to it and the prolixity of the unrevealable which would prevent it from belonging to itself' (244).

Arguably, Blanchot is both more *and* less radical than Heidegger in his resistance to organicism. On the one hand, he rebukes the German thinker for not going far enough, as Heidegger's notion of 'Being towards death' supposedly makes of death a possibility and resource for an understanding being, rather than an uncrossable limit and recurring stumbling block. In a similar vein, Heidegger's notion of 'earth' is almost completely diverted from its ties with nature (or *phusis*, as Heidegger designates his more origi-nary understanding of nature), made uninhabitable[10] and converted into a more neutral conception of an obscure worklesssness. Such gestures are, on the other hand, accompanied by a strategy that places Blanchot's discourse in a closer proximity with vitalism than Heidegger's. For Blanchot allows the artistic work a relation to both life and the body, even if it is only in the transcendence of these categories: art is closely related to, and articu-lated via, such given phenomena as death, impotence and the cadaver. There is a phenomenological remnant in Blanchot's approach here, which doesn't quite correspond to the radical transcendence of the ontic (and the vitalistic) called for by Heidegger.

In other texts, Blanchot gives a different formulation to the double movement expressed by the coexistence of the leap and suspension of movement in the 'bridge' of art, and in the process dissevers both the organic body and the hermeneutical circle. The finished work that readers confront as an aesthetic object is only the residue, and betrayal, of the unworking that the work must confront. In an essay on Heinrich Hölderlin, which constantly relates to Heidegger's reading of the same poet, Blanchot stresses that the compromise represented by the finished work in many respects saves one from actually facing the destructive immediacy of that same work's origin:

> The poem must exist, because without it the day would be there but it would not light up: without it everything would communicate, but this communication would also be at every moment the destruction of everything, lost into an always open infinity, refusing to return to its infinity.[11]

Since the origin of the work of art is a disastrous immediacy, it is both desired and denied. Here one encounters one of the more important consequences of Blanchot's divergence from Heidegger and the German hermeneutical tradition: namely, a complete transformation of the hermeneutical circle, of 'the circular procedure' that Blanchot deems to be 'characteristic' of Heidegger.[12] For if there is an ineradicable difference between the centre of the work and the decision of the poet to approach that centre, one cannot let these simply imply each other in a circular procedure.

Since the approach of the artist to the centre of the work always has to cross a line or bridge that is both suspended and unreal, a peculiar form of traffic will take place. Both a transgressive leap and a suspension or halt are equally in their place. Blanchot describes this 'double contrary movement' as one

that does not succeed either at conciliating itself, or pushing itself back, or penetrating itself; it is a double prohibition, a double demand rigorously contradictory. The unexpressed must be unveiled – it must, that is a duty – and yet it is an act that is not appropriate.[13]

What later poststructuralist thought will call (in accordance with psychoanalysis) a 'double bind' is thus born out of the ashes of the hermeneutical circle. It stems from the impossibility of any free, circular navigation between the part (often represented by a subjective agency) and the central immediacy that caps, or is the head, of the body of the whole. Blanchot will later formalise this ambivalent relation in the phrase 'le pas au delà', which means both 'the step beyond' and 'the not beyond'.[14] It identifies the task of the poet in a manner that is close to Coleridge's comparing of the reader's progress to the motion of a snake: 'at every step he pauses and half recedes, and from the retrogressive movement collects the force which again carries him onward.'[15] But in Blanchot's understanding, progression cannot fully include retrogression, since the two demands are not dialectically sublated but cancel each other out in a relation of unresolved tension.

This tension lies at the heart of Blanchot's understanding of the exigency of the absolute work. In his readings of Stéphane Mallarmé, he gives a new articulation to the task of a combined literary and philosophical work that would, as an absolute text, address or even fill the space left open by the modern critique of the Bible. We have already seen how Wordsworth's architectural sketch for *The Recluse* stranded on the aporias of organicism. Although Blanchot does not mention Wordsworth or Coleridge, he is both a historian and theoretician of how the notion of an absolute book 'begins with the Bible'[16] and, in a more transcendental guise, 'will later tend to be affirmed with the romantics (Novalis), then more rigorously with Hegel, then still more radically (though in a different way) with Mallarmé.'[17] The *impossibility* of the absolute work is given its peculiar form through the temporality that corresponds to the double demand laid before the poet.

To make the sacred present in a work of art would be to capture it in time, in the moment of the 'now' or self-present instant. Yet this cannot be done, since 'immediate presence is presence of what could not be present, presence of the non-accessible, presence excluding or exceeding any present'.[18] Time is itself a process of mediation, of structure, and cannot contain immediacy within its framework. Therefore, the exigency of the absolute work acquires a skewed and singular temporality. The work offers itself only in the form of 'The book to come',[19] as a promise of what cannot arrive, of what only presents itself as the coming of that which cannot ever make itself present. As we have seen previously, both Coleridge and Wordsworth were marked by this temporality in their aspirations for an absolute book. Rigorously applied, literature can take up the mantle of religion only if it grants the Book a status not entirely dissimilar that of a Messiah whose presence is both impossible and radically untimely.

In the extreme exigency represented by the absolute work one can glimpse the extremity of the aporia that gradually leads Blanchot, in his later writings, to repudiate the aesthetics of the work. If the work is, strictly speaking, impossible, then there cannot be any remnant or compromise constructions created by would-be Orpheuses fleeing the experience of death. To be sure, there are failed works of art, but there are no true works. This problem also affects Blanchot's view of the artist. Already in *The Space of Literature* we have seen him insist that the artist, or the writer, should confront the alien space of death. This confrontation brings with it the impersonality of death, which Blanchot finds a trace of in Franz Kafka's thoughts on the impersonal instance that embodies, through the pronoun '*il*', the narrative voice of his novels: 'The third person substituting for the 'I': such is the solitude that comes to the writer on account of the work' (28). Insofar as the writer can enter into this space, and yet create a completed work, (s)he is a successful mediator, and indeed in *The Space of Literature* it is stated that the poet of Hölderlin's hymns, for instance, is a 'mediator' (269). Here one is very close to the position previously encountered in the reading I made of Friedrich Schlegel. The writer is, as it were, the self-destructive surrogate representative for the sublime, for that beyond the work that cannot be represented. And insofar as the writer creates works of narrative, Blanchot claims (s)he is embodied by the neutrality of the narrative voice that is somewhere between a person and a thing (Blanchot's '*il*' can both be read as an 'it' and as a 'he'). Here something like a complex coexistence of the warring representatives of the sublime takes place, which is reminiscent of the quarrel we encountered early in chapter 3, between Schleiermacher and Schlegel, with regard to the contending merits of the natural and the personal sublime. In *The Space of Literature*, Blanchot does not choose between these two alternatives, but rather allows both to coexist in a radicalised reinterpretation of the sublime transposed onto the poetics of narrative.

Less than ten years later, when Blanchot goes over the same problems again, the situation is more complex, and the proximity to romanticism is considerably attenuated. Now the narrative voice 'cannot be embodied,' and although

> it may well borrow the voice of a judiciously chosen character, or even create the hybrid function of the mediator (the voice that ruins all mediation), it is always different from what utters it: it is the indifferent-difference that alters the personal voice. Let us (on a whim) call it spectral, ghostlike. ... it is thus neutral in the decisive sense that it cannot be central, does not create a center, does not speak from out of a center, but, on the contrary, at the limit, would prevent the work from having one: withdrawing from it every privileged point of interest (even afocal), and also not allowing it to exist as a completed whole, once and forever achieved.[20]

Now there is no true embodiment of the narrative voice, as it is separated from all identifiable signs and would-be agencies within the text. Even more fraught with consequences is the disappearance of the *centre* of the work, a disappearance here ascribed to the narrative voice. In a short, unpaginated fragment preceding the text proper of *The Space of Literature*, Blanchot had written that even a fragmentary book 'has a center which attracts it'. Here, too, a shift has taken place.

What has happened in the mean time, in between these two different approaches to the centre of the work? Arguably, a radicalisation of the understanding of textual fragmentation has taken place. This radicalisation causes Blanchot, in his later writings, to take an interest in, but ultimately dismiss, Friedrich Schlegel's theory of the fragment. Schlegel is taken to task for (a) considering the fragment to be a text that has its centre in itself, (b) neglecting the structuring function of the interval *between* the fragments, and (c) not realising that fragmentary writing escapes all forms of unity whatsoever.[21] Obviously Blanchot is here calling for a structure of fragmentation that will escape organicism and the aesthetics of the work altogether – something which never entered Schlegel's mind. If Blanchot did not leave romantic organicism completely behind in *The Space of Literature*, he certainly wants to do so here. But is this a feasible project? And how far can this movement be taken? In what follows, an explication of Derrida's critique of structured totalities will bring these issues into closer focus.

The text of mourning: Derrida

Jacques Derrida has been an important influence on the manner in which the preceding chapters have brought forth unarticulated tensions and underlying aporias in the various organicisms propounded. Derrida's critique of structured totalities, that led to the popularisation and reification of the term 'deconstruction', was aimed not only at French structuralism but also at organicist thought in general. As one critic has pointed out, one of the 'more striking and shocking features' of the work of Derrida and his contemporaries, has precisely been its 'fierce attack on the notion of organic unity'.[22] At least this is the received opinion. While it is a valid view with regard to Paul de Man's critique of organicism, it risks oversimplifying what in Derrida at least is a highly complex and multifaceted position. In order to present an outline of the latter, I will initially unfold some of the premises for Derrida's quite considerable resistance to the organicist heritage. I will then go on to identify some of its more hesitant notes, as well as some of the more affirmative tendencies – indicative, perhaps, of something like a state of mourning – struck by Derrida with regard to organic unity.

In the main, Derrida identifies organicism as simply one of many interrelated strands of Western metaphysics. It is cast in a different role than in romanticism, as it now no longer embodies the innovative means of liberation from the mechanical explanation. The onus of liberation now lies primarily on a new conception of the *text* (although Derrida also places much weight on the related terms such as 'writing', 'différance' and 'trace'). Textuality has to be extricated and separated from organicism (and the related paradigm of the work), its dilapidated or monstrous double.[23] In its unlimited application – encompassing language, the body and all articulation *per se* – the ontotypological figure of the text is effectively cast as a rival to dethrone the organism.[24] Despite Derrida's considerable stress on the singular and the idiomatic, one of the characteristics that most closely links him with figures such as Schlegel and Coleridge is how pervasively a consistent manner of approaching the question of structural totality informs his approach to a wide variety of issues. The difference is, of course, that in Derrida's case the 'totalitarian' figure of the organism is supplanted and replaced by the text. But the mechanics of this supplanting is not as straightforward as one might be led to believe, for instance, by Roland Barthes' polemical declarations in 'From Work to Text'.[25] Derrida ultimately approaches the notion of the text as a provisional manner of articulating the unspeakable, rather than as any kind of final word. This is evident, for instance, in the hesitation and use of quotation marks in the following formulation:

> What has happened, if it has happened, is a sort of overrun that spoils all these boundaries and divisions and forces us to extend the accredited concept, the dominant notion of a 'text,' of what I still call a 'text,' for strategic reasons, in part – a 'text' that is henceforth no longer a finished corpus of writing, some content enclosed in a book or its margins, but a differentiated network, a fabric of traces referring endlessly to something other than itself, to other differential traces.[26]

The provisional nature of the figure of the text is one of the reasons why organicism cannot be simply dismissed out of hand.

The main tendency of Derrida's thought has long been to present organicism as an assimilative structure that appropriates everything other into its own vital but dominating totality. A particularly important manner in which this totality has striven for summarisation and completion is 'the ontotheology of the great Book'.[27] The interwoven, repetitious, and frequently aphoristic manner of Derrida's many texts is a gesture towards another kind of writing, that would escape all dreams of comprehensiveness and unity. This gesture also renders any presentation of his thought both risky and necessarily piecemeal. Nevertheless, a strategic entry can be made through the introductory essay to *Margins of Philosophy*, entitled 'Tympan', in which the discourse of metaphysical tradition in general is identified in terms which are very close to those we have found central to romantic organicism. Metaphysics is said to be characterised by its ability to suppress, through the construction of a controlling centre, the plural field opened up by a diversity of organs. Metaphysics always attempts to produce 'the pacifying lure of organic indifference' [*l'effacement idéalisant de la différence organique*],[28] by appropriating what is other to it into its own presence. It does so by a controlled opening towards what is alien to it, all the while 'assuring itself mastery over the limit'.[29] For Derrida, Hegel's dialectical philosophy epitomises this tendency. Metaphysical appropriation of what is at the limit takes two forms: namely, 'hierarchy and envelopment.'[30] The former, hierarchical tendency is evident in the way in which philosophy grants itself access to a fundamental ontology at the head of all other activities, and it is also credited by Derrida as a means of *delimiting* the more specialised fields as subordinate members of the whole. The latter, enveloping strategy is deployed in order to ensure that 'the whole is implied, in the speculative mode of reflection and expression, in each part'.[31] It makes for a circular traffic between part and whole, which Derrida finds evidence of in Heidegger's hermeneutical circle and of course also is part and parcel of organicism.

The categories unfolded by Derrida in 'Tympan' correspond fairly closely to the principles of hierarchical totalisation, reciprocal interdependence and external delimitation (although the latter principle is not emphasised much), which I have pursued in some of their romantic and post-romantic inflections. A small difference is evident, though, between Derrida's understanding of 'envelopment' and the organicist tradition of reciprocity. For envelopment is always controlled, and always between part and whole, while romantic interdependence can take place in the relations between parts – and it can also (as in Coleridge's thought) be understood as subversive in its tendency to run riot.

One of the main ways in which the discourse of a metaphysical whole is regulated, according to Derrida, is by way of dichotomies. Binary oppositions such as inner–outer, intelligible–sensible, signified–signifier, subject–object, and so on, are employed both in order to centre a structure (in the privileged side of the dichotomies) and to give it an extension and an outside (through the repressed, but nevertheless included, elements). In order to surpass this logic, Derrida employs a strategy of considerable complexity. In an early formulation, he identifies 'a kind of *general strategy of deconstruction*' as consisting in the avoidance of 'both simply *neutralizing* the binary oppositions of metaphysics and simply *residing* within the closed field of these oppositions, thereby confirming it'.[32]

This desire to bypass the oppositions of metaphysics brings with it a close proximity to the radical organicism of romanticism (which also wanted to leave behind the relations of subject–object, active–passive, form–matter, and the like), yet in Derrida's resistance to a simple neutralisation of such oppositions there are grounds for difference. Wanting to circumvent the totalising unities evident in Hegel, Derrida both argues for a provisional but 'indispensable phase of *reversal*'[33] that will privilege the neglected terms of the dialectic, and for a more paradoxical relation between the terms. As he somewhat cryptically puts it on one occasion: 'Neither/nor, that is, *simultaneously* either *or*' [*Ni/ni, c'est* à la fois *ou bien* ou *bien*].[34]

One way to conceptualise this highly articulated and volatile stance, is that Derrida does not simply choose one way of relating metaphysical opposites, but instead utilises the possible combinations however he finds it strategically tenable. When faced with a given dichotomy, he can decide to favour one element over the other (in a gesture of recompense for traditional discrimination), or to transcend both elements, or retain both in a state of agonistic suspension. To hold all these possibilities as tenable is to grant a certain *undecidability* to structural configuration. The affirmation of undecidability puts all hierarchies into question.

Although the two notions have their own unique histories and articulations, romantic organicism's deployment of the principle of interdependent reciprocity has similar *effects* to that of undecidability. In both, the centring and teleological directing of structure is countered. Their closeness becomes even more pronounced when one observes how Derrida's own focus has changed over the years. In his early, influential lecture on 'Structure, Sign, and Play in the Discourse of the Human Discourses', he dismisses any decision between nostalgia for old metaphysical centring devices and an affirmative celebration of the absence of those devices. There are no grounds for a decision between the two, he claims, because

> although these two interpretations must acknowledge and accentuate their difference and define their irreducibility, I do not believe that today there is any question of *choosing* – in the first place because here we are in a region (let us say, provisionally, a region of historicity) where the category of choice seems particularly trivial; and, in the second,

because we must first try to conceive of the common ground, and the *différance* of this irreducible difference.[35]

In more recent texts, though, a less dismissive account is given of the act of decision, which now is deemed to be something that, at times, is inescapable: there is 'the necessity of deciding there where the decision seems imposs-ible'.[36] Deconstruction does not amount to a simple favouring of the tension among individual elements within a text. It cannot be reduced to a gesture of desisting to decide, as there often is an obligation to make a decision that cuts into relations of undecidability.

This indecision, so to speak, between pure decision and pure undecidability, renders Derrida's concept of structure ambivalent and torn in a manner that is very similar to that I have located in romantic organicism. On the one hand, his theoretical articulations of the cut, or act of severing, inherent in division links his thought to the principle of hierarchy so central to organicism. This is particularly true when this act is formulated in terms of a performative, foundational gesture. Such decisions (which Derrida is careful to describe as singular events rather than voluntary or subjective acts) are deemed to be heterogeneously and dissymmetrically related to all elements (or acts) within the articulated structure that they bring about. On the other hand, the *topos* of undecidability leads to a flat, non-regulated structure that is more akin to the effect produced by the organic principle of interdependence. Derrida's later texts have consistently traced this tension between the singularity of the heterogeneous (in political contexts described in terms of the impossible, revolutionary immediacy of the violent founding of a state) and the iterability of representation that escapes decision. This tension is also evident in how Derrida's search for a deconstructive logic that would no longer sacrifice alterity is offset by his admission that all transmission of tradition (and indeed all interpretation) is impossible without selective and quite often brutal interventions.[37] Just as was the case with Coleridge and Wordsworth, deconstruction both confirms and denies the sacrificing act of exclusion.

Although the clash between decision and undecidability is evocative of the tension between the principles of organicism, one cannot simply equate the former with the latter. Certainly, there is quite some distance from the clichés one usually ascribes to romantic and post-romantic thought. Derrida is careful to untangle the decision from voluntarism, and he is adamant that what he understands as effects of singularity are not signs of subjectivity or of the private domain. But of course the same goes for romanticism, which can seldom be reduced to the simple form of subjectivism its critics tend to confuse it with. A more fruitful means of gauging the distance separating deconstruction from organicism lies in Derrida's rather ambivalent stance towards the philosophy of life, that is, towards vitalism. Although he supports, and indeed at times even outbids

Heidegger's stress upon the ontological difference (between beings and their abyssal ground of Being), and also tends to endorse Blanchot's radicalisation of the 'Being towards death', he nevertheless draws back from any complete denunciation of the tradition of vitalism. Derrida uses the term *sur-vivre* to denote both a limit experience on the edge of life and death (simultaneously excluding and embracing both elements of this dichotomy, according to the complex logic mentioned earlier), as well as the survival of tradition through repetition and textuality. By this gesture, he resists any wholesale endorsement of Heidegger's distinction between organic and mortal beings. 'As justified as it may be from a certain point of view,' he demurs, 'Heidegger's obstinate critique of vitalism and of the philosophies of life, but also of any consideration of life in the structure of *Dasein*, is not unrelated to ... a "sacrificial structure".'[38] The vitalism we have seen insistent in romantic organicism and pantheism thus has the saving grace that it constitutes a rearguard against the excesses of what even in Heidegger constitutes 'the profoundest metaphysical humanism'.[39]

Derrida treats the structure of *sur-vivre* in the double-barrelled essay 'Living On: Borderlines', which offers parallel interpretations of Shelley's *The Triumph of Life* and Blanchot's *Death Sentence*. There one can trace another sign of deferral with regard to the tradition of organicism. It concerns the term 'invagination', which Derrida uses in order to conceptualise the folding of a border of a text. The use of this term amounts to more than a humorously subversive importation of gender-specific traits into the supposedly neutral, formalistic domain of literary criticism: it also represents a borrowing from the science of embryology.[40] In using this word to denote 'the inverted reapplication of the outer edge to the inside of a form where the outside thus opens a pocket',[41] Derrida is importing a term descriptive of the internal scission that generates the digestive system of vertebrates. He is also inscribing himself in a tradition – which includes Bataille and Coleridge – which has expressed literary productivity in terms borrowed from the biology of cellular division.

Some of the themes and motifs of 'Living On: Borderlines' recur in Derrida's later essay 'The Law of Genre', where Blanchot's short fiction *The Madness of the Day* is employed to subvert the possibility of unifying and closing the field of any literary genre. In a typical gesture, Derrida here uses something akin to the idealist theme of self-reflection in a manner which goes against the grain of the tradition of New Criticism: the text's mirroring of itself is not taken to provide a self-identical centre to its structure, but rather a point of overflowing and internal dissension. One of the words invoked to denote this point (along with the 're-mark') is 'invagination'. Any genre marker or title functions, for Derrida, as 'a pocket inside the corpus', which takes 'the form of an *invagination*' splitting, traversing, and bounding the corpus in one gesture.[42]

By stressing the insurmountable and infinite process opened up by such genre markers, Derrida is effectively subverting the closure promised by aesthetic self-referentiality and idealistic renderings of the intellectual intuition with something akin to the mobility and interminableness evident in the process of self-reflection as it was thematised by Friedrich Schlegel. The frequent structuralist and poststructuralist use of the concept of the 'mise en abyme' – that is, the infinite, deferring structure of referentiality opened up when one part of a text includes the whole within itself – is another version of this structure. Its close proximity to the traditional organicist paradox in which an element (a 'microcosm' of sorts) fully comprehends and instantiates the whole (the 'macrocosm') is undeniable. Derrida has noted this proximity, for instance in a reading of Hegel's introduction to his lectures on aesthetics, where the 'totality of philosophy, the encyclopaedic corpus is described *as* a living organism *or as* a work of art.'[43] In observing how close this kind of organicism is to the avant-garde practice of the 'mise en abyme', Derrida tries to articulate a distinction. Interestingly, the distinction does not depend upon whether the imbrication of part and whole is described in organic (or vitalistic) terms or not. The question cannot be settled simply on the basis of an ontological determination – it depends upon the relation between the movement of the abyss, and the possibility to put an end to that movement. Derrida claims that there is a 'comic effect' in the ambivalent manner in which this relation frequently is presented, as for instance in Heidegger's use of the hermeneutical circle:

> Interrogate the comic effect of this. One never misses it if the abyss is never sufficient, if it must remain – undecided – between the bottom-less and the bottom of the bottom. The *operation* of the *mise en abyme* always occupies itself (activity, busy positing. mastery of the subject) with somewhere filling up, full of abyss, filling up the abyss[.][44]

Insofar as it is an 'operation', then, the 'mise en abyme' tends to set terminate the abyssal movement of infinite reflection in an act of positing. Yet the opposite can also be true, if the act of mastery fails. A subversive movement occurs if the bottom is not closed up, and the effects of the trajectory are not collected in one unitary gathering, but are instead experienced as the adventure of the bottomless. This would be a form of repetition with and according to difference, a more radical kind of mise en abyme or '*contre-abyme*' that Derrida also evokes in his reading of Kafka in the text called 'Before the Law'.[45]

A deconstructive form of infinite reflection is not entirely dissociable, then, from subversive unworking that can be perpetrated when the organicist principle of interdependence is let loose. Deconstruction does not expel organicism entirely, like a virulent disease, but lets itself be touched by it at a certain border site where the text overlaps with the *ergon* in a *parergon*.[46] This is true, though, only as long as it does not lead to any complete form of hierarchical totalisation. Effects of dissymmetry and violence, as well as a *desire* for identity and totalisation, are ineluctable in all structures. But the unified act of gathering cannot be allowed by Derrida, whether it takes the form of Heideggerian *Versammlung* (evident in the 'rift' or 'design' (*Riß*) we encountered in his treatise on the origin of the work of art) or that of Friedrich Schlegel's hedgehog, rolling itself up into the delimited whole of a work of art: 'Whether in Schlegel or Heidegger, it is always a matter of this gathering together, of this being-one with oneself, in all these stories of the hedgehog, of indivisible individuality or of being always already with oneself, from the origin or the finish line of some *Bestimmung*.'[47]

Derrida's interventions into the field of inquiry opened up by recent work on the theory of reception are further evidence of this resistance against 'gathering' and closure. Whereas many theories of reception present the essence of reading as an act of gathering that makes the work whole, Derrida stresses all the factors that make such a position problematical. He counters theories of meaning which imply an organic teleology, where the self-presence of the author's intention (or the work's immanent meaning) traverses the process of communication and its media to be fulfilled in the goal of its reception. Against this view, he stresses that communication can always go wrong: the medium of writing, for instance, is not just a temporary stop between a vocal (or spiritual) source and destination, but an essential risk undergone by meaning. The same is true of the essential dispersal any message is subjected to through processes of reproductive iteration (whether the latter are merely potential or realised). Here Derrida (inspired by Blanchot) suggests that there is something like a 'Being towards death' at the very heart of communication: theories that do not take heed of such potential deformations are, he implies, thinking of meaning in terms that are only apposite to organic, and not truly mortal, beings. Obviously, this also constitutes a ground for disagreement with the brand of organic vitalism we saw dominating Gadamer's hermeneutics in the previous chapter.

Totalisation is thus what Derrida mainly objects to in organicism. Is it possible to think of an organicism without hierarchy or totalisation? And to what degree and extent would this omission or repression of hierarchy have to be carried out in order to attune organicism to the movement and drift of deconstruction? This question has particular relevance if we turn to Derrida's writings on the problem of *community*. On the matter of such a community, he basically echoes his general rejection of all forms of thought that impose a unified totality, however mediated and self-professedly inclusive that totality may be. His texts repeatedly deal with figures, such as the scapegoat and the outsider, who participate without fully belonging to a community. Yet at the same time, Derrida has always been highly suspicious of all forms of individualism, essentially seeing the same sacrificial mechanisms at work in the construction of the individual subject as in the larger 'subject' of an integrated collectivity. In his recent meditations on the classical problem of friendship, the transcendence of the individual is a point of departure. Derrida's interest and point of view comes as an extension of a modern tradition (or counter-tradition) that stems from Nietzsche, and includes Bataille, Blanchot and Nancy. The following statement by Blanchot illustrates how this line takes classical friendship as its starting point in order to formulate a notion of community that is based on difference and distance rather than identity:

> Friendship, this relation without dependence, without episode, yet into which all of the simplicity of life enters, passes by way of the recognition of the common strangeness that does not allow us to speak of our friends but only to speak to them, not to make of them a topic of conversations (or essays), but the movement of understanding in which, speaking to us, they reserve, even on the most familiar terms, an infinite distance, the fundamental separation on the basis of which what separates becomes relation.[48]

This distance which is so vast that it forbids one to use one's incidental knowledge of the other, even 'were it to praise him',[49] is not entirely dissimilar to that which I identified at the heart of Coleridge's conception of friendship. In the romantic idea of a friendship with God, there was a distance so vast that no praise or determination of the other could impinge upon the empty abyss separating the two 'friends' that communicated. There, too, a form of communication was opened in which one could not, to use Blanchot's words, 'pretend to carry on a dialogue'.[50] The thought of Blanchot and Derrida is frequently at its closest to romanticism when they formulate the radical event of such relations in a form close to that of negative theology: romanticism and deconstruction share a resistance to reducing the sacred to straightforwardly rational or socio-political terms.

Yet, in its most radical form, the differentially constituted form of community elaborated by these recent French thinkers is deemed (in the words of Nancy) to have 'nothing to do with communion, with fusion into a body'.[51] It is evidently anything but an organism. Furthermore, its distance from all forms of liberal individualism leads its proponents, as Blanchot puts it, 'to question the very notion of reciprocity'. Instead of interdependence, there is a relation of 'dissymmetry' with the Other.[52]

Such formulations implicitly suggest a dangerous proximity both to pure senselessness and to a nascent return of totalitarianism. Does not the radicalness of such relations risk either making them irrelevant to constructive, 'practical' political thought, or providing ideological justification for repressively dissymmetrical relations? In this context, it is illuminating to observe how roundabout an approach Derrida takes to these themes in his recent study *Politics of Friendship*. Unlike Nancy and Blanchot he devotes considerable time and space to the commentary of the 'the great discourses on friendship',[53] and the detour of these discourses significantly influences his thought. Critical to the latent male-centredness of this tradition of fraternity and fraternisation, Derrida vows to move 'out *beyond this* politics without ceasing to intervene therein to transform it'.[54] A recurring point in his non-chronological reinterpretation of the classics is that a certain unbounded and non-symmetrical responsibility is evident in the early Greek pronouncements on *philia*: this is not a heritage which was born with, or had any simple origin in, Christian *agape*. Yet this dissymmetry introduces an element of 'inegalitarian heteronomy',[55] which is hard to reconcile with democratic values of equality and reciprocity. Indeed, for Derrida the relation of reciprocity frequently acquires a rather problematical status. He generally ascribes an economical meaning to it, as for instance in the political friendship of Aristotle, wherein he detects 'a homology of reciprocity, as in the case of a contract, an agreement between two subscribing parties'.[56]

Yet Derrida wants to save a notion of democracy, of 'egality', that would preserve a politics of friendship with difference at its heart. He seeks to locate '*an alterity without hierarchical difference at the root of democracy*',[57] and thereby to enable himself to 'still speak of equality ... in the dissymmetry and boundlessness of infinite alterity'.[58] Needless to say, this is not easy. In effect, it means eradicating the very violence which Derrida, in other contexts, has claimed to be irreducible. This is why such a non-violent community of difference is, as he himself admits, another 'dream'.[59] Nevertheless, this does not prevent him from elaborating upon the premises of such a dream. One is to hear a spectral, messianic call for an impossible but necessary form of being-together, a negative community (without presence or fully present body) which is admitted to be

> always untenable at least for the reason that it calls for the infinite respect of the singularity *and* infinite alterity of the other as much as for the respect of the countable, calculable, subjectal equality between anonymous singularities.[60]

Despite being untenable, impossible and even self-contradictory, this promise remains urgent for Derrida as a quasi-transcendental call for an 'alliance of a *rejoining* without conjoined mate, without organization, without party, without nation, without State, without property'.[61] It will, in other words, be a community forever without body or materiality. Precisely this feature has provoked the ire of some traditionalistic marxists, who have seen in Derrida's self-proclaimed solidarity – in the tract *Specters of Marx* – with 'the *spirit of Marxism*'[62] nothing less than a desire to dismantle

Marx's thought from all effective political institutions and possibilities of action.[63] Yet this response may be a bit hasty, since *Specters of Marx* is not solely characterised by a wish to go beyond the concept of the organisation and its roots in organicism. For, in the same text, Derrida declares that his radicalisation of the Marxist heritage 'does not mean to give up every form of practical or effective organization', since it is 'exactly the contrary that matters to us here'.[64]

Derrida's dream of friendship is, then, both for and against organisation. Organicism is denied, strictly speaking, and yet (since organisations, however virtual or embattled they may be, *work*) also tolerated. A call is heard by deconstruction which proclaims the necessity of going beyond all 'things' and beings, and this call is responsible for both a singular messianism and for a new understanding of textuality. At the same time, the task at hand is always to supplement or probe into the body (or work) that faces one, tracing both its desire (its projected intention, centre or limit) and its lesions (the sites at which its lack becomes apparent). And even if Derrida partially embraces Heidegger's critique of the ontology inherent in all 'biologism', the very systematics of his thought frequently boil down to something very close to the organic strife between the principles of hierarchy (loosened from all relations to power) and the principle of interdependence with its attendant risk of dissevering the parts of the organism. It is hard to measure this proximity: on the one hand, deconstruction and organicism would seem to be separated by a difference that is both wide and all too familiar. On the other hand, though, one might conjecture that their difference does not exclude a relation, or touching closeness, that one might even call a form of friendship.

Although the thought of Derrida's fellow poststructuralist Gilles Deleuze has followed its own, separate trajectory, there are certain similarities on this matter. Like Derrida, Deleuze is consistently suspicious of hier-archical and unifying systems. In his early readings of Hegel and Leibniz, he seems to give them credit for something similar to the kind of opening up to diversity that we have seen at work in organicism. Yet their 'orgiastic' opening up of organicism only renders the suppressive forces of identity and representation stronger in their capability of configuring an infinity of elements.[65] Ultimately, Deleuze's vitalism denies any affiliation with organicism: 'the life in question is inorganic, germinal, and intensive, a powerful life without organs, a Body that is all the more alive for having no organs.'[66] Deleuze's politics have always been tied to a celebration of the uncontrollable revolutionary force which he links to this dynamic body, and he has gone further than Derrida in shying away from any form of institutional solidification.

Despite his aims, however, many of Deleuze's most central notions are closely related to organicism. There is the way in which form should grow out of matter rather than be extraneous to it, the 'reciprocity' between content and expression (so important for him to supersede structuralism's formalist schemas) in unified strata and assemblies, the related use of *bodily* relations of intervention to avoid static regimes of representation,[67] as well as the danger of the undifferentiated black hole. The latter, typically organicist motif of a grounding abyss of unity is dismissed in *Anti-Oedipus* as being a mystifying, psychoanalytical invention – drawing attention away from the multiplicity of intensities really behind the Unconscious – yet is considered a true risk of all transgressive movements in the later *A Thousand Plateaus* (both co-written with Félix Guattari). Most importantly, Deleuze's thought on multiplicity differs from Derridean *différance* by consistently having recourse to continuous unities: this usually takes the form of vague references to Cosmos, redeployments of the Kantian Idea, or references to the immanent unity of a body without organs. Derrida has recently expressed some curiosity about Deleuze's notion of immanence,[68] and it is precisely through this term that the latter's transcendence of the subject–object dichotomy comes closest to the absolute of romantic and idealist organicism. Deleuze has referred approvingly to Fichte's transcendence of the subject–object distinction, and presented it as an inspiration for his own understanding of 'the transcendental field as *a life*.'[69] It is an open question whether Deleuze suffers the same temptation as Fichte did, albeit in a different form: does his vitalism reify the absolute by making it into a continuous, material field that can be conceptually analysed? While his materialism seems to offer a way forward for a more politicised and affirmative poststructuralism,[70] there is always the risk of this constituting a too credulous alternative to Derrida's blend of sceptical deconstructions and deferred messianism.

Deleuze has constantly sought to blur the difference between living beings and machines. An added twist to the story of the clandestine, long-distance friendship between Derridean deconstruction and its déclassé double can be gleaned if one approaches the question of the machine. For it is possible that the premise of the preceding discussion – that is, that deconstruction must either deny or affirm this heritage – is wrong-headed. To both affirm and negate organicism, and in the process to transcend the terms of such a question, is indeed another path taken by Derrida. It is perhaps somewhat surprising that the machine should open this path, since Derrida frequently (and with some justification) has been cast as a thinker of the machine *in opposition* to organicism, as a eulogist of all that is artificial and not 'biodegradable'.[71]

Yet the entire opposition between mechanism and organism has to be transcended, if one is to believe one of his recent articles – a meditation on religion entitled (in a conscious echo of Kant and Bergson) 'Faith and Knowledge: the Two Sources of "Religion" at the Limits of Reason Alone'.[72] Here a new closeness to Deleuze is evident, as Derrida tries to resist thinking religion through the opposition between its vital kernel or source and its derivative (and potentially destructive) technical mediation:

> Instead of opposing them, as is almost always done, they ought to be thought *together*, as *one and the same possibility*: the machine-like and faith, and the same holds for the machinal and all the values entailed in the sacrosanct (*heilig*, holy, safe and sound, unscathed, intact, immune, free, vital, fecund, fertile, strong, and above all, as we will soon see, 'swollen') – more precisely in the sacrosanctity of the **phallic** effect.[73]

As with all the developments and concepts that have been briefly considered in this chapter, I cannot take time to place this line of thought (and the 'phallic effect' it refers to) fully in the context within which Derrida employs it. One interesting aspect of this context is that Derrida seems to localise his own notion of a 'spectralizing messianicity' in this juncture between 'the value of life ... and the theological machine',[74] while at the same time indicting the archaic violence and imperialistic force engendered by it.

Thus Derrida's early, compensatory privileging of the 'repressed' pole of a metaphysical dichotomy (the machine in opposition to the living body) is replaced by an attempted transcendence of both the poles of the equation. In the essay on 'Faith and Knowledge' this is made even more evident by the introduction of a new term, which reflects Derrida's changed view on organicism. Rather than using the organism as the figure of violent appropriation, it is now – with the introduction of the term 'auto-immunization' – used as a way of approaching a non-appropriating, welcoming logic:

> As for the process of auto-immunization, which interests us particularly here, it consists for a living organism, as is well known and in short, of protecting itself against its self-protection by destroying its own immune system. As the phenomenon of these antibodies is extended to a broader zone of pathology and as one resorts increasingly to the positive virtues of immuno-depressants destined to limit the mechanisms of rejection and to facilitate the tolerance of certain organ transplants, we feel ourselves authorized to speak of a sort of general logic of auto-immunization. It seems indispensable to us today for thinking the relations between faith and knowledge, religion and science, as well as the duplicity of sources in general.[75]

One might ask, not entirely facetiously, whether these words truly belong to Derrida. Is the man who formulates this quasi-organic 'principle of sacrificial self-destruction'[76] the same as he who, more than twenty years earlier, countered the Hegelian vision of an organically structured and absolute idealism with, precisely, the machine?[77] To be sure, already there one might have detected traces of an originary 'auto-immunisation' that straddles the machine and the work, the technical and the organic *ergon*. Yet, given all this (and given that the strategy for the overturning of such dichotomies was programmed early on in Derrida's discourse), 'Faith and Knowledge' strikes a different note – or a different march. Is Derrida making a *step beyond* himself (and deconstruction, and the 'text') in this gesture, in this auto-immunisation against his own leanings towards the technological? Or is he rather playing the ventriloquist for Deleuze, or even for the 'romantic scientist' Döllinger, who as early as in 1805 heralded the overcoming of the distinction between the mechanism and the organism?[78] To allow these questions to fully unfurl, one would have to step beyond the limits of this enquiry. It would entail crossing the outer rim of this text in order to dream of a space – perhaps fantastic, perhaps unthinkable and certainly impossible – beyond the ending and the automatic.

10
Ending the Automatic

I have pursued the organism at some length. In doing so, I have indulged in the ambivalent *ascesis* and pleasure that is commentary. Commentary is, of course, never innocent, especially not when it arrogates to itself large domains – extensive piles constituted by texts, authors and eras – under its rule. It can be said to feign the immediacy of anonymity in its translucent divesting of the inner truth of the matter at hand. Hiding the seams or scandals of its argument, the utopian ideal of commentary tends towards the state of the automatic. Everything comes off on its own, everything is pellucid in the clear light of this dream of day: it is a relentless mechanism, a divine machine. Yet the automaticity of an ideal commentary also represents, one might just as justifiably say, an ideal of an organic relation: a non-violent and essential inner connection between original and commentary is what is aimed at. One evolves, or flowers, into the other.

This complicity or proximity of the mechanical and organic is not fortuitous, nor has it escaped attention.[1] If romantic organicism berated the enlightenment and the developing natural sciences for being overly mechanical in their arbitrary linking of elements, then later eras have likewise found grounds for judging the romantic alternative to be too mechanical. Organicism is mechanical, the critique goes, due to its teleology. For is not the organicist dream of an entity that is driven exclusively from a spontaneous and inner force the very essence of *the automatic*? As Derrida implies, behind the bodywork of the living organism there would stand revealed an automaton. For if *automaton* is the common name, as etymology would seem to intimate, for all that generates movement through its own self (*autos*), then mechanism and organicism might be said to suffer from the same malaise, namely autism. To end the automatic would mean, then, to escape all means to an end. However human a transcendence of the ills of causality one might glimpse in the means-end relation, that relation must itself be transcended.

This manner of thinking renders any conception of a conclusion to the body of a text problematical, as the body of a text should not have any form of *ending*. To summarise or conclude entails the exclusion of new openings, passages and transitions. Yet at the same time, repetition (one strand of thought tells one) is never simply tautology. However much one repeats and abridges one's arguments, things will never be the same, and the tail end of a book will never represent its teleological maturation.

However much one tries to end, then, one cannot. The snake may want to coil its tail into its mouth, but the tail, as Coleridge puts it, 'is too big to be taken up into the Coiler's Mouth'.[2] Both heartened and chastened by this realisation, let me cut matters short and own up: the *ending* of organicism, and a certain folding or repetition of that ending, is the closest one comes to a central theme of this study. In this latter statement, two different modalities of the end, of closure, are implied. First, in the study of German idealism, Jena romanticism and the texts of Coleridge and Wordsworth, I have focused on the problems organicism has with coming to a final end in the sense of a final (and external) delimitation as well as a terminal and teleological goal. This was true whether the church, the community of friends or the more quasi-transcendental realms of theory were the main concern, and it also informed the subsequent reading of Richards. In the other studies of recent thinkers such as Bataille, Gadamer, Blanchot and Derrida, it was another (but certainly not unrelated) problem that came to the fore. There I instead turned to the problems that face any thought that wants to terminate and transcend the horizon of organicism: the survival, even if it is only in a piecemeal or latent fashion, of organicism.

Another name for this survival is 'afterlife'. I have focused on the afterlife of organicism in at least four different ways. There is (a) the continuation of the tradition in British romanticism even after the origin of its conception of organicism, German idealism, revealed its underlying aporias. Organicism also has an afterlife in terms of (b) its more general survival, despite much opposition, in twentieth-century thought and philosophy. This survival is of course closely related to (c) a certain reconsideration of organicism in the scholarly commentaries of romanticism in recent years, despite its supposed demise at the hands of deconstruction. As I indicated in the introduction, my own study is a continuation of the work undertaken by scholars such as Murray Krieger and Kathleen Wheeler in this respect. Such scholarship cannot pretend to complete any full resuscitation of the idea of organicism, but nevertheless addresses (as a protracted mourning) its still insistent relevance. For even if the life of this idea has become increasingly evanescent, the system-organism has repeatedly proven to be a surprisingly resilient being. One of the main reasons for this resilience, is that organicism also essentially has an 'afterlife' in the sense of (d) transcending the status of the ontic, of living substances or subjects. This is the paradox latent in Abrams' words, when he claims that organicism is 'derived' from vital phenomena: 'Organicism may be defined as the philosophy whose major categories are derived from the attributes of living things.'[3] For although it often overlaps with vitalism, organicism is far from being simply identical to it.[4] The same is true with regard to its relation to the aesthetic conception of an autonomous work. In addition, organicism often takes the more transcendental guise of a form or law that is the grounds of possibility for the very life of living beings. There is, one might say, something spectral or ghostly about the body of organicism that is frequently missed by simplistic dismissals of it on the grounds that it represents a too materialistic paradigm.[5]

In its conditional accords with general theories such as vitalism and the aesthetic of the work, one glimpses something of the mobility of organicism – a mobility that is insistent, even if I have, consistently and almost mechanically, stilled it somewhat in this study for the sake of cohesion and accessibility. Let me put an end to such pretences and admit it: the organism is a wandering spectre. From one definition to the other, it submits itself to metamorphosis, to a profound conceptual instability, displaying itself as a necessarily virtual phenomenon in the process. All too easily it can, like some irritating flea one shrugs off while barely noticing it, be dismissed as a mere *example* belonging to a set of more important conceptual apparatuses. One moment it is only an epiphenomenon of the crucial conflict between matter and form, another moment it is declared to be a rhetorical trope, soon it is subsumed to the subject–object relation or to the old Greek conundrum of the one of the many. All these approaches would set up another centre in the totality of the logic or discursive field in which organicism, cut down to size, is only a subordinate member. To halt their mobility and common contamination, insisting that organicism is not on its last limb, is indeed to go out on a limb.

On the other hand, there is the opposite risk: the relative ubiquity of organicism as a *modus operandi* in the romantic era shows that it is susceptible to being reduced to just that: a *modus*, or formal schema, rather than a fully-fledged theory or phenomenon. Not only in aesthetic criticism, but also in ontology and political theory, it cannot be said to fully generate its own content, as the idealists demanded of it. This is the weakness inherent in its strength, and the reason why it can be accused of being an empty formalism.

The main aporia of organicism pursued in this study has been another one: the more 'internal' one of its clashing of principles, the arbitrariness of its inner articulation. This problem has been attacked via several different routes. In the introduction, I suggested that three privileged points of interest were going to be (a) the notion of an absolute literary-philosophical work, (b) the limit-experience, and (c) the problem of community. In all these concerns, romanticism constitutes an important precedent to modern literary theory. In the Jena romantics, as well as in Coleridge and Wordsworth's *Recluse* project, one sees literature turning to address the lacuna opened up by the enlightenment critique of the Bible. A work of art would be able to fill that gap if it were to achieve the immediacy and total harmony previously ascribed to the divine. Yet quickly an absolute scission is experienced between the centre of the organic structure and the representational field inhabited by all singular efforts of signification and cognition. No simple traffic between the two is possible, and hence literature (as Blanchot shows) suffers a double bind both demanding and delaying the fulfilment of the absolute exigency.

On the question of community, both the romantic and modern theories show dissatisfaction with the enlightenment heritage of isolated, rational subjects. But as romantic organicism was caught between the competing principles of reciprocity and hierarchical organisation, modern theories capsize on the aporia opened up between alterity and equal relations of reciprocity. Roughly speaking, dependency and sharing come into conflict with the need for autonomy and control. Even if the Heideggerian conception of finitude pulls the carpet under any theory of an autonomous subject, the nature of *Dasein*'s responsiveness remains a contentious question. How radically is one constituted by one's 'others', and which 'others' does this involve? Derrida's deconstruction would open this responsiveness to an unlimited affirmation, not exclusive of death or other living beings, while Gadamer's hermeneutics represents, like Richards, a more delimited and humanistic stance.

The limit-experience can be understood as a formalisation of the encounter between a ruptured 'subjectivity' (if one can keep such a term) and its heterogeneous ground. It is thus itself a radical form of community. Already for the romantics, the identity of that ground was unstable and open to debate. In Blanchot's notion of impersonality, the challenge to subjectivity is not entirely different from the form of self-sacrifice which Friedrich Schlegel demanded of the artist. In somewhat different fashion, my reading of Bataille disclosed that new conceptions of a heterogeneous bodily mobility are far closer to organicism than one is often led to expect.

Has this, then, been a *defence* of organicism? Although I am wary of the clichéd predictability of arguments which simplistically counter innovative radicalisations with reminders of the richness and ineluctability of tradition, there is certainly something of an apology of organicism latent in the later stages of this study. To say the least, the rumours of its demise (as the saying goes) are very exaggerated. It is not hard to conjure up considerable evidence against such rumours: within the more theoretical kinds of questioning, one is struck by the persistent use of holistic categories such as 'epoch', 'era' or 'case' in even the most particularising forms of historicism (often accompanied by implicit assumptions of a pre-critical or sociological nature concerning the unity of societies and humanity). There is also the lingering presence of an aesthetics of the work, the need for a regulative idea of totality or perfection (in Kantian or hermeneutic guises), in addition to the image of the whole aimed for by desire (in recent French theory). Even the most circumspect theories, it seems, cannot do without some kind of a dream of cohesion. In a wider context, there is the compelling evidence of the environmental question and its necessary challenge to narrow-minded humanism, the various organisations projected by communitarianisms (radical or liberal) critical of atomistic individualism, and even the recurring necessity of relating to a much-maligned 'romantic' sense of immediacy (orgiastic or more religiously oriented). On the whole, inflections of organicism seem to be so inherent in our culture that a wholesale sacrifice of its tradition seems not only foolhardy but also impossible. We cannot ever rid us of this tradition. However much we cleanse or delouse ourselves there will always remain the ghost of this flea. This does not mean that there can be any simple return of the repressed. Not only must organicism submit to historical transformation, and compete with other models, but it must also be tempered by a general suspicion towards large-scale schematics. This is not only due to pragmatic reasons, but also simply because – as my study has shown in some detail – the organicist approach is beset with self-contradiction and insuperable aporias.

In short, if organicism's afterlife promises to continue to be an embattled site suspect to radical revisions and denunciations, things are as they should be. Would it be out of place to end this study with one more singular vision to battle with others on this site? Would a sketch of yet another kind of organic afterlife be totally amiss? However inscrutable and arcane such a sketch might seem, let me venture it. Allow me to once again summon the awkward action, or passion, of the *dream* (encountered earlier in Wordsworth, Coleridge and Derrida), and dream of a new and other organ-icism, an organicism that does not mean 'work', nor teleological closure. This would be an organicism that would finally end the reign of the automatic, ushering in another logic where heterogeneity does not exclude re-ciprocity. Is such a dream merely laughable, like the ass young Coleridge wanted to befriend? Is it negligible like a flea, or does it – despite everything – sting like a bee? Perhaps one should instead be attuned to the poss-ibility of apocalyptic monstrosity inherent in a return of organicism, and picture – as a warning – the rough beast conjured up by Yeats in his vision of the second coming? Whatever possibilities one conjures up, and however much they provoke earnestness or irony, the obsession seems to be ineluctable: the dream continues.

Notes

Chapter 1

1. Lines 56–7 of 'Ode: Intimations of Immortality from the Recollections of Early Childhood'. Unless otherwise is stated, all quotations from Wordsworth's poetry (apart from *The Prelude*) will be taken from William Wordsworth, *The Poems*, two volumes (edited by John O. Hayden, Harmondsworth: Penguin Books, 1977).
2. Jean-François Lyotard, *The Postmodern Condition: A Report on Knowledge* (translated by Geoff Bennington and Brian Massumi, Manchester: Manchester University Press, 1984), xxiv.
3. 'Dust as we are, the immortal spirit grows / Like harmony in music; there is a dark / Inscrutable workmanship that reconciles / Discordant elements, makes them cling together / In one society' (Lines 340–4 of the 1850 edition of *The Prelude*. Unless otherwise is stated, all subsequent references to *The Prelude* will be taken from the *1805* version as it presented in William Wordsworth, *The Prelude: The Four Texts (1798, 1799, 1805, 1850)* (edited by Jonathan Wordsworth, London: Penguin Books, 1995).
4. Maurice Blanchot, 'The Athenaeum', 359 (translation modified), in *The Infinite Conversation* (translated by Susan Hanson, Minnesota: University of Minneapolis Press, 1993). ('L'Athenaeum', 527, in *L'Entretien infini* [Paris: Gallimard, 1969].)
5. 'The Origin of the Work of Art', 38, in Martin Heidegger, *Poetry, Language, Thought* (translated by Alfred Hofstadter, New York: Harper & Row, 1971).
6. For an influential interpretation of English romanticism in terms of the problem of subjectivity, see 'The Internalization of Quest Romance', in Harold Bloom, *The Ringers in the Tower: Studies in Romantic Tradition* (Chicago: The University of Chicago Press, 1971), 13–35. Mark Kipperman has made a study of the intersection between German idealism and English romantic poetry, building upon Bloom's thematisation of the self and the quest romance, in *Beyond Enchantment: German Idealism and English Romantic Poetry* (Philadelphia: University of Pennsylvania Press, 1986).
7. Charles Taylor, *Human Agency and Language: Philosophical Papers 1* (Cambridge: Cambridge University Press, 1985), 257.
8. My use of the term 'radical organicism' has a precedent in Richard Shusterman, who has shown how G. E. Moore's *Principia Ethica* attacks a 'radical notion of organic unity' that 'requires that any individual part we distinguish as contributing to form the whole cannot be so distinguished' ('Organic Unity: Analysis and Deconstruction', 99, in Reed Way Dasenbrock (ed.), *Redrawing the Lines: Analytic Philosophy, Deconstruction, and Literary Theory* [Minneapolis: University of Minnesota Press, 1989]).
9. Frederick Burwick, 'Introduction', ix, in Burwick (ed.), *Approaches to Organic Form: Permutations in Science and Culture* (Dordrecht: D. Reidel Publishing Company, 1987).
10. For an extended meditation on the question of figuration and 'ontotypology' in Heidegger, see the essay 'Typography' in Philippe Lacoue-Labarthe, *Typography: Mimesis, Philosophy, Politics* (translated by Christopher Fynsk, Stanford, CA: Stanford University Press, 1998).

11. William K. Wimsatt, 'Organic Form: Some Questions about a Metaphor', 62, in G. S. Rousseau (ed.), *Organic Form: The Life of an Idea* (London: Routledge & Kegan Paul, 1972).
12. 'The Rhetoric of Temporality', 197, in Paul de Man, *Blindness and Insight: Essays in the Rhetoric of Contemporary Criticism* (second and revised edition, London: Routledge, 1983 [1971]).
13. 'The Rhetoric of Blindness: Jacques Derrida's Reading of Rousseau', 104, in ibid.
14. On the 'mechanical' nature of de Man's conception of language, see, for instance, the descriptions of grammar in Paul de Man, *Allegories of Reading: Figural Language in Rousseau, Nietzsche, Rilke, and Proust* (New Haven, CT: Yale University Press, 1979), 15–16 and 293–4.
15. Although one can question whether the distinction inner/outer has any absolute value in this context, it is nevertheless true that deconstructive readings generally have aspired towards achieving a rigorous intimacy with the structures that they want to unravel. See, for instance, Jacques Derrida, *Of Grammatology* (translated by Gayatri Chakravorty Spivak, Baltimore: The Johns Hopkins University Press, 1976), 24.
16. On Schlegel's complicated anticipation of Schelling's later work, see for instance note 12 on pp. 255–6 of Werner Hamacher, *Premises: Essays on Philosophy and Literature from Kant to Celan* (translated by Peter Fenves, Stanford, CA: Stanford University Press, 1996).
17. Such is the consequence of the following programmatic statement: 'Philosophy, then, controls romanticism' [*La philosophie, donc, commande le romantisme*] (Philippe Lacoue-Labarthe and Jean-Luc Nancy, *The Literary Absolute: The Theory of Literature in German Romanticism* [translated by Philip Barnard and Cheryl Lester, Albany: State University of New York Press, 1988]), 29. (*L'absolu littéraire: Théorie de la littérature du romantisme allemand* [Paris: Éditions du Seuil, 1978], 42]).
18. Lacoue-Labarthe and Nancy minimise the importance of nature for Schlegel and the German romantics, stressing instead their link to Kantian transcendentalism and insisting that their romanticism 'represents nothing other than the final repetition of Western eidetics in the element of subjectivity. From now on, in the axis of a certain Plato, or rather, of a certain Platonism, eidetics will always be able to shift into aesthetics' (ibid., 37). For a later, more endorsing reading of German idealism and romanticism through the prism of aesthetic subjectivity, see Andrew Bowie, *Aesthetics and Subjectivity: From Kant to Nietzsche* (Manchester: Manchester University Press, 1990).
19. Murray Krieger, *A Reopening of Closure: Organicism Against Itself* (New York: Columbia University Press, 1989), 2.
20. Ibid., 8.
21. Ibid., 28.
22. Ibid., 64.
23. Ibid., 40.
24. Ibid., 49.
25. Kathleen M. Wheeler, *Romanticism, Pragmatism and Deconstruction* (Oxford: Blackwell, 1993), xiv.
26. See for instance ibid., 4–5 and 230–1.
27. Ibid., 198–9.
28. M. H. Abrams, for one, has claimed that, by 'Coleridge's analysis, organic form is inherently teleological' (M. H. Abrams, 'Archetypal Analogies in the Language of Criticism', 324, *University of Toronto Quarterly*, Volume 18, 1949).
29. Seamus Perry, *Coleridge and the Uses of Division* (Oxford: Clarendon Press, 1999).

Chapter 2

1. A. W. Schlegel, 'Die Gemälde', 14, in *Athenaeum: Ein Zeitschrift von August Wilhelm Schlegel und Friedrich Schlegel*, volume II (edited by Curt Grützmacher, Reinbek bei Hamburg: Rowohlt, 1969); my translation.
2. Johann Wolfgang Goethe, *Faust/Part One* (translated by Philip Wayne, Harmondsworth: Penguin Books, 1981), 95 ['Wer will was Lebendings erkennen und beschreiben, / Sucht erst den Geist heraus zu treiben, / Dann hat er die Teile in seiner Hand, / Fehlt leider! nur das geistige Band' *(Faust: Der Tragödie erster und zweiter Teil.* Urfaust (edited by Erich Trunz, Munich: Verlag C. H. Beck, 1986, ll. 1936–39), 63)].
3. Immanuel Kant, *Critique of Pure Reason* (translated by Norman Kemp, London: Macmillan, 1929), 22 (*Kritik der reinen Vernunft* [edited by Ingeborg Heidemann, Stuttgart: Philipp Reclam Jun., 1966], B XVII). I will follow the standard practice of referring to the page numbers of the first and second editions of the German original with the letters 'A' and 'B', respectively. These will be supplied even where quotations are only given in English translation.
4. According to Thomas McFarland, although 'we should beware of underestimating the continuity of the organic tradition, at least as far back as Leibniz and actually as far as classical antiquity, it was Kant who most authoritatively channelled this underground current into the great river that flowed into the historical ocean of Romanticism' (*Romanticism and the Forms of Ruin: Wordsworth, Coleridge, and the Modalities of Fragmentation* [Princeton, NJ: Princeton University Press, 1981], 36). He is here consciously opposing the position of such critics as James Benziger (see his 'Organic Unity: Leibniz to Coleridge', in *Modern Language Association of America*, Volume 66, Number 2, March 1951, 24–48) and Ernst Cassirer (cf. *The Philosophy of the Enlightenment* [translated by Fritz C. A. Koelln and James P. Pettegrove, Princeton, NJ: Princeton University Press, 1979], 28–36). Both Benziger and Cassirer give Leibniz credit for inaugurating eighteenth-century organicist thought. For a recent interpretation which follows McFarland in claiming that Kant's thought on organic systems quickly surpassed its Leibnizian precedent, see the second chapter of Susan Meld Shell, *The Embodiment of Reason: Kant on Spirit, Generation and Community* (Chicago: The University of Chicago Press, 1996).
5. See Nicolai Hartmann, *Die Philosophie des deutschen Idealismus* (Berlin: Walter de Gruyter, 1974), 4, and Martin Heidegger, *Schellings Abhandlung über das Wesen der menschlichen Freiheit* (Tübingen: Max Niemeyer Verlag, 1971), 42 ff.
6. See Immanuel Kant, *Anthropology from a Pragmatic Point of View* (translated by Mary J. Gregor, The Hague: Martinus Nijhoff, 1974), 4 (*Anthropologie im pragmatischer Hinsicht*, 120, in *Gesammelte Schriften*, volume VII [Berlin: Königlich Preußischen Akademie der Wissenschaften, 1917]).
7. See M. H. Abrams, *The Mirror and the Lamp: Romantic Theory and the Critical Tradition* (New York: Norton, 1958), 35.
8. Henry Fuseli's translation of Johann Joachim Winckelmann's 'Description of the Torso Belvedere in Rome' is reproduced in Timothy Webb (ed.), *English Romantic Hellenism, 1700–1824* (Manchester: Manchester University Press, 1982), 124–7.
9. Immanuel Kant, *The Critique of Judgement* (translated by James Creed Meredith, Oxford: Clarendon Press, 1952 [1928]), part II, 24 (in subsequent references Roman numerals will indicate which *part* of the work is cited) (*Kritik der Urteilskraft*, 376, in *Gesammelte Schriften*, volume V [Berlin: Königlich Preußischen Akademie der Wissenschaften, 1913]).

10. Immanuel Kant, *Opus Postumum* (edited by Eckart Förster, translated by Eckart Förster and Michael Rosen, Cambridge: Cambridge University Press, 1993), 85 (*Opus Postumum*, volume II, in *Gesammelte Schriften*, volume XXII [Berlin: Königlich Preußischen Akademie der Wissenschaften, 1938], 548). A similarly bifurcated definition is given on p. 64.

11. Immanuel Kant, *The Metaphysics of Morals* (translated by Mary Gregor, Cambridge: Cambridge University Press, 1996), 97.

12. The *Critique of Pure Reason* seems to claim that the finished work of metaphysics will be a 'science' and a 'system' in a way which the critical edifice cannot be, on p. 659 [A 841/B 869]. Yet Kant later counters Fichte's claim that he provides only a preparation and not the finished system of metaphysics in the brief 'Erklärung in Beziehung auf Fichtes Wissenschaftslehre' (*Gesammelte Schriften*, volume XII [Berlin: Königlich Preußischen Akademie der Wissenschaften, 1922], 370–1).

13. Jacques Derrida makes this point in his reading of the *Critique of Judgement*. See *The Truth in Painting* (translated by Geoff Bennington and Ian McLeod, Chicago: The University of Chicago Press, 1987), 40–1.

14. See for instance pp. 188–9 of Friedrich Schiller, *On the Aesthetic Education of Man in a Series of Letters* (edited and translated by Elizabeth M. Wilkinson and L. A. Willoughby, Oxford: Clarendon Press, 1967).

15. Quoted from pp. 151–2 of Johann Gottfried Herder, *Ueber die neuere Deutsche Literatur* in *Sämmtliche Werke*, volume I (edited by Bernhard Suphan, Hildesheim: Georg Olms Verlag, 1887); my translation.

16. See F. W. J. Schelling, *Bruno, or, On the Natural and the Divine Principle of Things* (translated by Michael G. Vater, Albany: State University of New York Press, 1984), 150–1 and 177.

17. F. W. J. Schelling, *The Philosophy of Art* (translated by Douglas W. Stott, Minneapolis: University of Minnesota Press, 1989), 157 (*Philosophie der Kunst*, 215, in Schelling, *Werke*, dritter Ergänzungsband [edited by Manfred Schröter, Munich: C. H. Beck und R. Oldenburg, 1959 (1927)]).

18. Fichte often berates Kant's lack of unity, for instance in the following reference to the trivium of the critical edifice: 'Now, *Kant* ... also lacked unity. His three beginnings [Kanten *fehlte es nun ... auch an der Einheit. Sein dreimahliges Ansätzen*]' (Vorlesungen der Wissenschaftslehre im Winter 1804', 64, in J. G. Fichte, *Gesamtausgabe*, volume II, 7 [edited by Reinhard Lauth and Hans Gliwitzky, Stuttgart: Friedrich Frommann Verlag, 1989]; my translation).

19. I follow Daniel Breazeale's practice of keeping the original German term, rather than transposing it into some misleading English term. See Breazeale's comment on p. XV of his 'Note on Translation' in J. G. Fichte, *Early Philosophical Writings* (translated and edited by Daniel Breazeale, Ithaca, NY: Cornell University Press, 1988).

20. Dieter Heinrich, 'Fichtes ursprüngliche Einsicht', in Dieter Heinrich and Hans Wagner (eds.), *Subjektivität und Metaphysik: Festschrift für Wolfgang Cramer* (Frankfurt am Main: Vittorio Klostermann, 1966).

21. I will place Gadamer's notion of a 'melting of horizons', and its relation to organicism, under scrutiny in chapter 8.

22. See Walter Benjamin, *The Concept of Criticism in German Romanticism*, translated by David Lachterman, Howard Eiland and Ian Balfour, in *Selected Writings*, volume 1 (edited by Marcus Bullock and Michael W. Jennings, Cambridge, MA: Belknap Press/Harvard University Press, 1996).

23. For Kant's definition of the intellectual intuition, see *Critique of Pure Reason*, 88 [B 68].

24. 'Vorlesungen der Wissenschaftslehre im Winter 1804', 135; my translations (Fichte's editors indicate that the reading of 'inner [*innere*]' is uncertain – Fichte may have written 'always [*immer*]').

25. The use of organicism marks Fichte's most central theses on natural right in 1797. Before that, the earliest formulations of the *Wissenschaftslehre* insist upon the foundation's transcendence of the subject–object distinction, while nevertheless applying a more hierarchical notion of the gradually more determined series, inherited from Spinoza's causality-based systematics, to the subordinate elements of the system (see, for instance, *Concerning the Concept of the Wissenschaftslehre*, 110, in Fichte, *Early Philosophical Writings* [translated and edited by Daniel Breazeale, Ithaca, NY: Cornell University Press, 1988]). A few years later, in texts such as *Sonnenklarer Bericht an das grössere Publikum über das eigentliche Wesen der neuesten Philosophie*, such a series is replaced by a model of mutually determining elements.

26. *Grundlage zur gesamten Wissenschaftslehre*, 399, in J. G. Fichte, *Gesamtausgabe*, volume I, 2 (edited by Reinhard Lauth and Hans Jacob, Stuttgart: Friedrich Frommann Verlag, 1965); my translation.

27. 'For let an intelligence combine and link together continually, as long as it likes, then there will arise aggregation, or alligation [*sic*], but never a melting together, the latter presupposing an inner force in nature itself' [*Denn mag eine Intelligenz zusammensetzen und verknüpfen immerfort, so lange sie will, so entsteht daraus Aggregation, Alligation, aber nimmermehr Verschmelzung, welche letztere eine innere Kraft in der natur selbst voraussetzt*] (*Das System der Sittenlehre*, 116, in J. G. Fichte, *Gesamtausgabe*, volume I, 5 [edited by Reinhard Lauth and Hans Gliwitzky, Stuttgart: Friedrich Frommann Verlag, 1977]; my translation).

28. Bowie presents a straightforwardly symbolic account of Schelling's view on language (see *Aesthetics and Subjectivity from Kant to Nietzsche*, 106) and does not challenge his organicism – instead Bowie insists that 'organicism is vital to sustaining the aesthetic as a sphere whose value lies in itself' (ibid., 99). Paul de Man locates evidence of tension between the symbolic and allegorical modes in both Fichte and Hegel, claiming, for instance, that the latter 'both espouses and undoes' what he calls 'the ideology of the symbol' (de Man, 'Sign and Symbol in Hegel's *Aesthetics*', 101, in *Aesthetic Ideology* [edited by Andrzej Warminski, Minneapolis: University of Minnesota Press, 1996]).

29. See ibid., 172.

30. Fichte, *The Vocation of Man* (edited by Roderick M. Chisholm, translated by William Smith, New York: The Liberal Arts Press, 1956), 82 and 76; translation modified.

31. Ibid., 99.

32. Ibid., 143.

33. *Early Philosophical Writings*, 133 (*Gesamtausgabe*, I, 2, 149).

34. Ibid.

35. In *System des transcendentalen Idealismus* (in Schelling, *Werke*, zweiter Hauptband [edited by Manfred Schröter, Munich: C. H. Beck, 1958 (1927)]; all translations of this text are mine), Schelling grants absolute status to the 'primordial act of self-consciousness' (390) and sees the philosopher's act as a '*free imitation [freie Nachahmung]* of this action. ... The 'I', once it is transposed into time, is in constant transition from representation to representation; yet it is in its power to interrupt this series through reflection, [and] with the absolute interruption of that succession [*der absoluten Unterbrechung jener Succession*] all philosophising begins' (395–6).

36. 'My *absolute I* is obviously not the *individual*, though this is how offended courtiers and irate philosophers have interpreted me, in order that they may falsely attribute to me the disgraceful theory of practical egoism' (Letter to Jacobi, 30 August 1795, in Fichte, *Early Philosophical Writings*, 411). Nevertheless, an individualist reading of Fichte is attempted in Frederick Neuhouser, *Fichte's Theory of Subjectivity* (Cambridge: Cambridge University Press, 1990), 143 ff.
37. *Grundlage zur gesamten Wissenschaftslehre*, 332; my translation.
38. 'Vorlesungen der Wissenschaftslehre im Winter 1804', 203; my translation.
39. *Early Philosophical Writings*, 131.
40. G. W. F. Hegel, *Differenz der Fichte'schen und Schelling'schen Systems der Philosophie* (Hamburg: Felix Meiner, 1962), 73.
41. It is only by overlooking this fundamental possibility of idealism, that Seamus Perry can claim that Coleridge's 'muddle' of idealism and realism represents an original feature that transcends the thought of his German predecessors. See, for instance, pp. 240–1 of Perry's *Coleridge and the Uses of Division*.
42. For the reference to 'deconstruction', see Schelling, *Darstellung meines Systems der Philosophie*, 65–6, in *Werke*, dritter Hauptband.
43. Quoted from p. 97, and a note on p. 103, of Fichte's 'Von der Sprachfähigkeit und dem Urprung der Sprache', in *Gesamtausgabe*, volume I, 3 (edited by Reinhard Lauth and Hans Jacob, Stuttgart: Friedrich Frommann Verlag, 1966); my translation.
44. *The Philosophy of Art*, 100.

Chapter 3

1. Friedrich Schleiermacher, *On Religion: Speeches to its Cultured Despisers* (translated and edited by Richard Crouter, Cambridge: Cambridge University Press, 1988), 5.
2. See ibid., 23.
3. In *Coleridge and the Concept of Nature* (London: Macmillan, 1985), 75, Raimonda Modiano points out that Coleridge's conception of love transforms the idealist conception of self-consciousness into an intersubjective phenomenon. Anthony John Harding has claimed this transformation entails that Coleridge moves beyond what he has 'learned from Kant's followers', in *Coleridge and the Idea of Love: Aspects of Relationship in Coleridge's Thought and Writing* (London: Cambridge University Press, 1974), 118.
4. The source of the original German is Friedrich Schleiermacher, *Über die Religion: Reden an die Gebildeten unter ihnen Verächtern* (Hamburg: Felix Meiner Verlag, 1958), 124.
5. The sublime in its typical eighteenth-century version of an overpowering encounter with nature (a natural object), is implicitly denigrated in the second of Schleiermacher's five speeches on religion. See *On Religion*, 35.
6. *Ideas*, no. 105, in Friedrich Schlegel, *Philosophical Fragments* (translated by Peter Firchow, Minneapolis: University of Minnesota Press, 1991). All references to Schlegel's *Ideas* and *Athenaeum* fragments will be to this edition, with German references from *Charakteristiken und Kritiken I*, in *Kritische Friedrich-Schlegel-Ausgabe*, volume 2 (edited by Hans Eichner, Paderhorn: Verlag Ferdinand Schöningh, 1967).
7. Friedrich Schlegel, Review of Schleiermacher's *On Religion* in 'Notizen', in *Athenaeum: Ein Zeitschrift von August Wilhelm Schlegel und Friedrich Schlegel*, volume II (edited by Curt Grützmacher, Reinbek bei Hamburg: Rowohlt, 1969), 118; my translation.

8. I have modified Firchow's translation here. He translates 'preisgibt' with 'reveal' rather than 'sacrifices', on this occasion. In the translation of the 44th of the *Ideas*, quoted immediately above, Firchow too uses 'sacrifice'.
9. See *On Religion*, 37–8.
10. Pronouncements such as these surely show Lacoue-Labarthe and Nancy's polemical claim that 'romanticism effectuates the Subject's decisive break with all "naturality"' (*The Literary Absolute*, 104) to be a bit too emphatic.
11. Friedrich Schlegel, *Charakteristiken und Kritiken II*, in *Kritische Friedrich-Schlegel-Ausgabe*, volume 3 (edited by Hans Eichner, Paderhorn: Verlag Ferdinand Schöningh, 1975), 10, emphasis added; my translation.
12. Ibid.
13. Friedrich Schlegel, *Studien des klassischen Altertums*, in *Kritische Friedrich-Schlegel-Ausgabe*, volume 1 (edited by Ernst Behler, Paderhorn: Verlag Ferdinand Schöningh, 1979), 206; all translations of this work are mine.
14. Ibid.
15. Ibid., 305.
16. Ibid., 326.
17. Ibid., 288.
18. Ibid., 269.
19. Ibid.
20. Ibid., 306.
21. Ibid., note 2 on p. 640.
22. Ibid., 631.
23. Ibid., 217.
24. Cf. pp. clii–clv of Ernst Behler's 'Einleitung' in Friedrich Schlegel, *Studien des klassischen Altertums*.
25. *Studien des klassischen Altertums*, 131.
26. Ibid., 125.
27. Ibid.
28. Ibid., 124.
29. Ibid., 131. The reference is to the point at which Aristotle – comparing the plots of tragedy and epic, and finding the latter 'less unified' – states that the epic sometimes 'comprises a number of actions. The *Iliad* and *Odyssey* have many parts of this kind, which possess magnitude in their own right; and yet the construction of these poems could not be improved upon, and they are an imitation of a single action to the greatest possible degree' (Aristotle, *Poetics* [translated with an introduction and notes by Malcolm Heath, Penguin Books, London: 1996], 47 (62b)).
30. 'On Goethe's *Meister*', 63, in Kathleen M. Wheeler (ed.), *German Aesthetic and Literary Criticism: The Romantic Ironists and Goethe* (Cambridge: Cambridge University Press, 1984).
31. See *Studien des klassischen Altertums*, 325.
32. Ibid., 42.
33. Ibid., 40.
34. 'Über die Griechen und Römer,' 215, in ibid.
35. 'Versuch über den Begriff des Republikanismus', 16, in *Kritische Friedrich-Schlegel-Ausgabe*, volume 7 (edited by Ernst Behler, Paderhorn: Verlag Ferdinand Schöningh, 1966); my translation.
36. 'Versuch über den Begriff des Republikanismus', 25, in *Studien zur Geschichte und Politik;* translations from this text are mine.
37. Ibid., 19.

38. *Athenaeum* fragment, no. 214. Compare Novalis' 'Vermischte Bemerkungen', no. 122: 'Where the majority decides – force rules over form – while the contrary is true where the minority has the upper hand. ... It has not struck anyone to find out whether monarchy – and downright democracy, as elements of a true and universal state, must and can be unified?' (Novalis, *Das philosophische Werk I*, in *Schriften*, volume 2 [edited by Richard Samuel, Darmstadt: Wissenschaftliche Buchgesellschaft, 1965], 466–8; my translation).
39. In *The Literary Absolute*, Nancy and Lacoue-Labarthe link organicism and the fragment in Schlegel, without relating these themes to his early work.
40. *Studien des klassichen Altertums*, 98.
41. *Athenaeum* fragment, no. 97.
42. *The Literary Absolute*, 50.
43. *Athenaeum* fragment, no. 259.
44. Cf. the 77th *Athenaeum* fragment – and the note on it – in *Charakteristiken und Kritiken I*, 176.
45. *Athenaeum* fragment, no. 77.
46. Ibid., no. 206.
47. Ibid., no. 297.
48. Critical fragment no. 65, from Friedrich Schlegel, *Philosophical Fragments*.
49. In the review of Herder's 'Briefe zu Beförderung der Humanität', 47, in *Charakteristiken und Kritiken I*.
50. *Athenaeum* fragment no. 383.
51. Critical fragment, no. 32, in *Philosophical Fragments*.
52. See, for instance, pp. 202–11 of Maurice Blanchot's *The Infinite Conversation*, and the discussion of Bataille's notion of scissiparity in Denis Hollier, *Against Architecture: The Writings of Georges Bataille* (translated by Betsy Wing, Cambridge, MA: MIT Press, 1989), 68.
53. *Studien des klassischen Altertums*, 29–30.
54. See critical fragment, no. 34, in *Philosophical Fragments*.
55. Ibid., no. 90 [158]. Simon Critchley describes the play of synthesis and dissolution in Schlegel's concepts of irony and wit in *Very Little ... Almost Nothing: Death, Philosophy, Literature* (London: Routledge, 1997), 112–15.
56. *Athenaeum* fragment, no. 12.
57. It is also referred to in the 95th of the *Ideas*, and may also have inspired Coleridge, who at one stage planned to write a biography on Lessing. Coleridge's notes on Lessing indicate knowledge of this particular text. See the reference on p. 683 of *Marginalia III: Irving to Oxlee*, in Collected *Works*, volume 12:3 (edited by H. J. Jackson and George Whalley, London: Routledge, 1992). Lessing's most emphatic statement is in the 86th paragraph of *Erziehung des Menschengeschlechts*, where the scriptures of the New Testament are interpreted as presaging such a work: 'The time of a *new, eternal gospel*, promised to us even in the elementary books of the New Testament, will certainly come [*Sie wird gewiß kommen, die Zeit eines* neuen ewigen Evangeliums, *die uns selbst in den Elementarbüchern des Neuen Bundes versprochen wird*]' (Gotthold Ephraim Lessing, *Erziehung des Menschengeschlechts. Gespräche über Freimaurer* [Hamburg: Hamburg Kulturverlag, 1948, 57]; my translation).
58. *Athenaeum* fragment, no. 357.
59. *Ideas*, no. 74.
60. Ibid., no. 96.
61. Ibid.
62. Ibid., no. 46.

63. *Athenaeum* fragment, no. 419.
64. *Ideas*, no. 34.
65. *Charakteristiken und Kritiken II*, 7.
66. *Athenaeum* fragment, no. 216.
67. Cited in Wolfgang Hecht's 'Einleitung', XXV, in Friedrich Schlegel, *Werke in zwei Bänden*, volume 1 (edited by Wolfgang Hecht, Berlin: Aufbau-Verlag, 1988); my translation.
68. *Athenaeum* fragment, no. 76; my translation. Peter Firchow's translation of this fragment, obviously based on another interpretation of Schlegel's words, is as follows: 'An intellectual intuition is the categorical imperative of any theory.'
69. Ibid., no. 384.
70. *Charakteristiken und Kritiken II*, 60; my translation.
71. Ibid.
72. *Athenaeum* fragment, no. 281.

Chapter 4

1. De Quincey made the first charges of plagiarism in 1834. Recently, one of the most vigorous attacks on Coleridge on this score has been Norman Fruman's *Coleridge: The Damaged Archangel* (London: Allen and Unwin, 1972).
2. Cf. McFarland's *Coleridge and the Pantheist Tradition* (Oxford: Clarendon Press, 1969).
3. Walter Jackson Bate, *Coleridge* (London: Macmillan, 1969), 148. See also M. H. Abrams, *Natural Supernaturalism: Tradition and Revolution in Romantic Literature* (New York: Norton, 1971), 268, and Inger Christensen, *The Shadow of the Dome: Organicism and Romantic Poetry* (Bergen: Studia Anglistica Norvegica 3, 1985), 38.
4. Samuel Taylor Coleridge, *Biographia Literaria, or Biographical Sketches of My Literary Life and Opinions*, volume I, in *Collected Works*, volume 7:1 (edited by James Engell and W. Jackson Bate. London: Routledge & Kegan Paul, 1983), 25.
5. Samuel Taylor Coleridge, *Biographia Literaria, or Biographical Sketches of My Literary Life and Opinions*, volume II, in *Collected Works*, volume 7:2 (edited by James Engell and W. Jackson Bate. London: Routledge & Kegan Paul, 1983), 65.
6. As argued by Kathleen Wheeler in *Sources, Processes and Methods in Coleridge's 'Biographia Literaria'* (Cambridge: Cambridge University Press, 1980), 122.
7. *Biographia Literaria*, I, 305.
8. Ibid., 294.
9. Ibid., 304.
10. Ibid.
11. *Biographia Literaria*, II, 20.
12. Samuel Taylor Coleridge, *Shorter Works and Fragments*, volume I, in *Collected Works*, volume 11:1 (edited by H. J. Jackson and J. R. de J. Jackson, London: Routledge & Kegan Paul, 1995), 372.
13. Ibid., 378 (in cursive in the original). In 'Coleridge and Organic Form: The English Tradition' (*Studies in Romanticism*, Volume 6, 1967, 89–97), Daniel Stempel points out how there is some precedent for Coleridge's organicism within British empiricism. Nevertheless, as G. N. G. Orsini has made clear (in 'The Ancient Roots of a Modern Idea', note 8 on pp. 21–2, in G. S. Rousseau, *Organic Form: The Life of an Idea*), the mere fact that Coleridge uses means-end

relations rather than causal relations to define organicism is sufficient to show a debt to German philosophy.

14. *Phaedrus* (264C) in Plato, *Euthyphro/Apology/Crito/Phaedo/Phaedrus* (translated by Harold North Fowler, London: William Heinemann Ltd., 1914), 528–9. The precedence and authority of this passage is explored at length in G. N. G. Orsini, *Organic Unity in Ancient and Later Poetics: The Philosophical Foundations of Literary Criticism* (Carbondale, IL: Southern Illinois University Press, 1975).
15. *Biographia Literaria*, II, 13–14.
16. *Athenaeum* fragment, no. 206.
17. 'Über Goethes 'Meister'', 131, in *Charakteristiken und Kritiken I*.
18. *Biographia Literaria*, I, 234. Philip C. Ritterbush has noted the similarity between Coleridge's conception of organic unity in Shakespeare and Schlegel's reading of *Wilhelm Meister*, without mentioning this crucial difference (see 'Aesthetics and Objectivity in the Study of Form in the Life Sciences', 43, in G. S. Rousseau, *Organic Form: The Life of an Idea*).
19. *Biographia Literaria*, II, 72.
20. Ibid., 193.
21. Ibid.
22. Ibid., 122–3.
23. Ibid., 15.
24. The similarity between the critical thought of Coleridge and Roman Jacobson is discussed in Emerson R. Marks, *Taming the Chaos: English Poetic Diction Theory Since the Renaissance* (Detroit: Wayne State University Press, 1998), 142–3.
25. *Biographia Literaria*, I, 302–3; emphasis added.
26. Ibid., 136.
27. *Biographia Literaria*, II, 156.
28. Ibid., 25–6.
29. Harold Bloom, *The Western Canon: The Books and School of the Ages* (New York: Harcourt Brace & Company, 1994).
30. *Biographia Literaria*, I, 283.
31. Ibid., 228.
32. David Jasper has distinguished Coleridge's stance on this matter from those of some of his less obviously Christian contemporaries, in *The Sacred and the Secular Canon in Romanticism: Preserving the Sacred Truths* (London: Macmillan, 1999), 37.
33. *Biographia Literaria*, I, 136.
34. Samuel Taylor Coleridge, *Lay Sermons*, in *Collected Works*, volume 6 (edited by R. J. White, London: Routledge & Kegan Paul, 1972), 18.
35. Ibid.
36. Ibid., 19.
37. Ibid., 30.
38. Ibid., 70.
39. Although my interpretation of Coleridge and Friedrich Schlegel has in some respects a similar focus to that of Stephen Prickett, we differ on precisely this point. Although the organic body is hardly a ubiquitous metaphor having absolute dominion within romanticism (indeed, part of my aim has been to show the impossibility of any form of absolute dominion), I cannot follow Prickett when he grants the Bible – rather than, for instance, organicism – the status of what he calls a 'metatype': 'From offering a typological insight into contemporary affairs, it [i.e. the Bible] was increasingly seen in terms of what one might call a 'metatype': not so much a form with limited and specific

meanings, as a universal and absolute category giving meaning and shape to the rest of literature' (Stephen Prickett, *Origins of Narrative: The Romantic Appropriation of the Bible* [Cambridge: Cambridge University Press, 1996], 216).
40. 'A Lay Sermon', 182, in *Lay Sermons*.
41. Samuel Taylor Coleridge, *Shorter Works and Fragments*, volume II, in *Collected Works*, volume 11:2 (edited by H. J. Jackson and J. R. de J. Jackson, London: Routledge & Kegan Paul, 1995), 1134.
42. Ibid., 1160.
43. Ibid., 1156.
44. Ibid., 1139.
45. Ibid., 1151.
46. Ibid., 1149 and 1152.
47. Ibid.
48. *Lay Sermons*, 197
49. *Biographia Literaria*, II, 150.
50. Ibid., 126.
51. Ibid., 148.
52. Ibid., 120.
53. *Biographia Literaria*, I, 304.
54. *Biographia Literaria*, II, 128.
55. *Shorter Works and Fragments*, II, 1121.
56. Ibid.
57. Samuel Taylor Coleridge, *Aids to Reflection*, in Collected *Works*, volume 9 (edited by John Beer, London: Routledge & Kegan Paul, 1993), 45.
58. *Biographia Literaria*, II, 147.
59. For an account of how Coleridge's *Theory of* Life is influenced by the *Naturphilosophen* and other scientific controversies of his day, see Trevor H. Levere, *Poetry Realized in Nature: Samuel Taylor Coleridge and Early Nineteenth-Century Science* (Cambridge: Cambridge University Press, 1981), especially pp. 42–5 and 215–19. For more recent work on Coleridge and life, see the essays collected in Nicholas Roe (ed.), *Samuel Taylor Coleridge and the Sciences of Life* (Oxford: Oxford University Press, 2001).
60. *Shorter Works and Fragments*, I, 492–3.
61. Ibid., 502–3.
62. Ibid., 510.
63. Ibid., 512.
64. On the importance of polarity for Coleridge, see for instance chapters 3 and 4 of Owen Barfield, *What Coleridge Thought* (London: Oxford University Press, 1972).
65. *Shorter Works and Fragments*, I, 517.
66. Ibid., 516.
67. Ibid.
68. Cf. the editor's remark in ibid., note 1, p. 514.
69. In a notebook entry, Coleridge imagines beginning 'a poem of Spinoza' with the following scenario: 'I would make a pilgrimage to the burning sands of Arabia, or &c &c to find the Man who could explain to me there can be *oneness*, there being infinite Perceptions – yet there must be a *one*ness, not an intense Union but an Absolute Unity, for &c' (Entry number 556 in Samuel Taylor Coleridge, *The Notebooks*, volume 1 [edited by Kathleen Coburn, London: Routledge & Kegan Paul, 1957]).

70. Raimonda Modiano has pointed this out, with a slightly different emphasis: 'Coleridge took a hard look at the underside of the most appealing concepts proposed by the *Naturphilosophen*. He saw, for example, that due to their unqualified exuberance for the notion of organic unity and polarity, the *Naturphilosophen* elevated sameness of essence over important hierarchical differences between lower and higher forms of life and consciousness. In interpreting the works of his predecessors, Coleridge was undoubtedly helped by his Christian beliefs, although he stretched them far enough to include the tenets of dynamic philosophy. ... Coleridge attempted to construct a system in which he could demonstrate not the identity but the continuity between the ideal and the real based on a structure of mediation which preserved their hierarchical separateness and their mutual dependence' (*Coleridge and the Concept of Nature*, 140). Modiano goes on to claim that Coleridge shows an 'unwillingness to sacrifice [hierarchical] distinctions for the sake of the ideal of organic unity' (ibid., 149). As I claim that both unity and hierarchical distinction are part of the legacy of organicism, the crucial point instead becomes Coleridge's choosing to privilege a conservative form of organicism over a radical one.
71. See Samuel Taylor Coleridge, *Logic*, in *Collected Works*, volume 13 (edited by J. R. de J. Jackson, London: Routledge & Kegan Paul, 1981), 80.
72. *Aids to Reflection*, 77.
73. *Shorter Works and Fragments*, I, 509.
74. Ibid., 557.
75. Ibid., 542.
76. Ibid., 547.
77. Ibid., 548.
78. Ibid., 549.
79. *Biographia Literaria*, II, 14.
80. Samuel Taylor Coleridge, *The Philosophical Lectures* (edited by Kathleen Coburn, London: Pilot Press, 1949), 359.
81. A fine analysis is given in G. N. G. Orsini, *Coleridge and German Idealism: A Study in the History of Philosophy with Unpublished Materials from Coleridge's Manuscripts* (Carbondale: Southern Illinois University Press, 1969), 136 ff.
82. *The Philosophical Lectures*, 226.
83. Coburn, 'Introduction', in ibid., 40–1.
84. Ibid., 41.
85. *The Philosophical Lectures*, 174.
86. Ibid., 204–5.
87. Ibid., 244.
88. Ibid., 266.
89. Ibid.
90. Ibid., 267.
91. Ibid., 312–13.
92. Ibid., 316.
93. 'Patriotism' is presumed to have been written in 1819, while 'On Election' is dated to somewhere between 1816 and 1823 by Coleridge's editors (*Shorter Works and Fragments*, I, 802 and 433).
94. Ibid., 433.
95. Ibid., 802–3.
96. Ibid., 803.

97. Ibid.
98. Samuel Taylor Coleridge, *On the Constitution of Church and State*, in *Collected Works*, volume 10 (edited by John Colmer, London: Routledge & Kegan Paul, 1976), 84–5.
99. Ibid., 23.
100. Ibid., 107.
101. Ibid., 54.
102. *Marginalia III*, 677–8. In *Table Talk*, Coleridge is cited as saying (on 17 December 1831) that in organic structures 'the whole is ... in fact every thing, and the parts nothing' (Samuel Taylor Coleridge, *Table Talk*, volume I, in *Collected Works*, volume 14:1 [edited by Carl Woodring, London: Routledge, 1990], 258).
103. *The Philosophical Lectures*, 196.
104. Ibid.
105. Bate, *Coleridge*, 226.
106. *On the Constitution of Church and State*, 77.
107. Ibid., 118.
108. Ibid., 121.
109. Ibid., 133.
110. Ibid., 120.
111. Ibid.
112. Ibid., 5–6 (the emphasis on 'friend' is added).
113. Ibid., 114.
114. McFarland, *Coleridge and the Pantheist Tradition*, 110.
115. Quoted on p. 114 of *Lay Sermons*.
116. To Thomas Curtis, 29 April, 1817, in Coleridge, *Collected Letters*, volume IV (edited by Earl Leslie Griggs, Oxford: Clarendon Press, 1959), 728.
117. *Biographia Literaria*, I, 302–3.
118. Ibid., 304.
119. Quoted on p. lvi of John Colmer, 'Editor's Introduction', in Coleridge, *Church and State*.
120. Ibid.
121. *Aids to Reflection*, 534.
122. Ibid., 32–3.
123. Ibid., 42.
124. Ibid., 268.
125. Letter to Thomas Poole, 9 October, 1809, in *Collected Letters*, volume III (edited by Earl Leslie Griggs, Oxford: Clarendon Press, 1959), 235.
126. Ibid.
127. Samuel Taylor Coleridge, *The Friend*, volume I, in *Collected Works*, volume 4:1 (edited by Barbara E. Rooke, London: Routledge & Kegan Paul, 1969), 150.

Chapter 5

1. Cf. Richard Holmes' note to the conversation poems on p. 31 of Samuel Taylor Coleridge, *Selected Poems* (edited by Richard Holmes, London: Penguin Books, 1996).
2. Kelvin Everest, *Coleridge's Secret Ministry: The Context of the Conversation Poems 1795–1798* (Hassocks: The Harvester Press, 1979), 71.

3. See for instance Richard Holmes, *Coleridge: Early Visions* (London: Penguin Books, 1990), 78.
4. References given directly in the text of this chapter refer to Samuel Taylor Coleridge, *Collected Letters*, volume I (edited by Earl Leslie Griggs, Oxford: Clarendon Press, 1956).
5. In making friendship essential to the internal cohesiveness of the body politic, Coleridge is in agreement with Aristotle's *Nicomachean Ethics*. The equivalence between Aristotle's 'philia' and the modern term 'friendship' has been disputed, though. David Konstan claims that Aristotle's use of the word designates a wider sphere of affectionate relationships than the more limited application of 'friendship' (David Konstan, *Friendship in the Classical World* [Cambridge: Cambridge University Press, 1997], 68). One might argue that a similar semantic extension occurs in Coleridge's use of the modern term.
6. Compare Wordsworth's pronouncement, fifteen years later, in *The Convention of Cintra*: 'The outermost and all-embracing circle of benevolence has inward concentric circles which, like those of a spider's web, are bound together by links, and rest upon each other; making one frame, and capable of one tremor; circles narrower and narrower, closer and closer, as they lie more near to the centre of self from which they proceeded, and which sustains the whole' (*The Prose Works of William Wordsworth*, volume I [edited by W. J. B. Owen and Jane Worthington Smyser, Oxford: Clarendon Press, 1974], 340). Although James K. Chandler has pointed out that the latter passage resembles part of Burke's argument against French rationalism, in *Wordsworth's Second Nature: A Study of the Poetry and Politics* (Chicago: The University of Chicago Press, 1984), 37 and 43, this should not mislead one to believe that this view is necessarily or simply a conservative one. Chandler does not, for instance, note the strong similarity between Wordsworth's later view and Coleridge's pantisocratic philosophising. Indeed, the idea of ever-widening circles of social benevolence spreading from a centre was articulated by Frances Hutcheson as early as in 1725 and was later adopted by a number of liberal thinkers. See Allan Silver, 'Friendship in Commercial Society: Eighteenth-Century Social Theory and Modern Sociology', particularly pp. 1489 and 1491, in *American Journal of Sociology*, Volume 95, Number 6, 1990.
7. 'Summary of the History of Philosophy', 842, in *Shorter Works and Fragments II*.
8. As Alan Liu suggests, Coleridge's understanding of friendship has another, biographical side to it: Coleridge wished to be integrated into Wordsworth's extended family, and his expanding of the confines of the family concept can be interpreted as a ploy to this end. For the relationship between romantic friendship and the family, see Liu's *Wordsworth: The Sense of History* (Stanford, CA: Stanford University Press, 1989), 280–6. For readings of the creative friendship between Coleridge and Wordsworth, see, for instance, Thomas McFarland's chapter on 'The Symbiosis of Coleridge and Wordsworth' (*Romanticism and the Forms of Ruin*, 56–103), Paul Magnuson's *Coleridge and Wordsworth: A Lyrical Dialogue* (Princeton, NJ: Princeton University Press, 1988), and pp. 174–82 of Seamus Perry's *Coleridge and the Uses of Division*.
9. Cf., for instance, the letter to Robert Southey, 21 October, 1794 (*Letters*, I, 118).
10. See Everest, *Coleridge's Secret Ministry*, 10.
11. See, for instance, p. 188 of Cicero's dialogue 'Laelius: On Friendship', in *On the Good Life* (translated by Michael Grant, London: Penguin Books, 1971), and pp. 83 and 86 of Michel Eyquem de Montaigne's 'On Friendship', in *The Essays* (translated by Charles Cotton, Chicago: Encyclopaedia Britannica, 1952).

12. Here, too, there is classical precedent for Coleridge's interpretation of friendship. For instance, in Cicero's dialogue on friendship, Laelius warns friends against confusing their relationship with more exclusively amatory affections, insisting that 'besides loving and cherishing each other, they will also feel mutual respect. Remove respect from friendship, and you have taken away the most splendid ornament it possesses' (Cicero, *On the Good Life*, 217).
13. Quoted from paragraph 46 (p. 215) of the second part of Kant's *The Metaphysics of Morals*.
14. Translation: 'Best wishes, my dear brother – a brother whose love and care towards me are truly paternal' (*Letters*, I, 57).
15. See the letter to Joseph Cottle, 28 March, 1798 (ibid., 412).
16. Edmund Burke, *A Philosophical Enquiry into the Origin of Our Ideas of the Sublime and Beautiful* (edited by James T. Boulton, Notre Dame: University of Notre Dame Press, 1968 [1958]), 111.
17. Ibid.
18. A list of the conversation poems is given on page 191 of G. M. Harper's essay 'Coleridge's Conversation Poems', of 1928, included in M. H. Abrams (ed.), *English Romantic Poets: Modern Essays in Criticism* (Oxford: Oxford University Press, 1975).
19. Kelvin Everest omits 'To William Wordsworth' from his list: see *Coleridge's Secret Ministry*, 4.
20. See the contents, on p. v, of Samuel Taylor Coleridge, *Selected Poetry and Prose* (edited by Donald A. Stauffer, New York: Random House, 1951).
21. 'Dejection' is included by G. M. Harper, as well as by A. Gérard in his essay 'The Systolic Rhythm: The Structure of Coleridge's Conversation Poems', in Kathleen Coburn (ed.), *Coleridge: A Collection of Critical Essays* (Englewood Cliffs, NJ: Prentice-Hall, 1967), 78.
22. Everest states that 'To the Reverend George Coleridge' is 'in many respects a conversation poem' (*Secret Ministry*, 151), but omits it from his list. It is, however, included by Richard Holmes in his edition of Coleridge's *Selected Poetry*.
23. The latter poem is included among the conversation poems in Holmes' edition of the *Selected Poetry*.
24. 'If remarks of belonging belong without belonging, participate without belonging, then *genre-designations cannot be simply part of the corpus*' (Jacques Derrida, 'The Law of Genre', 230, in *Acts of Literature* [edited by Derek Attridge, London: Routledge, 1992]).
25. See the 'General Introduction; or, A Preliminary Treatise on Method', in Coleridge, *Shorter Works and Fragments*, I.
26. All references to Coleridge's poetry are taken from Samuel Taylor Coleridge, *The Complete Poems* (edited by William Keach, London: Penguin Books, 1997).
27. In chapter 9, I will return to the theme of the 'parergon' (a term frequently used by Jacques Derrida) and the related transcendence of the aesthetics of the work.
28. This, and the subsequent quote, is found in a letter to Wordsworth, dated 10 May 1798 (*Letters*, I, 406).
29. Cf. the note to the poem on p. 522 of Keach's Penguin edition of *The Complete Poems*.
30. William Godwin, *Enquiry Concerning Political Justice and its Influence on Morals and Happiness*, Volume I (edited by F. E. L. Priestly, Toronto: University of Toronto, 1946), 296.
31. Schleiermacher, *On Religion*, 90.

32. Francis Bacon, *The Essays* (edited by John Pitcher, London: Penguin Books, 1985), 144.
33. This and the following quote is from the letter to Thomas Poole, 6 February 1797 (*Letters*, I, 302).
34. Cicero, *On the Good Life*, 193.
35. Ibid., 221.
36. Rosemary Ashton notes that the poem's 'tone, appropriately for a celebration of poetic success in his friend by one who feels himself a failure, is Wordsworthian' (*The Life of Samuel Taylor Coleridge: A Critical Biography* [Oxford: Blackwell, 1996], 240).
37. On Coleridge's distinction between understanding and reason, see G. N. G. Orsini, *Coleridge and German Idealism*, 139 ff., and Rosemary Ashton, *The German Idea: Four English Writers and the Reception of German Thought, 1800–1860* (Cambridge: Cambridge University Press, 1980), 46–8.
38. 'My Heart Leaps Up', line 7. This line was later used as part of an epigraph to 'Ode: Intimations of Immortality'.
39. Cf. the following notebook entry, written a couple of years earlier: 'Our quaint metaphysical opinions in an hour of anguish like playthings by the bedside of a child deadly sick' (Entry number 181 in *Notebooks*, I).
40. Cf. p. 668 of 'General Introduction, or, A Preliminary Treatise on Method', in *Shorter Works and Fragments*, I.
41. *Aids to Reflection*, 25.
42. While copying entails attempting to make the reproduction completely the *same* as the original, imitation 'consists either in the interfusion of the SAME throughout the radically DIFFERENT, or of the different throughout a base radically the same' (*Biographia Literaria*, II, 72).
43. According to Socrates, true friendship can only be lasting if it is between virtuous persons. But a good individual has no need of a friend: 'What place then is there for friendship, if, when absent, good men have no need of one another (for even when alone they are sufficient for themselves), and when present have no use of one another? How can such persons ever be induced to value one another?' (*The Works of Plato* [edited by Irwin Erdman, translated by Benjamin Jowett, New York: Random House, 1956 (1928)], 20).
44. To Thomas Poole, 12 December, 1796 (*Letters*, I, 270).
45. Ibid.
46. 'Lectures on Revealed Religion, its Corruptions and Political Views', 163, in Samuel Taylor Coleridge, *Lectures 1795: On Politics and Religion*, in *Collected Works*, volume 1 (edited by Lewis Patton and Peter Mann, London: Routledge & Kegan Paul, 1971). Even late in life, Coleridge did not deem it inadmissible to write of '*God – the Friend*' (see Coleridge, *The Notebooks*, volume IV [edited by Kathleen Coburn and Merton Christensen, London: Routledge, 1990], 4632).
47. Paul Ricoeur, *Oneself as Another* (translated by Kathleen Blamey, Chicago: The University of Chicago Press, 1992), 187.
48. Coleridge cited in McFarland, *Coleridge and the Pantheist Tradition*, 318.
49. Ibid.
50. For this distinction, see Jacques Derrida, 'How to Avoid Speaking: Denials', translated by Ken Frieden, 111, in Harold Coward and Toby Foshay (eds.), *Derrida and Negative Theology* (Albany: State University of New York Press, 1992). Elsewhere, Derrida has tied friendship to the prayer: 'Friendship is never a present given, it belongs to the experience of expectation, promise, or engagement. Its discourse

is that of prayer, it inaugurates, but reports nothing, it is not satisfied with what is, it moves out to this place where a responsibility opens up a future' (*Politics of Friendship* [translated by George Collins, London: Verso, 1997], 236).
51. 'The Nightingale', ll. 81–2, emphasis added.
52. 'Reflections on Having Left a Place of Retirement', ll, 39–40. The emphasis on 'Seem'd' is mine.
53. Gillray's drawing is one of the images reproduced between pp. 128 and 129 in Holmes, *Coleridge: Early Visions*.
54. For an account the earliest stirrings of organicism in Coleridge, see John Beer, *Coleridge's Poetical Intelligence* (London: Macmillan, 1977).

Chapter 6

1. All page references given directly in the text of this chapter, unless context suggests otherwise, refer to book and line number of *The Excursion*, as rendered in *The Poems*, II, 35–289.
2. Later, in conversation with Isabella Fenwick, Wordsworth identified the local Grasmere church of St Oswald's as the model for the church in *The Excursion*, book five. Strictly speaking, this is a Norman church, rather than a gothic cathedral – nevertheless it is linked to Wordsworth's pervading interest in sacred architecture. Throughout this chapter, I have tried to be inclusive (including other forms of churches, buildings, and so on, as far as the argument has warranted it) in my contextualisation of his use of the gothic cathedral as a metaphor, in an attempt to touch upon some of the outer limits evoked by the architectural and religious motifs of his later writings.
3. Lines 552–4 of *The Tuft of Primroses*, in Wordsworth, *The Tuft of Primroses with Other Late Poems for 'The Recluse'* (edited by Joseph F. Kishel, Ithaca, NY: Cornell University Press, 1986).
4. This chapter is inspired, throughout, by Jacques Derrida's many explorations of space and spatial paradox, as for instance in 'Tympan', in *Margins of Philosophy* (translated by Alan Bass, New York: Harvester Wheatsheaf, 1982), ix-xxix) and *'Fors: The Anglish Words of Nicolas Abraham and Maria Torok'*, which is the foreword to Nicolas Abraham and Maria Torok, *The Wolf Man's Magic Word: A Cryptonymy* (translated by Nicholas Rand, Minnesota: University of Minneapolis Press, 1986).
5. *Concerning the Concept of the Wissenschaftslehre or, of So-called 'Philosophy'*, 104–5, in *Early Philosophical Writings*.
6. For an account of architecture as a master science, see Denis Hollier, *Against Architecture*, 33.
7. *The Poems*, II, 36.
8. Dora Wordsworth in a letter to Miss Kinnaird (17 February 1832), cited on p. 49 of Harvey and Gravil (eds.), *Wordsworth: The Prelude. A Casebook*.
9. Kenneth R. Johnston, *Wordsworth and 'The Recluse'* (New Haven, CT: Yale University Press, 1984), xxiii.
10. Ibid., 121.
11. See ibid., 346.
12. Letter to Wordsworth, 30 May 1815 (*Letters*, IV, 573).
13. Ibid. (574).
14. See, for instance, Christopher Wilson, *The Gothic Cathedral: The Architecture of the Great Church 1130–1530* (London: Thames and Hudson, 1990), 8 and 32, Paul

Frankl, *Gothic Architecture* (translated by Dieter Pevsner, Harmondsworth: Penguin Books, 1962), 231, and Otto von Simson, *The Gothic Cathedral: Origins of Gothic Cathedral and the Medieval Concept of Order* (Princeton, NJ: Princeton University Press, 1988 [1956]), 8.

15. In *The Gothic Cathedral*, Otto von Simson draws upon the mathematical proportion of St Augustine's theory of music. Erwin Panofsky has linked the cathedrals to scholastic logic in *Gothic Architecture and Scholasticism* (Latrobe: Archabbey Press, 1951).

16. Andrew Martindale, *Gothic Art* (London: Thames and Hudson, 1967), 17.

17. See Alain Erlande-Brandenburg, *The Cathedral: The Social and Architectural Dynamics of Construction* (translated by Martin Thom, Cambridge: Cambridge University Press, 1994), 216.

18. Johann Wolfgang Goethe, 'Von Deutscher Baukunst. D. M. Erwini a Steinbach', 210, in Heinz Kindermann (ed.), *Von Deutscher Art und Kunst* (Leipzig: Philipp Reclam Jun., 1935); my translation.

19. See 'Briefe auf einer Reise durch die Niederlande, Rheingegenden, die Schweiz, und einen Teil von Frankreich', in Friedrich Schlegel, *Ansichten und Ideen von der christlichen Kunst*, in *Kritische Friedrich-Schlegel-Ausgabe*, volume 4 (edited by Hans Eichner, Munich: Verlag Ferdinand Schöningh, 1959), 191–2. All translations from this source are my own.

20. 'Briefe auf einer Reise ...', 200. The richness and unruliness of the ornamentation was the basis on which John Ruskin would later declare 'variety' to be characteristic of gothic. See the famous chapter on 'The Nature of Gothic', in *The Stones of Venice* (3 volumes, London: Dent, 1907).

21. 'Brief auf einer Reise ...', 161.

22. See, for example, Kenneth Clark, *The Gothic Revival: An Essay in the History of Taste* (Harmondsworth: Penguin Books, 1962 [1928]), 81.

23. *The Prelude*, II, 295–6.

24. For Violett-le-Duc's 'ideal cathedral', see Erlande-Brandenburg, *The Cathedral*, 18.

25. The sonnet is to be found in *The Poems*, II, 637.

26. 'For a Seat in the Groves of Coleorton', 17–20. Recent historicist readings try to locate a historical 'primal scene', of sorts (replacing earlier psychoanalytical ones, as well as interpretations focusing on Wordsworth's presumed sense of guilt towards Annette Vallon), in Wordsworth's early exposure to the French Revolution. See, for instance, David Bromwich, *Disowned by Memory: Wordsworth's Poetry of the 1790s* (Chicago: The University of Chicago Press, 1998), 17. According to this view, Wordsworth's later poetry is a site of expiation for his early, revolutionary sins. My reading can be adjusted so as to comply with this kind of scenario: Wordsworth's construction of gothic cathedral of poetry can be read as an act seeking absolution for his complicity in the revolutionary violence that led to the destruction of such edifices as the Grande Chartreuse. (On Wordsworth's later poetry as an act of mourning for his early political transgressions, see Marilyn Butler, *Romantics, Rebels and Reactionaries: English Literature and its Background 1760–1830* [Oxford: Oxford University Press, 1981], 65.) It must be stressed that this is a complex act of attempted absolution, as Wordsworth also *repeats* the destruction of the pre-Revolutionary church, by replacing it with a quasi-transcendent edifice akin to that of the pure reason invoked by the revolutionaries. As Gregory Dart has pointed out in *Rousseau, Robespierre and English Romanticism* (Cambridge: Cambridge University Press, 1999), Wordsworth's recanting of his revolutionary ideals is far less straightforward than it usually is made out to be.

27. Lines 7–10 of 'Cathedrals, etc.'.
28. In *A Guide through the District of the Lakes*, indicates that the local churches of the area are almost transparent signifiers for the virtues of the place, See *The Prose Works of William Wordsworth*, volume II (edited by W. J. B. Owen and Jane Worthington Smyser, Oxford: Clarendon Press, 1974), 205.
29. 'Cathedrals, etc.', line 1.
30. Lines 1–2 of 'Continued' (poem XLV of part three of *Ecclesiastical Sonnets*).
31. The friend has been identified as Beaumont. See *The Poems*, II, 997.
32. 'Church to be erected', ll. 1–4.
33. 'New church-yard', ll. 8–9.
34. 'Continued' (sonnet XL of part three), ll. 12–13.
35. Lines 127–8 of *The Tuft of Primroses*, emphasis added.
36. 'Composed in One of the Valleys of Westmoreland, on Easter Sunday', l. 12.
37. See John Dixon Hunt on an early example of this feature in the gardens at Stowe, in *Gardens and the Picturesque: Studies in the History of Landscape Architecture* (Cambridge, MA: MIT Press, 1992), 99.
38. See for instance pp. 200–4 of 'The Rhetoric of Temporality', in Paul de Man, *Blindness and Insight*.
39. 'A Little Onward Lend Thy Guiding Hand', ll. 33–9.
40. *The Tuft of Primroses*, l. 583.
41. 'Cave of Staffa', ll. 12–14.
42. 'Composed in Roslin Chapel, During a Storm', l.1.
43. Ibid., ll. 8–14.
44. William Gilpin, *Observations, Relative Chiefly to Picturesque Beauty, Made in the Year 1772, on Several Parts of England; Particularly the Mountains, and Lakes of Cumberland, and Westmoreland*, volume II (Richmond: The Richmond Publishing Co., 1973), 188.
45. There are two different poems entitled 'At Furness Abbey'. I refer to the poem of that name that opens with the words 'Here, where, of havoc tired' and is printed in *The Poems*, II, 838.
46. Malcolm Andrews identifies five different eighteenth-century responses to ruins: sentimental, antiquarian, aesthetic, moral (in terms of a *memento mori*) and political, in *The Search for the Picturesque: Landscape Aesthetics and Tourism in Britain, 1760–1800* (Aldershot: Scolar Press, 1989), 45–6.
47. See the note dictated to Isabella Fenwick in *The Poems*, II, 1066.
48. 'In Lombardy', ll. 14 and 12, respectively.
49. Cf. Umberto Eco, *The Open Work* (translated by Anna Cancogni, Cambridge, MA: Harvard University Press, 1989).
50. *The Prelude*, VI, 602–5.
51. 'Stanzas Suggested in a Steamboat off Saint Bees' Heads, on the Coast of Cumberland', ll. 154 and 157.
52. Ibid., l. 84.
53. Here one can see some general anticipations of both Victor Hugo's vision of the medieval church building as the locus of a democratic revolt against the hierarchies of feudalism (see chapter 2 of book V, *Notre-Dame of Paris* [translated by John Sturrock, London: Penguin Books, 1978]), and the still widespread understanding of it as a centring force at the middle of the medieval city (Erlande-Brandenburg, *The Cathedral*, 166). A very different view is suggested by Michael Camille, when he claims that the 'medieval town, although it stood for freedom from the feudal obligations of the land, was the most policed of all medieval spaces' (*Gothic Art: Visions and Revelations of the Medieval World* [London:

Calmann and King, 1996], 60–1). The latent oppressiveness of Wordsworth's emancipatory rhetoric in the poem on St Bees is documented by Peter J. Manning in *Reading Romantics: Texts and Contexts* (Oxford: Oxford University Press, 1990), chapter 12, where he demonstrates how the poem is related to Wordsworth's private connection with the aristocratic legacy of Lord Lowther.

54. *The White Doe of Rylstone*, ll. 37–8.
55. For the paradoxical instantiation of organic community in the blind beggar episode of *The Prelude*, see Charles I. Armstrong, 'Begging Questions: The Urban Vision of Wordsworth's *Prelude*', in Jan Arnald et al., *Slöja & spegel – Romantikens Former* (Stockholm: Aiolos, 2000).
56. Ibid., ll. 43–9 and 56–8.
57. Alison Hickey's reading of *The Excursion* alludes to this interpretation by evoking 'the mansion (or gothic cathedral) of language' (*Impure Conceits: Rhetoric and Ideology in Wordsworth's 'Excursion'* [Stanford, CA: Stanford University Press, 1997], 46). In Wordsworth's most orthodox pronouncements, increasingly prominent in the later years, he of course subscribes to a Christian ontology (dismissed by both Heidegger and de Man) where the divine house of being is the gift of God.
58. Jacques Derrida, '"The Almost Nothing of the Unpresentable"', 79, in *Points ... Interviews, 1974–1994* (edited by Elizabeth Weber, Stanford, CA: Stanford University Press, 1995)
59. See *A Guide through the District of the Lakes*, 206, in *The Prose Works*, II.
60. 'As faith thus sanctified the warrior's crest', ll. 10–11.
61. *The Excursion*, II, 858–9. Hickey places the vision in the context of its agent (the Solitary) in *Impure Conceits*, 64–8.

Chapter 7

1. John Paul Russo, *I. A. Richards: His Life and Work* (London: Routledge, 1989), xvi-xvii.
2. 'How does a Poem know when it is Finished?', 108, in I. A. Richards, *Sciences and Poetries: A Reissue of Science and Poetry (1926, 1935) with Commentary* (London: Routledge & Kegan Paul, 1970).
3. See, for instance, the introduction to René Wellek and Austin Warren's classic *Theory of Literature*, where one is cautioned that thinking of a literary works in terms of organicism 'leads to biological parallels not always relevant' (*Theory of Literature* [Harmondsworth: Penguin Books, 1956 (1942)], 27). The New Critics were more adamantly opposed to Richards' psychological bias.
4. I. A. Richards, *Principles of Literary Criticism* (London: Routledge & Kegan Paul, 1924), 3. Subsequent citations from this work will be given directly in the text.
5. 'The Future of Poetry', 174, in I. A. Richards, *So Much Nearer: Essays Toward a World English* (New York: Harcourt, Brace & World, 1968 [1960]).
6. The notion of mental clearing-houses does however make an appearance in Ogden's *The Meaning of Psychology*. See Russo, *I. A. Richards: His Life and Work*, 180.
7. W. H. N. Hotopf, *Language, Thought and Comprehension: A Case Study of the Writings of I. A. Richards* (London: Routledge & Kegan Paul, 1965), 100.
8. I. A. Richards, *Coleridge on Imagination* (London: Routledge & Kegan Paul, 1962 [1934]), 57.

9. *Sciences and Poetries*, 45.
10. I. A. Richards, *Practical Criticism: A Study of Literary Judgment* (London: Routledge & Kegan Paul, 1929), 332.
11. Ibid., 356.
12. See *Coleridge on Imagination*, 87–8.
13. See Jerome P. Schiller, *I. A. Richards' Theory of Literature* (New Haven, CT: Yale University Press, 1969), 53.
14. *Practical Criticism*, 212–13.
15. Ralph Waldo Emerson, *Selected Essays* (New York: Penguin Books, 1982), 262.
16. Terry Eagleton finds Richards' conception of the mind 'not far from the Victorian belief that organizing the lower classes will ensure the survival of the upper ones, and indeed [it] is significantly related to it' (*Literary Theory: An Introduction* [Minneapolis: University of Minnesota Press, 1983], 46).
17. I. A. Richards, *The Philosophy of Rhetoric* (London: Oxford University Press, 1965), 103.
18. *Practical Criticism*, 323. Thirty-six years later, Richards was still eagerly waiting for the final, scientific revelation of the mind: see *Sciences and Poetries*, 96.
19. Ibid., 36.
20. The dismissal of Yeats as a minor poet is in *Principles of Literary Criticism*, note 1 on p. 197. Richards later revoked this assessment.
21. Both poems and the mind are described as 'would-be' systems in 'The Future of Poetry', 176, in *So Much Nearer*.
22. *Practical Criticism*, 259.
23. Ibid., 286.
24. 'The "Old Mole" and the Prefix *Sur*', 37, in Georges Bataille, *Visions of Excess: Selected Writings, 1927–1939* (edited by Allan Stoekl, translated by Allan Stoekl, with Carl R. Lovitt and Donald M. Leslie, Jr, Manchester: Manchester University Press, 1985).
25. 'Materialism', 15, in *Visions of Excess*.
26. On the topic of the polymorphously perverse, see especially Freud's *Three Essays on the Theory of Sexuality*, in *The Standard Edition*, volume VII (edited by James Strachey, London: Hogarth Press, 1971).
27. 'The Sacred Conspiracy', 181, in *Visions of Excess*.
28. 'The Jesuve', 76, in *Visions of Excess*.
29. See Denis Hollier, 'The Use-Value of the Impossible', 148, in Carolyn Bailey Gill (ed.), *Bataille: Writing the Sacred* (London: Routledge, 1995).
30. 'The Solar Anus', 5, in *Visions of Excess*.
31. Ibid.
32. Georges Bataille, 'Autobiographical Note', 222, in *My Mother, Madame Edwarda, The Dead Man* (translated by Austryn Wainhouse, London: Marion Boyars, 1995).
33. Richards quoted in Russo, *I. A. Richards: His Life and Work*, 107.
34. 'Sacrifices', 132, emphasis added, in *Visions of Excess* ('Sacrifices', 92, in Bataille, *Œuvres complètes*, volume I [Paris: Gallimard, 1973]).
35. 'Sacrificial Mutilation and the Severed Ear of Vincent Van Gogh', 66, in *Visions of Excess*.
36. Ibid., 67.
37. 'Rotten Sun', 57–8, in ibid.
38. On this topic, see for instance the essay 'The Labyrinth', which raises the issue of the metaphorical use of the divisibility of animalcula, which is one of the clear-

est links between Bataille and romantic organicism. It is particularly important to Bataille in his later study *Erotism: Death and Sensuality* (translated by Mary Dalwood, San Francisco: City Lights, 1986).

39. The essay is included in *Visions of Excess*, 137–60. The quotes given directly in the text in the remainder of this chapter refers to this edition. Throughout this essay, Bataille writes the terms 'homogeneous' and 'heterogeneous' in cursive.

40. See ibid., 141. Bataille also draws on Freud's text *Group Psychology and the Analysis of the 'Ego'* (cf. notes 8 and 11 in ibid., 160).

41. The original is cited from Bataille, *Œuvres complètes*, I, 343 and 353.

42. See 'Base Materialism and Gnosticism', in *Visions of Excess*, 45–52, as well as Denis Hollier, 'The Dualist Materialism of Georges Bataille', in Allan Stoekl (ed.), *On Bataille*, Yale French Studies, Number 78 (New Haven, CT: Yale University Press, 1990).

43. See the preface (without pagination) to *The Philosophy of Rhetoric*, where Richards asks that 'anything that seems extreme in these lectures be thought accidental or be taken as a speaker's device'.

44. *Practical Criticism*, 217. This passage might be compared with Bataille's description of poetical sensibility and feeling in 'From the Stone Age to Jacques Prévert', in Georges Bataille, *The Absence of Myth: Writings on Surrealism* (edited and translated by Michael Richardson, London: Verso, 1994).

45. Theodor W. Adorno, *Aesthetic Theory* (edited and translated by Robert Hullot-Kentor, London: The Athlone Press, 1997), 144.

46. See 'Counter attack: Call to action', translated by Annette Michelson, 27, in *October*, Number 36, Spring 1986.

47. This is the eighth point in Bataille's 'Program (Relative to *Acéphale*)', translated by Annette Michelson, 79, in *October*, Number 36, Spring 1986 ('Programme', 273, in Bataille, *Œuvres complètes*, volume II [Paris: Gallimard: 1972]).

48. 'To those organizations of coherent and disciplined forces which reconstitute the foundations of the structure of authority within a democracy in the process of decomposition, we can give the generic name of organic movements' ('Toward Real Revolution', translated by Annette Michelson, 38, in *October*, Number 36, Spring 1986). For differing interpretations of Bataille's complicated stance towards fascism in the 1930s, see the following readings of his controversial novel *The Blue of Noon* (written at this time): Susan Rubin Suleiman, 'Bataille in the Street: The Search for Virility in the 1930s', in Carolyn Bailey Gill (ed.), *Bataille: Writing the Sacred* (London: Routledge, 1995), and Leo Bersani, *The Culture of Redemption* (Cambridge, MA: Harvard University Press, 1990), 109–23.

49. The transcendence of all dichotomies is surely a more feasible explanation for why Coleridge swings between opposite political stances than that of mere opportunism. Compare Liu, *Wordsworth: The Sense of History*, 421–5.

50. The suppression of explicit politics in Richards and New Criticism has been explained as a product of liberalism. The belief in 'the priority and efficacy of autonomous individual action' has, as Pamela McCallum has pointed out, its own covert politics (Pamela McCallum, *Literature and Method: Towards a Critique of I. A. Richards, T. S. Eliot and F. R. Leavis* [Dublin: Gill and Macmillan, 1983], 11). See also Geoffrey H. Hartman on the implications of Richards' 'evasion of the sociological issue' ('The Dream of Communication', 162, in Brower, Vendler and Hollander (eds.), *I. A. Richards: Essays in His Honor* [New York: Oxford University Press, 1973]). Richards makes a rare foray into politics in the introduction to his own translation of Plato, where the latter is defended against all charges of totalitarianism and credited with the 'discovery of Justice as Order'

('Introduction', 11, in Plato, *Plato's Republic* [edited and translated by I. A. Richards, Cambridge: Cambridge University Press, 1966]).

51. *Coleridge on Imagination*, 81.
52. While the first view is not all that dissimilar to that presented by Paul de Man in *Aesthetic Ideology*, the latter is to be found in the writings of Jean-Luc Nancy.

Chapter 8

1. See the 48th and 49th paragraphs of Martin Heidegger, *Being and Time: A Translation of 'Sein und Zeit'* (translated by Joan Stambaugh, Albany: State University of New York Press, 1996).
2. See p. 552 of the 'Afterword' to Hans-Georg Gadamer, *Truth and Method*, revised edition (translated by Joel Weinsheimer and Donald G. Marshall, London: Sheed & Ward, 1996 [1989]). Unless otherwise is stated, all references in the body of this chapter will be to the English edition, while references to the German original will be to *Wahrheit und Methode: Grundzüge einer philosophischen Hermeneutik*, in *Gesammelte Werke*, volume 1 (Tübingen: J. C. B. Mohr (Paul Siebeck), 1975).
3. With the word 'mortality' I here refer to what Jacques Derrida has called 'this properly *in-finite* movement of radical destruction' that is beyond any conception of 'finitude as limit' (*Archive Fever: A Freudian Impression* [translated by Eric Prenowitz, Chicago: The University of Chicago Press, 1996], 94).
4. Hans-Georg Gadamer, 'Rhetoric, Hermeneutics, and the Critique of Ideology: Metacritical Comments on *Truth and Method*', translated by Jerry Dibble, 275, in Kurt Mueller-Vollmer (ed.), *The Hermeneutics Reader: Texts of the German Tradition from the Enlightenment to the Present* (New York: Continuum, 1994). Although Dilthey is, strictly speaking, a post-romantic thinker, he remains the closest link between Gadamer and organicist thought. Gadamer's most direct – and most debated – critique of romantic hermeneutics occurs through his confrontation with Schleiermacher, and the latter's alleged tendency to ground textual interpretation in an act of intuitive psychological identification with the genius of the author. But after much opposition, from Manfred Frank in particular, Gadamer has later partially admitted that this critique is based on a simplification of Schleiermacher's thought: see page 565 of the afterword to *Truth and Method*.
5. Wilhelm Dilthey, *Die Geistige Welt: Einleitung in die Philosophie des Lebens. Erste Hälfte: Abhandlungen zur Grundlegung der Geisteswissenschaften*, in *Gesammelte Schriften*, volume V (Stuttgart: B. G. Teubner Verlagsgesellschaft, 1957), 237; my translation.
6. From the conclusion to *The Renaissance*, in Walter Pater, *Selected Writings of Walter Pater* (edited by Harold Bloom, New York: Columbia University Press, 1974), 60.
7. This argument is amplified in Gadamer's essay 'Das Problem Diltheys: Zwischen Romantik und Positivismus', in Gadamer, *Neuere Philosophie II: Probleme, Gestalten*, in *Gesammelte Werke*, volume 4 (Tübingen: J. C. B. Mohr (Paul Siebeck), 1987).
8. *Letter on Humanism*, translated by Frank A. Capuzzi and J. Glenn Gray, 237, in Heidegger, *Basic Writings*, revised and expanded edition (edited by David Farrell Krell, London: Routledge, 1993) (Heidegger, *Über den Humanismus* [Frankfurt am Main: Vittorio Klostermann, 1947], 21). For a more recent example of Gadamer overemphasising Heidegger's connection to the philosophy of life,

see p. 422 of the essay 'Der eine Weg Martin Heideggers', in Gadamer, *Neuere Philosophie I: Hegel, Husserl, Heidegger*, in *Gesammelte Werke*, volume 3 (Tübingen: J. C. B. Mohr [Paul Siebeck], 1987). This does not mean that Heidegger remains untouched by organicism. Gadamer's own direct endorsement of organic vitalism is strongly linked to his more unequivocal championing of unity and continuity, yet, as David Farrell Krell has shown, 'however much Heidegger inveighs against life-philosophy his own fundamental ontology and poetics of being thrust him back onto *Lebensphilosophie* again and again' (*Daimon Life: Heidegger and Life-Philosophy* [Bloomington: Indiana University Press, 1992], xi).

9. Georgia Warnke has noted Gadamer's 'oscillation' in *Gadamer: Hermeneutics, Tradition and Reason* (Cambridge: Polity Press, 1987), 99. Warnke claims that this oscillation is sublated by the notion of a dialogical fusion of horizons, but her account of that fusion shows how it reproduces the oscillation it was meant to supersede. For, according to Warnke, there is 'a "fusion of horizons" in a two-fold sense: on the one hand we understand the object from the point of view of our assumptions and situation; on the other, our final perspective reflects the education we have received through our encounter with the object' (ibid., 107).

10. On this topic, see also Gadamer's 'Zur Fragwürdigkeit des ästhetischen Bewußtseins', in Dieter Heinrich and Wolfgang Iser (eds.), *Theorien der Kunst* (Frankfurt am Main: Suhrkamp, 1992 [1982]). Gadamer's tendency to counter aesthetic formalism with an emphasis on the inalienable unity of form and content in works of art repeats, of course, a traditional operation of organicism.

11. Gadamer's use of the theory of emanation is arguably his most significant innovation, in this context, compared to the important precedent of Heidegger's *On the Origin of the Work of Art*. On the link between emanation and organicism, see A. Hilary Armstrong, *Plotinian and Christian Studies* (London: Variorum Reprints, 1979), 66. As Dag Andersson has pointed out to me in conversation, Gadamer's characteristic German phrase for describing the result of emanation – '*Zuwachs an sein*' (which means 'increase in being', but more literally signifies something akin to 'growth in being') – more than nods towards the notion of organic development.

12. Gadamer, 'Rhetoric, Hermeneutics, and the Critique of Ideology: Metacritical Comments on *Truth and Method*', 279.

13. Here Gadamer, significantly enough, signals solidarity with Friedrich Schlegel's conception of the work, and notes that 'I have had long to defend myself against the spirit of the times, which wants to set aside the hermeneutical concept of the work. Here a feeling for the history of concepts can be helpful. "Work" does not mean anything different from the Greek word "*ergon*". It is characterised – just like "*ergon*" – by the fact that it is detached both from the producer and the activity of production. ... It stands, so to speak, only for itself and in itself' ('Hermeneutics and Logocentrism', translated by Richard Palmer and Diane Michelfelder, 123, in Michelfelder and Palmer (eds.), *Dialogue and Deconstruction: The Gadamer–Derrida Encounter* [Albany: State University of New York Press. 1989]).

14. *Praise of Theory: Speeches and Essays* (translated by Chris Dawson, New Haven: Yale University Press, 1998), 80.

15. Gadamer, *The Enigma of Health: The Art of Healing in a Scientific Age* (translated by Jason Gaiger and Nicholas Walker, Cambridge: Polity Press, 1996), 139.

16. Ibid., 80.

17. Hans-Georg Gadamer, *The Relevance of the Beautiful and Other Essays* (edited by Robert Bernasconi, translated by Nicholas Walker, Cambridge: Cambridge

University Press, 1986), 42 (*Ästhetik und Poetik I: Kunst als Aussage*, in *Gesammelte Werke*, volume 8 [Tübingen: J. C. B. Mohr (Paul Siebeck), 1993], 133).

Chapter 9

1. Georges Bataille, *Theory of Religion* (translated by Robert Hurley, New York: Zone Books, 1992), 19.
2. These lines were first published in 1829. On their origin and title ('What is life?') see the note on p. 567 of Coleridge, *The Complete Poems*.
3. Although it has not placed in the context of romantic organicism, Blanchot's proximity to Heidegger is well known. Gerald L. Bruns, for instance, writes of *The Space of Literature* that its 'theory is a rewriting of Heidegger's "Der Ursprung des Kunstwerkes"' (*Maurice Blanchot: The Refusal of Philosophy* [Baltimore: The Johns Hopkins University Press, 1997], 62).
4. 'The Origin of the Work of Art', 79. Although the treatise was first presented as a lecture in 1935, it was later revised, and an addendum was added in 1956.
5. See, for instance, this passage: 'World and earth are always intrinsically and essentially in conflict, belligerent by nature. Only as such do they enter into the conflict of clearing and concealing' (ibid., 55). Heidegger's understanding of a struggle between world and earth stands in some debt to Schelling's treatise on the essence of human freedom. See Heidegger's *Schellings Abhandlung über das Wesen der menschlichen Freiheit*.
6. Ibid., 63. Here is Heidegger's original, German wording: 'Dieser Rißt die Gegenwendigen in die Herkunft ihrer Einheit aus dem einigen Grunde zusammen. Er ist Grundriß. Er ist Auf-riß, der die Grundzüge des Aufgehens der Lichtung des Seienden zeichnet. Dieser Riß läßt die Gegenwendigen nicht auseinanderbersten, er bringt das Gegenwendige von Maß und Grenze in den einigen Umriß' (Heidegger, *Der Urprung des Kunstwerkes* (Stuttgart: Philipp Reclam Jun., 1977), 71).
7. Ibid., 64 [71].
8. Maurice Blanchot, *The Space of Literature* (translated by Ann Smock, Lincoln: University of Nebraska Press, 1982), 125. Subsequent page numbers given directly in the body of this chapter will refer to this book.
9. Blanchot has accused the author of *Being and Time* of fallaciously appropriating death as a heroic possibility of *Dasein*. Derrida has attempted to throw light upon the ambivalence inherent in the Heideggerian phrase 'possibility of impossibility' that is the bone of contention in this matter: see 'Awaiting (at) the Arrival,' 72–7, in Jacques Derrida, *Aporias* (translated by Thomas Dutoit, Stanford, CA: Stanford University Press, 1993).
10. See Blanchot's disagreement with Heidegger in 'The Book to Come', 240, in Maurice Blanchot, *The Sirens' Song* (edited by Gabriel Josipovici, translated by Sacha Rabinovitch, Bloomington: Indiana University Press, 1982).
11. 'The "Sacred" Speech of Hölderlin', 125–6, in Maurice Blanchot, *The Work of Fire* (translated by Charlotte Mandell, Stanford, CA: Stanford University Press, 1995).
12. Ibid., 111.
13. Ibid., 128.
14. For a discussion of this phrase, see pages xvi–xx of Lycette Nelson's 'Introduction' to Maurice Blanchot, *The Step Not Beyond* (translated by Lycette Nelson, New York: State University of New York Press, 1992).
15. *Biographia Literaria*, II, 14.

16. 'The Absence of the Book', 427, in *The Infinite Conversation*.
17. Ibid., 423.
18. 'The Great Refusal', 38, in ibid.
19. See the essay of this name, a translation of 'Le livre à venir', included in *The Sirens' Song*, 227–48.
20. 'The Narrative Voice (the "he," the neutral)', 386, in *The Infinite Conversation*.
21. See 'The Athenaeum', 359, in ibid.
22. Richard Shusterman, 'Organic Unity: Analysis and Deconstruction', 92.
23. With the term 'monstrous double', I here allude to René Girard's theory of sacrifice. According to Girard, there is an unrecognised reciprocity between the sacrificer and the victim (despite the latter's alleged monstrosity) of the sacrificial process. See for instance pages 160–5 of his book *Violence and the Sacred* (translated by Patrick Gregory, London: The Athlone Press, 1988).
24. On the imbrication of the body, language, and articulation in general, see Jacques Derrida, *Monolingualism of the Other; or, The Prosthesis of the Origin* (translated by Patrick Mensah, Stanford, CA: Stanford University Press, 1998), 26–7.
25. Roland Barthes, 'From Work to Text', in *Image, Music, Text* (edited and translated by Stephen Heath, London: Fontana Press, 1977).
26. Derrida, 'Living On / Borderlines', translated by James Hulbert, 83–4, in Harold Bloom, Paul de Man, Jacques Derrida, Geoffrey H. Hartman and J. Hillis Miller, *Deconstruction and Criticism* (London: Routledge & Kegan Paul, 1979).
27. Jacques Derrida, *Dissemination* (translated by Barbara Johnson, London: The Athlone Press, 1981), 45.
28. 'Tympan', xvii, in *Margins of Philosophy* (*Marges de la philosophie* [Paris: Minuit, 1972], X).
29. Ibid., x.
30. Ibid., xx.
31. Ibid.
32. Jacques Derrida, *Positions* (translated by Alan Bass, Chicago: The University of Chicago Press, 1981), 41.
33. 'Outwork, Prefacing', 6, in *Dissemination*.
34. *Positions*, 43 (*Positions: Entretiens avec Henri Ronse, Julia Kristeva, Jean-Louis Houdebine, Guy Scarpetta* [Paris: Minuit, 1972], 59).
35. 'Structure, Sign, and Play in the Discourse of the Human Sciences', 293, in Jacques Derrida, *Writing and Difference* (translated by Alan Bass, Chicago: The University of Chicago Press, 1978).
36. 'Sauf le nom (Post-Scriptum)', 83, in Derrida, *On the Name* (edited by Thomas Dutoit, translated by David Wood, John P. Leavey, Jr. and Ian McLeod, Stanford, CA: Stanford University Press, 1995).
37. On Derrida's desire to transcend sacrifice, see '"Eating Well," or the Calculation of the Subject', in *Points* .... For an admission of the selectivity of interpretation, see for instance 'The Law of Genre', 232, in Derrida, *Acts of Literature*. On the selectivity of historical transmission, see Derrida's '*Specters of Marx': The State of the Debt, the Work of Mourning, & the New International* (translated by Peggy Kamuf, New York: Routledge, 1994), 91–2.
38. ''Eating Well', or the Calculation of the Subject,' 280, in *Points* ... .
39. Jacques Derrida, *Of Spirit: Heidegger and the Question* (translated by Geoffrey Bennington and Rachel Bowlby, Chicago: The University of Chicago Press, 1989), 12.

40. On the term 'invagination', see Geoff Bennington, 'Derridabase', 226, in Bennington and Derrida, *Jacques Derrida* (translated by Bennington, Chicago: The University of Chicago Press, 1993).
41. 'Living On: Borderlines', 97.
42. 'The Law of Genre', 236, in *Acts of Literature*.
43. 'Parergon', 27, in Derrida, *The Truth in Painting*.
44. Ibid. (the text has no final stop or punctuation mark).
45. See 'Before the Law', 217, in Derrida, *Acts of Literature*.
46. The term 'parergon' recurs in Derrida's texts (often with special reference to Kant), and is very close to that of Blanchot's *désœuvrement*: 'A parergon comes against, beside, and in addition to the *ergon*, the work done, the fact, the work, but it does not fall to one side, it touches and cooperates within the operation, from a certain outside. Neither simply outside nor simply inside' ('Parergon', 54, in *The Truth in Painting*).
47. '*Istrice 2. Ich bünn all hier*', 305, in *Points* ... .
48. Maurice Blanchot, *Friendship* (translated by Elizabeth Rottenberg, Stanford, CA: Stanford University Press, 1997), 291.
49. Ibid.
50. Ibid., 292.
51. Jean-Luc Nancy, *The Inoperative Community* (edited by Peter Connor, translated by Peter Connor, Lisa Garbus, Michael Holland and Simona Sawhney, Minneapolis: University of Minnesota Press, 1991), xxxviii.
52. Maurice Blanchot, *The Unavowable Community* (translated by Pierre Joris, Barrytown: Station Hill Press, 1988), 3.
53. Derrida, *Politics of Friendship*, 229.
54. Ibid., 159.
55. Ibid., 196.
56. Ibid., 204.
57. Ibid., 232.
58. Ibid., 233.
59. See Jacques Derrida, 'Remarks on Deconstruction and Pragmatism', translated by Simon Critchley, 83, in Critchley, Derrida, Ernesto Laclau and Simon Rorty, *Deconstruction and Pragmatism* (edited by Chantal Mouffe, London: Routledge, 1996).
60. Jacques Derrida, '*Specters of Marx*', 65.
61. Ibid., 29.
62. Ibid., 59.
63. This point recurs in the essays by Terry Eagleton ('Marxism without Marxism', cf. p. 86), Aijaz Ahmad (p. 98 of 'Reconciling Derrida: 'Specters of Marx' and Deconstructive Politics'), and Tom Lewis ('The Politics of 'Hauntology' in Derrida's '*Specters of Marx*', 147–8) that are collected in Michael Sprinker (ed.), *Ghostly Demarcations: A Symposium on Jacques Derrida's 'Specters of Marx'* (London: Verso, 1999). In the same volume, Derrida responds such criticism in an essay entitled 'Marx & Sons' (translated by G. M. Goshgarian). Although he does not dwell at length upon the subject of organisation, he distances himself from detects 'those Marxists who would like to reproduce the present obsolete forms of organization represented by the state, Party and International' (245). Here the stress is upon a transformation of existing organisations, rather than a general critique (which lies behind many of the formulations in *Specters of Marx*) of the concept of organisation.

64. *'Specters of Marx'*, 89.
65. See Gilles Deleuze, *Difference and Repetition* (translated by Paul Patton, London: The Athlone Press, 1994), 263. A more detailed account of Leibniz' thought is presented by Deleuze in *The Fold: Leibniz and the Baroque* (translated by Tom Conley, Minneapolis: University of Minnesota Press, 1993).
66. Gilles Deleuze and Félix Guattari, *A Thousand Plateaus* (translated by Brian Massumi, London: The Athlone Press, 1988), 499.
67. Ibid., 86.
68. See p. 195 of the eulogy 'I'm Going to Have to Wander All Alone', translated by Leonard Lawler, in Derrida, *The Work of Mourning* (edited by Pascale-Anne Brault and Michael Naas, Chicago: The University of Chicago Press, 2001).
69. Gilles Deleuze, *Pure Immanence: Essays on A Life* (translated by John Rajchman, New York: Zone Books, 2001), 27.
70. This view has recently been propounded by John Protevi in *Political Physics: Deleuze, Derrida and the Body Politic* (London: The Athlone Press, 2001).
71. On this last term, see Jacques Derrida, 'Biodegradables: Seven Diary Fragments' (translated by Peggy Kamuf, *Critical Inquiry*, Volume 15, Number 1, Summer 1989).
72. The essay is an expanded version of a lecture held at Capri in 1994.
73. 'Faith and Knowledge: the Two Sources of "Religion" at the Limits of Reason Alone', translated by Samuel Weber, 13–14, in Jacques Derrida and Gianni Vattimo (eds.), *Religion* (Cambridge: Polity Press, 1998), 48. The use of cursive and boldface is Derrida's own.
74. Ibid., 51.
75. Ibid., note 27 on p. 73.
76. Ibid., 51.
77. See 'The Pit and the Pyramid: Introduction to Hegel's Semiology', 107, in *Margins of Philosophy*.
78. See Dietrich von Engelhardt, 'Vitalism between Science and Philosophy in Germany around 1800', 170, in Guido Cimino and François Duchesneau (eds.), *Vitalisms: From Haller to the Cell Theory* (Florence: Leo S. Olschki Editore, 1997).

Chapter 10

1. See, for instance, G. W. Leibniz, *Monadology: An Edition for Students* (translated by Nicholas Rescher, London: Routledge, 1991), 221, and Immanuel Kant, *Opus Postumum*, 64–5.
2. Letter to John Kenyon, 3 November 1814 (*Letters*, III, 542).
3. M. H. Abrams, 'Archetypal Analogies in the Language of Criticism', 320.
4. As Frederick Burwick has pointed out, according to one possible taxonomy it is even possible to argue that organicism was formulated in deliberate opposition to vitalism. See 'Introduction', ix–x, in Burwick (ed.), *Approaches to Organic Form*.
5. Here I allude to Derrida's notion of the spectral. See, for example, *'Specters of Marx'*, 126.

Bibliography

Abrams, M. H., 'Archetypical Analogies in the Language of Criticism', *University of Toronto Quarterly*, Volume 18, 1949, 313–27.

—— *The Mirror and the Lamp: Romantic Theory and the Critical Tradition* (New York: Norton, 1958).

—— *Natural Supernaturalism: Tradition and Revolution in Romantic Literature* (New York: Norton, 1971).

Adorno, Theodor W., *Aesthetic Theory* (translated and edited by Robert Hullot-Kentor, London: The Athlone Press, 1997).

Ahmad, Aijaz, 'Reconciling Derrida: "*Specters of Marx*" and Deconstructive Politics', in Michael Sprinker (ed.), *Ghostly Demarcations: A Symposium on Jacques Derrida's 'Specters of Marx'* (London: Verso, 1999), 88–109.

Andrews, Malcolm, *The Search for the Picturesque: Landscape Aesthetics and Tourism in Britain, 1760–1800* (Aldershot: Scolar Press, 1989).

Aristotle, *The Nicomachean Ethics* (translated by H. Rackham, Cambridge, MA: Harvard University Press, 1926).

—— *Poetics* (translated by Malcolm Heath, London: Penguin Books, 1996).

Armstrong, A. Hilary, *Plotinian and Christian Studies* (London: Variorum Reprints, 1979).

Armstrong, Charles I., 'Begging Questions: The Urban Vision of Wordsworth's *Prelude*', in Jan Arnald et al., *Slöja & spegel – Romantikens Former* (Stockholm: Aiolos, 2000), 163–77.

Ashton, Rosemary, *The German Idea: Four English Writers and the Reception of German Thought, 1800–1860* (Cambridge: Cambridge University Press, 1980).

—— *The Life of Samuel Taylor Coleridge: A Critical Biography* (Oxford: Blackwell, 1996).

Bacon, Francis, *The Essays* (edited by John Pitcher, London: Penguin Books, 1985).

Barfield, Owen, *What Coleridge Thought* (London: Oxford University Press, 1972).

Barthes, Roland, *Image, Music, Text* (edited and translated by Stephen Heath, London: Fontana Press, 1977).

Bataille, Georges, *Œuvres complètes*, 12 volumes (Paris: Gallimard, 1970–88).

—— *Visions of Excess: Selected Writings, 1927–1939* (edited by Allan Stoekl, translated by Allan Stoekl, with Carl R. Lovitt and Donald M. Leslie, Jr, Manchester: Manchester University Press, 1985).

—— *Erotism: Death and Sensuality* (translated by Mary Dalwood, San Francisco: City Lights, 1986).

—— 'Counter attack: Call to action', translated by Annette Michelson, in *October*, Number 36, Spring 1986, 26–7.

—— 'Program (Relative to *Acéphale*)', translated by Annette Michelson, in *October*, Number 36, Spring 1986, 79.

—— 'Toward Real Revolution', translated by Annette Michelson, in *October*, Number 36, Spring 1986, 32–41.

—— *Theory of Religion* (translated by Robert Hurley, New York: Zone Books, 1992).

—— *The Absence of Myth: Writings on Surrealism* (edited and translated by Michael Richardson, London: Verso, 1994).

—— 'Autobiographical Note', in Bataille, *My Mother, Madame Edwarda, The Dead Man* (translated by Austryn Wainhouse, London: Marion Boyars, 1995).

Bate, Walter Jackson, *Coleridge* (London: Macmillan, 1969).

Beer, John, *Coleridge's Poetical Intelligence* (London: Macmillan, 1977).

Behler, Ernst, 'Einleitung', in Friedrich Schlegel, *Studien des klassischen Altertums, in Kritische Friedrich-Schlegel-Ausgabe*, volume 1 (edited by Ernst Behler, Munich: Verlag Ferdinand Schöningh, 1979).

Benjamin, Walter, *The Concept of Criticism in German Romanticism*, in Benjamin, *Selected Writings*, volume 1 (translated by David Lachterman, Howard Eiland and Ian Balfour, edited by Marcus Bullock and Michael W. Jennings, Cambridge, MA: Belknap Press/Harvard University Press, 1996).

Bennington, Geoffrey, 'Derridabase', in Geoffrey Bennington and Jacques Derrida, *Jacques Derrida* (translated by Geoffrey Bennington, Chicago: The University of Chicago Press, 1993), 3–316.

Benziger, James, 'Organic Unity: Leibniz to Coleridge', in *Modern Language Association of America*, Volume 66, Number 2, March 1951, 24–48.

Bersani, Leo, *The Culture of Redemption* (Cambridge, MA: Harvard University Press, 1990).

Blanchot, Maurice, *L'Entretien infini* (Paris: Gallimard, 1969); translated by Susan Hanson, *The Infinite Conversation* (Minnesota: University of Minneapolis Press, 1993).

—— *The Space of Literature* (translated by Ann Smock, Lincoln: University of Nebraska Press, 1982).

—— *The Sirens' Song* (edited by Gabriel Josipovici, Bloomington: Indiana University Press, 1982).

—— *The Unavowable Community* (translated by Pierre Joris, Barrytown: Station Hill Press, 1988).

—— *The Work of Fire* (translated by Charlotte Mandell, Stanford, CA: Stanford University Press, 1995).

—— *Friendship* (translated by Elizabeth Rottenberg, Stanford, CA: Stanford University Press, 1997).

Bloom, Harold, *The Ringers in the Tower: Studies in Romantic Tradition* (Chicago: The University of Chicago Press, 1971).

—— *The Western Canon: The Books and School of the Ages* (New York: Harcourt Brace & Company, 1994).

Bowie, Andrew, *Aesthetics and Subjectivity: From Kant to Nietzsche* (Manchester: Manchester University Press, 1990).

Breazeale, Daniel, 'Note on Translation', in J. G. Fichte, *Early Philosophical Writings* (translated and edited by Daniel Breazeale, Ithaca, NY: Cornell University Press, 1988).

Bromwich, David, *Disowned by Memory: Wordsworth's Poetry of the 1790s* (Chicago: The University of Chicago Press, 1998).

Bruns, Gerald L., *Maurice Blanchot: The Refusal of Philosophy* (Baltimore: The Johns Hopkins University Press, 1997).

Burke, Edmund, *A Philosophical Enquiry into the Origin of Our Ideas of the Sublime and Beautiful* (edited by James T. Boulton, Notre Dame: University of Notre Dame Press, 1968 [1958]).

Burwick, Frederick, 'Introduction', in Burwick (ed.), *Approaches to Organic Form: Permutations in Science and Culture* (Dordrecht: D. Reidel Publishing Company, 1987), ix–xvii.

Butler, Marilyn, *Romantics, Rebels and Reactionaries: English Literature and its Background 1760–1830* (Oxford: Oxford University Press, 1981).

Camille, Michael, *Gothic Art: Visions and Revelations of the Medieval World* (London: Calmann and King, 1996).

Cassirer, Ernst, *The Philosophy of the Enlightenment* (translated by Fritz C. A. Koelln and James P. Pettegrove, Princeton, NJ: Princeton University Press, 1979 [1951]).

Chandler, James K., *Wordsworth's Second Nature: A Study of the Poetry and Politics* (Chicago: The University of Chicago Press, 1984).

Christensen, Inger, *The Shadow of the Dome: Organicism and Romantic Poetry* (Bergen: Studia Anglistica Norvegica 3, 1985).

Cicero, *On the Good Life* (translated by Michael Grant, London: Penguin Books, 1971).

Clark, Kenneth, *The Gothic Revival: An Essay in the History of Taste* (Harmondsworth: Penguin Books, 1962 [1928]).

Coburn, Kathleen, 'Introduction', in Samuel Taylor Coleridge, *The Philosophical Lectures* (edited by Kathleen Coburn, London: Pilot Press, 1949).

Coleridge, Samuel Taylor, *The Philosophical Lectures* (edited by Kathleen Coburn, London: Pilot Press, 1949).

—— *Selected Poetry and Prose* (edited by Donald A. Stauffer, New York: Random House, 1951).

—— *Collected Letters*, 6 volumes (edited by Earl Leslie Griggs, Oxford: Clarendon Press, 1956–71).

—— *The Notebooks*, 8 volumes (edited by Kathleen Coburn. Bollingen Series 50. London: Routledge & Kegan Paul, 1957–90).

—— *The Collected Works*, 16 volumes (general editor Kathleen Coburn. Bollingen Series 75. London: Routledge & Kegan Paul, 1969–).

—— *Selected Poems* (edited by Richard Holmes, London: Penguin Books, 1996).

—— *The Complete Poems* (edited by William Keach, London: Penguin Books, 1997).

Colmer, John, 'Editor's Introduction', in Samuel Taylor Coleridge, *On the Constitution of Church and State*, in *Collected Works*, volume 10 (edited by John Colmer, London: Routledge & Kegan Paul, 1976).

Critchley, Simon, *Very Little … Almost Nothing: Death, Philosophy, Literature* (London: Routledge, 1997).

Dart, Gregory, *Rousseau, Robespierre and English Romanticism* (Cambridge: Cambridge University Press, 1999).

Deleuze, Gilles, *The Fold: Leibniz and the Baroque* (translated by Tom Conley, Minneapolis: University of Minnesota Press, 1993).

—— *Difference and Repetition* (translated by Paul Patton, London: The Athlone Press, 1994).

—— *Pure Immanence: Essays on A Life* (translated by John Rajchman, New York: Zone Books, 2001)

Deleuze, Gilles, and Guattari., Félix, *A Thousand Plateaus* (translated by Brian Massumi, London: The Athlone Press, 1988).

De Man, Paul, *Allegories of Reading: Figural Language in Rousseau, Nietzsche, Rilke, and Proust* (New Haven, CT: Yale University Press, 1979).

—— *Blindness and Insight: Essays in the Rhetoric of Contemporary Criticism*, second and revised edition (London: Routledge, 1983).

—— *Aesthetic Ideology* (edited by Andrzej Warminski, Minneapolis: University of Minnesota Press, 1996).

Derrida, Jacques, *Positions: Entretiens avec Henri Ronse, Julia Kristeva, Jean-Louis Houdebine, Guy Scarpetta* (Paris: Minuit, 1972); translated by Alan Bass, *Positions* (Chicago: The University of Chicago Press, 1981).

—— *Marges de la philosophie* (Paris: Minuit, 1972); translated by Alan Bass, *Margins of Philosophy* (New York: Harvester Wheatsheaf, 1982).

—— *Of Grammatology* (translated by Gayatri Chakravorty Spivak, Baltimore: The Johns Hopkins University Press, 1976).

—— *Writing and Difference* (translated by Alan Bass, Chicago: The University of Chicago Press, 1978).

—— 'Living On / Borderlines', translated by James Hulbert, in Harold Bloom, Paul de Man, Jacques Derrida, Geoffrey H. Hartman and J. Hillis Miller, *Deconstruction and Criticism* (London: Routledge & Kegan Paul, 1979), 75–156.

—— *Dissemination* (translated by Barbara Johnson, London: The Athlone Press, 1981).

—— 'Fors: The Anglish Words of Nicolas Abraham and Maria Torok', in Nicolas Abraham and Maria Torok, *The Wolf Man's Magic Word: A Cryptonymy* (translated by Nicholas Rand, Minnesota: University of Minneapolis Press, 1986), xi–xlviii.

—— *The Truth in Painting* (translated by Geoffrey Bennington and Ian McLeod, Chicago: The University of Chicago Press, 1987).

—— *Of Spirit: Heidegger and the Question* (translated by Geoffrey Bennington and Rachel Bowlby, Chicago: The University of Chicago Press, 1989).

—— 'Biodegradables: Seven Diary Fragments', translated by Peggy Kamuf, *Critical Acts of Literature* (edited by Derek Attridge, London: Routledge, 1992).

—— 'How to Avoid Speaking: Denials', translated by Ken Frieden, in Harold Coward and Toby Foshay (eds.), *Derrida and Negative Theology* (Albany: State University of New York Press, 1992), 73–142.

—— *Aporias* (translated by Thomas Dutoit, Stanford, CA: Stanford University Press, 1993).

—— 'Specters of Marx': The State of the Debt, the Work of Mourning, & the New International* (translated by Peggy Kamuf, New York: Routledge, 1994).

—— *Points …: Interviews, 1974–1994* (translated by Peggy Kamuf and others, edited by Elisabeth Weber, Stanford, CA: Stanford University Press, 1995).

—— 'Sauf le nom (Post-Scriptum)', translated by John P. Leavey Jr., in Derrida, *On the Name* (edited by Thomas Dutoit, Stanford, CA: Stanford University Press, 1995).

—— *Archive Fever: A Freudian Impression* (translated by Eric Prenowitz, Chicago: The University of Chicago Press, 1996).

—— 'Remarks on Deconstruction and Pragmatism', translated by Simon Critchley, in Critchley, Derrida, Ernesto Laclau and Simon Rorty, *Deconstruction and Pragmatism* (edited by Chantal Mouffe, London: Routledge, 1996), 77–88.

—— *Politics of Friendship* (translated by George Collins, London: Verso, 1997).

—— 'Faith and Knowledge: The Two Sources of "Religion" at the Limits of Reason Alone', translated by Samuel Weber, in Derrida and Vattimo (eds.), *Religion* (Cambridge: Polity Press, 1998), 1–78.

—— *Monolingualism of the Other; or, The Prosthesis of the Origin* (translated by Patrick Mensah, Stanford, CA: Stanford University Press, 1998).

—— 'Marx & Sons', translated by G. M. Goshgarian, in Michael Sprinker (ed.), *Ghostly Demarcations: A Symposium on Jacques Derrida's 'Specters of Marx'* (London: Verso, 1999), 213–69.

—— 'I'm Going to Have to Wander All Alone', translated by Leonard Lawler, in Derrida, *The Work of Mourning* (edited by Pascale-Anne Brault and Michael Naas, Chicago: The University of Chicago Press, 2001).

Dilthey, Wilhelm, *Die Geistige Welt: Einleitung in die Philosophie des Lebens. Erste Hälfte: Abhandlungen zur Grundlegung der Geisteswissenschaften*, in *Gesammelte Schriften*, volume V (Stuttgart: B. G. Teubner Verlagsgesellschaft, 1957).

Eagleton, Terry, *Literary Theory: An Introduction* (Minneapolis: University of Minnesota Press, 1983).

—— 'Marxism without Marxism', in Michael Sprinker (ed.), *Ghostly Demarcations: A Symposium on Jacques Derrida's 'Specters of Marx'* (London: Verso, 1999), 83–7.

Eco, Umberto, *The Open Work* (translated by Anna Cancogni, Cambridge, MA: Harvard University Press, 1989).

Emerson, Ralph Waldo, *Selected Essays* (New York: Penguin Books, 1982).

Engelhardt, Dietrich von, 'Vitalism between Science and Philosophy in Germany around 1800', in Guido Cimino and François Duchesneau (eds.), *Vitalisms: From Haller to the Cell Theory* (Florence: Leo S. Olschki Editore, 1997), 157–74.

Erlande-Brandenburg, Alain, *The Cathedral: The Social and Architectural Dynamics of Construction* (translated by Martin Thom, Cambridge: Cambridge University Press, 1994).

Everest, Kelvin, *Coleridge's Secret Ministry: The Context of the Conversation Poems 1795–1798* (Hassocks: The Harvester Press, 1979).

Fichte, J. G., *The Vocation of Man* (edited by Roderick M. Chisholm, translated by William Smith, New York: The Liberal Arts Press, 1956).

—— *J. G. Fichte: Gesamtausgabe der Bayerischen Akademie der Wissenschaften*, 15 volumes (edited by Reinhard Lauth, Hans Jacob and Hans Gliwitsky. Stuttgart-Bad Cannstatt: Friedrich Frommann Verlag-Holzboog, 1964–).

—— *Early Philosophical Writings* (translated and edited by Daniel Breazeale, Ithaca, NY: Cornell University Press, 1988).

Frankl, Paul, *Gothic Architecture* (translated by Dieter Pevsner, Harmondsworth: Penguin Books, 1962).

Freud, Sigmund, *Three Essays on the Theory of Sexuality*, translated by James Strachey, in *The Standard Edition*, volume VII (edited by James Strachey, London: Hogarth Press, 1971).

Fruman, Norman, *Coleridge: The Damaged Archangel* (London: Allen and Unwin, 1972).

Gadamer, Hans-Georg, *Wahrheit und Methode: Grundzüge einer philosophischen Hermeneutik* (Tübingen: J. C. B. Mohr (Paul Siebeck), 1975); translated by Joel Weinsheimer and Donald G. Marshall, *Truth and Method*, revised edition (London: Sheed & Ward, 1996 [1989]).

—— *Gesammelte Werke*, 10 volumes (Tübingen: J. C. B. Mohr (Paul Siebeck), 1985–95).

—— *The Relevance of the Beautiful and Other Essays* (edited by Robert Bernasconi, translated by Nicholas Walker, Cambridge: Cambridge University Press, 1986).

—— 'Hermeneutics and Logocentrism', translated by Richard Palmer and Diane Michelfelder, in Diane P. Michelfelder and Richard E. Palmer (eds.), *Dialogue and Deconstruction: The Gadamer-Derrida Encounter* (Albany: State University of New York Press. 1989), 114–25.

—— 'Zur Fragwürdigkeit des ästhetischen Bewußtseins', in Dieter Heinrich and Wolfgang Iser (eds.), *Theorien der Kunst* (Frankfurt am Main: Suhrkamp, 1992 [1982]), 59–69.

—— 'Rhetoric, Hermeneutics, and the Critique of Ideology: Metacritical Comments on *Truth and Method*', translated by Jerry Dibble, in Kurt Mueller-Vollmer (ed.), *The Hermeneutics Reader: Texts of the German Tradition from the Enlightenment to the Present* (New York: Continuum, 1994), 274–92.

—— *The Enigma of Health: The Art of Healing in a Scientific Age* (translated by Jason Gaiger and Nicholas Walker, Cambridge: Polity Press, 1996).

—— *Praise of Theory: Speeches and Essays* (translated by Chris Dawson, New Haven, CT: Yale University Press, 1998).

Gérard, A., 'The Systolic Rhythm: The Structure of Coleridge's Conversation Poems', in Kathleen Coburn (ed.), *Coleridge: A Collection of Critical Essays* (Englewood Cliffs, NJ: Prentice-Hall, 1967), 78–87.

Gilpin, William, *Observations, Relative Chiefly to Picturesque Beauty, Made in the Year 1772, on Several Parts of England; Particularly the Mountains, and Lakes of Cumberland, and Westmoreland*, volume II (Richmond: The Richmond Publishing Co., 1973).

Girard, René, *Violence and the Sacred* (translated by Patrick Gregory, London: The Athlone Press, 1988).

Godwin, William, *Enquiry Concerning Political Justice and its Influence on Morals and Happiness*, Volume I (edited by F. E. L. Priestly, Toronto: University of Toronto, 1946).

Goethe, Johann Wolfgang, 'Von Deutscher Baukunst. D. M. Erwini a Steinbach', in Heinz Kindermann (ed.), *Von Deutscher Art und Kunst* (Leipzig: Philipp Reclam Jun., 1935), 209–16.

—— *Faust: Der Tragödie erster und zweiter Teil. Urfaust* (edited by Erich Trunz, Munich: Verlag C. H. Beck, 1986); translated by Philip Wayne, *Faust/Part One* (Harmondsworth: Penguin Books, 1981).

Hamacher, Werner, *Premises: Essays on Philosophy and Literature from Kant to Celan* (translated by Peter Fenves, Stanford, CA: Stanford University Press, 1996).

Harding, Anthony John, *Coleridge and the Idea of Love: Aspects of Relationship in Coleridge's Thought and Writing* (London: Cambridge University Press, 1974).

Harper, G. M., 'Coleridge's Conversation Poems', in M. H. Abrams (ed.), *English Romantic Poets: Modern Essays in Criticism* (Oxford: Oxford University Press, 1975), 188–201.

Hartman, Geoffrey H., 'The Dream of Communication', in Reuben Brower, Helen Vendler and John Hollander (eds.), *I. A. Richards: Essays in His Honor* (New York: Oxford University Press, 1973), 157–77.

Hartmann, Nicolai, *Die Philosophie des deutschen Idealismus* (Berlin: Walter de Gruyter, 1974).

Hecht, Wolfgang, 'Einleitung', in Friedrich Schlegel, *Werke in zwei Bänden*, volume 1 (edited by Wolfgang Hecht, Berlin: Aufbau-Verlag, 1988).

Hegel, G. W. F., *Differenz der Fichte'schen und Schelling'schen Systems der Philosophie* (Hamburg: Felix Meiner, 1962).

Heidegger, Martin, *Über den Humanismus*. Frankfurt am Main: Vittorio Klostermann, 1947; translated by Frank A. Capuzzi and J. Glenn Gray, *Letter on Humanism*, in Heidegger, *Basic Writings*, revised edition (edited by David Farrell Krell, London: Routledge, 1993).

—— *Schellings Abhandlung über das Wesen der menschlichen Freiheit* (Tübingen: Max Niemeyer Verlag, 1971).

—— *Poetry, Language, Thought* (translated by Alfred Hofstadter, New York: Harper & Row, 1971).

—— *Der Ursprung des Kunstwerkes* (Stuttgart: Philipp Reclam Jun., 1977).

—— *Being and Time: A Translation of 'Sein und Zeit'* (translated by Joan Stambaugh, Albany: State University of New York Press, 1996).

Heinrich, Dieter, 'Fichtes ursprüngliche Einsicht', in Dieter Heinrich and Hans Wagner (eds.), *Subjektivität und Metaphysik: Festschrift für Wolfgang Cramer* (Frankfurt am Main: Vittorio Klostermann, 1966), 188–232.

Herder, Johann Gottfried, *Sämmtliche Werke*, volume I (edited by Bernhard Suphan, Hildesheim: Georg Olms Verlag, 1887).

Hickey, Alison, *Impure Conceits: Rhetoric and Ideology in Wordsworth's 'Excursion'* (Stanford, CA: Stanford University Press, 1997).

Hollier, Denis, *Against Architecture: The Writings of Georges Bataille* (translated by Betsy Wing, Cambridge, MA: MIT Press, 1989).

—— 'The Dualist Materialism of Georges Bataille', in Allan Stoekl (ed.), *On Bataille* (Yale French Studies, Number 78. New Haven, CT: Yale University Press, 1990), 124–39.

—— 'The Use-Value of the Impossible', in Carolyn Bailey Gill (ed.), *Bataille: Writing the Sacred* (London: Routledge, 1995), 133–53.

Holmes, Richard, *Coleridge: Early Visions* (London: Penguin Books, 1990).

Hotopf, W. H. N., *Language, Thought and Comprehension: A Case Study of the Writings of I. A. Richards* (London: Routledge & Kegan Paul, 1965).

Hugo, Victor, *Notre-Dame of Paris* (translated by John Sturrock, London: Penguin Books, 1978).

Hunt, John Dixon, *Gardens and the Picturesque: Studies in the History of Landscape Architecture* (Cambridge, MA: The MIT Press, 1992).

Jasper, David, *The Sacred and the Secular Canon in Romanticism: Preserving the Sacred Truths* (London: Macmillan, 1999).

Johnston, Kenneth R., *Wordsworth and 'The Recluse'* (New Haven, CT: Yale University Press, 1984).

Kant, Immanuel, *Kants Gesammelte Schriften* (Berlin: Königlich Preußischen Akademie der Wissenschaften/Walter de Gruyter, 1900–).

—— *The Critique of Judgement* (translated by James Creed Meredith, Oxford: Clarendon Press, 1952 [1928]).

—— *Kritik der reinen Vernunft* (edited by Ingeborg Heidemann, Stuttgart: Philipp Reclam Jun., 1966); translated by Norman Kemp, *Critique of Pure Reason* (London: Macmillan, 1929).

—— *Anthropology from a Pragmatic Point of View* (translated by Mary J. Gregor, The Hague: Martinus Nijhoff, 1974).

—— *Opus Postumum* (edited by Eckart Förster, translated by Eckart Förster and Michael Rosen, Cambridge: Cambridge University Press, 1993).

—— *The Metaphysics of Morals* (translated by Mary Gregor, Cambridge: Cambridge University Press, 1996).

Kipperman, Mark, *Beyond Enchantment: German Idealism and English Romantic Poetry* (Philadelphia: University of Pennsylvania Press, 1986).

Konstan, David, *Friendship in the Classical World* (Cambridge: Cambridge University Press, 1997).

Krell, David Farrell, *Daimon Life: Heidegger and Life-Philosophy* (Bloomington: Indiana University Press, 1992).

Krieger, Murray, *A Reopening of Closure: Organicism Against Itself* (New York: Columbia University Press, 1989).

Lacoue-Labarthe, Philippe, *Typography: Mimesis, Philosophy, Politics* (translated by Christopher Fynsk, Stanford, CA: Stanford University Press, 1998).

Lacoue-Labarthe, Philippe, and Nancy, Jean-Luc, *L'absolu littéraire: Théorie de la littérature du romantisme allemand* (Paris: Seuil, 1978); translated by Philip Barnard and Cheryl Lester, *The Literary Absolute: The Theory of Literature in German Romanticism* (Albany: State University of New York Press, 1988).

Leibniz, G. W., *Monadology: An Edition for Students* (translated by Nicholas Rescher, London: Routledge, 1991).

Lessing, Gotthold Ephraim, *Erziehung des Menschengeschlechts, Gespräche über Freimaurer* (Hamburg: Hamburg Kulturverlag, 1948).

Levere, Trevor H., *Poetry Realized in Nature: Samuel Taylor Coleridge and Early Nineteenth-Century Science* (Cambridge: Cambridge University Press, 1981).

Lewis, Tom, 'The Politics of 'Hauntology' in Derrida's *Specters of Marx'*, in Michael Sprinker (ed.), *Ghostly Demarcations: A Symposium on Jacques Derrida's 'Specters of Marx'* (London: Verso, 1999), 134–67.

Liu, Alan, *Wordsworth: The Sense of History* (Stanford, CA: Stanford University Press, 1989).

Lyotard, Jean-François, *The Postmodern Condition: A Report on Knowledge* (translated by Geoffrey Bennington and Brian Massumi, Manchester: Manchester University Press, 1984).

McCallum, Pamela, *Literature and Method: Towards a Critique of I. A. Richards, T. S. Eliot and F. R. Leavis* (Dublin: Gill and Macmillan, 1983).

McFarland, Thomas, *Coleridge and the Pantheist Tradition* (Oxford: Clarendon Press, 1969).

—— *Romanticism and the Forms of Ruin: Wordsworth, Coleridge, and the Modalities of Fragmentation* (Princeton, NJ: Princeton University Press, 1981).

Magnuson, Paul, *Coleridge and Wordsworth: A Lyrical Dialogue* (Princeton, NJ: Princeton University Press, 1988).

Manning, Peter J., *Reading Romantics: Texts and Contexts* (Oxford: Oxford University Press, 1990).

Marks, Emerson R., *Taming the Chaos: English Poetic Diction Theory Since the Renaissance* (Detroit: Wayne State University Press, 1998).

Martindale, Andrew, *Gothic Art* (London: Thames and Hudson, 1967).

Modiano, Raimonda, *Coleridge and the Concept of Nature* (London: Macmillan, 1985).

Montaigne, Michel Eyquem de, *The Essays* (translated by Charles Cotton, Chicago: Encyclopaedia Britannica, 1952).

Nancy, Jean-Luc, *La communauté désœuvrée* (Paris: Christian Bourgois Editeur, 1986); translated by Peter Connor, Lisa Garbus, Michael Holland and Simona Sawhney, *The Inoperative Community* (edited by Peter Connor, Minneapolis: University of Minnesota Press, 1991).

Nelson, Lycette, 'Introduction', in Maurice Blanchot, *The Step Not Beyond* (translated by Lycette Nelson, New York: State University of New York Press, 1992).

Neuhouser, Frederick, *Fichte's Theory of Subjectivity* (Cambridge: Cambridge University Press, 1990).

Novalis, *Das philosophische Werk I*, in *Schriften*, volume 2 (edited by Richard Samuel, Darmstadt: Wissenschaftliche Buchgesellschaft, 1965).

Orsini, G. N. G., *Coleridge and German Idealism: A Study in the History of Philosophy with Unpublished Materials from Coleridge's Manuscripts* (Carbondale: Southern Illinois University Press, 1969).

—— 'The Ancient Roots of a Modern Idea', in G. S. Rousseau, *Organic Form: The Life of an Idea* (London: Routledge & Kegan Paul, 1972), 8–23.

—— *Organic Unity in Ancient and Later Poetics: The Philosophical Foundations of Literary Criticism* (Carbondale, IL: Southern Illinois University Press, 1975).

Panofsky, Erwin, *Gothic Architecture and Scholasticism* (Latrobe: Archabbey Press, 1951).

Pater, Walter, *Selected Writings of Walter Pater* (edited by Harold Bloom, New York: Columbia University Press, 1974).

Perry, Seamus, *Coleridge and the Uses of Division* (Oxford: Clarendon Press, 1999).

Plato, *Euthyphro, Apology, Crito, Phaedo, Phaedrus* (translated by Harold North Fowler, London: William Heinemann Ltd., 1914).

—— *The Works of Plato* (edited by Irwin Erdman, translated by Benjamin Jowett, New York: Random House, 1956 (1928)).

Prickett, Stephen, *Origins of Narrative: The Romantic Appropriation of the Bible* (Cambridge: Cambridge University Press, 1996).

Protevi, John, *Political Physics: Deleuze, Derrida and the Body Politic* (London: The Athlone Press, 2001).

Richards, I. A., *Principles of Literary Criticism* (London: Routledge & Kegan Paul, 1924).

—— *Practical Criticism: A Study of Literary Judgment* (London: Routledge & Kegan Paul, 1929).

—— *Coleridge on Imagination* (London: Routledge & Kegan Paul, 1962 [1934]).

—— *The Philosophy of Rhetoric* (London: Oxford University Press, 1965).

—— 'Introduction', in Plato, *Plato's Republic* (edited and translated by I. A. Richards, Cambridge: Cambridge University Press, 1966).

—— *So Much Nearer: Essays Toward a World English* (New York: Harcourt, Brace & World, 1968 [1960]).

—— *Sciences and Poetries: A Reissue of Science and Poetry (1926, 1935) with Commentary* (London: Routledge & Kegan Paul, 1970).

Ricoeur, Paul, *Oneself as Another* (translated by Kathleen Blarney, Chicago: The University of Chicago Press, 1992).

Ritterbush, Philip C., 'Aesthetics and Objectivity in the Study of Form in the Life Sciences', in G. S. Rousseau, *Organic Form: The Life of an Idea* (London: Routledge & Kegan Paul, 1972), 25–59.

Roe, Nicholas (ed.), *Samuel Taylor Coleridge and the Sciences of Life* (Oxford: Oxford University Press, 2001).

Ruskin, John, *The Stones of Venice*, three volumes (London: Dent, 1907).

Russo, John Paul, *I. A. Richards: His Life and Work* (London: Routledge, 1989).

Schelling, F. W. J., *Schellings Werke* (edited by Manfred Schröter, Munich: C. H. Beck, 1927–54).

—— *Bruno, or, On the Natural and the Divine Principle of Things* (translated by Michael G. Vater, Albany: State University of New York Press, 1984).

—— *The Philosophy of Art* (translated by Douglas W. Stott, Minneapolis: University of Minnesota Press, 1989).

Schiller, Friedrich, *On the Aesthetic Education of Man in a Series of Letters* (edited and translated by Elizabeth M. Wilkinson and L. A. Willoughby, Oxford: Clarendon Press, 1967).

Schiller, Jerome P., *I. A. Richards' Theory of Literature* (New Haven: Yale University Press, 1969).

Schlegel, August Wilhelm, 'Die Gemälde', in *Athenaeum: Ein Zeitschrift von August Wilhelm Schlegel und Friedrich Schlegel*, volume II (edited by Curt Grützmacher, Reinbek bei Hamburg: Rowohlt, 1969), 7–72.

Schlegel, Friedrich, *Kritische Friedrich-Schlegel-Ausgabe* (edited by Ernst Behler, with Jean-Jacques Anstett and Hans Eichner, Paderhorn/Munich/Wien/Zürich: Verlag Ferdinand Schöningh and Thomas-Verlag, 1958–).

—— Review of Schleiermacher's *On Religion* in 'Notizen', in *Athenaeum: Ein Zeitschrift von August Wilhelm Schlegel und Friedrich Schlegel*, volume II (edited by Curt Grützmacher, Reinbek bei Hamburg: Rowohlt, 1969), 112–18.

—— 'On Goethe's *Meister*', in Kathleen M. Wheeler (ed.), *German Aesthetic and Literary Criticism: The Romantic Ironists and Goethe* (Cambridge: Cambridge University Press, 1984).

—— *Philosophical Fragments* (translated by Peter Firchow, Minneapolis: University of Minneapolis Press, 1991).

Schleiermacher, Friedrich, *Über die Religion: Reden an die Gebildeten unter ihnen Verächtern* (Hamburg: Felix Meiner Verlag, 1958); translated and edited by Richard Crouter, *On Religion: Speeches to its Cultured Despisers* (Cambridge: Cambridge University Press, 1988).

Shell, Susan Meld, *The Embodiment of Reason: Kant on Spirit, Generation and Community* (Chicago: The University of Chicago Press, 1996).

Shusterman, Richard, 'Organic Unity: Analysis and Deconstruction', in Reed Way Dasenbrock (ed.), *Redrawing the Lines: Analytic Philosophy, Deconstruction, and Literary Theory* (Minneapolis: University of Minnesota Press, 1989), 92–115.

Silver, Allan, 'Friendship in Commercial Society: Eighteenth-Century Social Theory and Modern Sociology', in *American Journal of Sociology*, Volume 95, Number 6, 1990, 1474–1504.

Simson, Otto von, *The Gothic Cathedral: Origins of Gothic Cathedral and the Medieval Concept of Order* (Princeton, NJ: Princeton University Press, 1988 (1956)).

Stempel, Daniel, 'Coleridge and Organic Form: The English Tradition', in *Studies in Romanticism*, Volume 6, 1967.

Suleiman, Susan Rubin, 'Bataille in the Street: The Search for Virility in the 1930s', in Carolyn Bailey Gill (ed.), *Bataille: Writing the Sacred* (London: Routledge, 1995), 26–45.

Taylor, Charles, *Human Agency and Language: Philosophical Papers 1* (Cambridge: Cambridge University Press, 1985).

Warnke, Georgia, *Gadamer: Hermeneutics, Tradition and Reason* (Cambridge: Polity Press, 1987).

Wellek, René, and Warren, Austin, *Theory of Literature* (Harmondsworth: Penguin Books, 1956 [1942]).

Wheeler, Kathleen M., *Sources, Processes and Methods in Coleridge's 'Biographia Literaria'* (Cambridge: Cambridge University Press, 1980).

—— *Romanticism, Pragmatism and Deconstruction* (Oxford: Blackwell, 1993).

Wilson, Christopher, *The Gothic Cathedral: The Architecture of the Great Church 1130–1530* (London: Thames and Hudson, 1990).

Winckelmann, Johann Joachim, 'Description of the Torso Belvedere in Rome', translated by Henry Fuseli, in Timothy Webb (ed.), *English Romantic Hellenism, 1700–1824* (Manchester: Manchester University Press, 1982).

Wimsatt, William K., 'Organic Form: Some Questions About a Metaphor', in G. S. Rousseau (ed.), *Organic Form: The Life of an Idea* (London: Routledge & Kegan Paul, 1972), 62–81.

Wordsworth, William, *The Prose Works of William Wordsworth*, 3 volumes (edited by W. J. B. Owen and Jane Worthington Smyser, Oxford: Clarendon Press, 1974).

—— *The Poems*, two volumes (edited by John O. Hayden, Harmondsworth: Penguin Books, 1977).

—— *The Tuft of Primroses with Other Late Poems for 'The Recluse'* (edited by Joseph F. Kishel, Ithaca, NY: Cornell University Press, 1986).

—— *The Prelude: The Four Texts (1798, 1799, 1805, 1850)* (edited by Jonathan Wordsworth, London: Penguin Books, 1995).

Index